HOT Springs
& Hot Pools
of the Southwest

HOT Springs & Hot Pools of the Southwest

Jayson Loam's Original Guide

Marjorie Gersh-Young

AQUA THERMAL ACCESS

Grateful acknowledgements

Ilene Bonomo, Jan Stiles, and Bruce Saltzman—all of whom went beyond their job description to offer advice and suggestions. All of the regional contributors who always went above and beyond their assignment to make this book interesting and accurate. Staff members at state parks, national forests, national parks, and hot springs resorts for their cooperation and encouragement. All of you who have written in with updates and information. Henry Young (my husband) for acting as my sounding board and making the computer run right.

Front Cover - Lil' Hot Creek, Central California
Justine Hill

Back Cover - Little Eden, Central California
Justine Hill

Hot Springs and Hot Pools of the Southwest: Jayson Loam's Original Guide

Copyright 1995 by Marjorie Gersh-Young

Design, layout and production
by Marjorie Gersh-Young

ISBN 0-9624830-8-7

Manufactured in the United States

Published by: **Aqua Thermal Access**
55 Azalea Lane
Santa Cruz, CA 95060
408 426-2956

Photo Credits

Bill and Pam Burt: 86R; Dave Bybee: 137; Clarissa Drake: 91L; Mark Gillespie: 115T; Luis Gonzales: 100, 149; Susan Harris: 133, 149R; Steve Hereema and Shara Biggs: 77, 79; Justine Hill: 10-12, 14 L, RT, RB, 15B, 23-26R, 27, 49LB, 50RB, 51, 52R, 53, 63-68, 70, 72R, 78, 82-85, 92, 118, 119, 121, 124B, 125, 126T, 128-130L, 131, 132, 140L, 143-145R, T&B, 146, 158-160, 162R, 163, 164L, 170-175T, 181R, 186; Jayson Loam: 8R, 28T, 29, 31, 32B, 33R, 34L, 36, 46, 55L, 61, 95, 101, 102, 104, 105L, RB, 106L, 107R, 112, 123, 137, 138R, 145L, 147, 150-152, 157, 162L, 164R, 165, 177-179; Marguerite Molk: 71R; Nancy Moyers: 74RB; Bill Pennington: 14LM; Melanie Sohler: 175R; Mark Stover: 138L, 141; Camilla Van Sickle: 86; Phil Wilcox: 19-22, 26L, 32T, 35, 37B, 39, 41L, 42, 43R, 44, 49R, TB, 52L, 56R, 57, 96-99, 110-111RM, 113L, 139, 140R; Rob Williams: 183-185, 187-199; Henry Young: 8L; Marjorie Young: 5, 13, 69LB; 87, 88T, 89L, 90, 91R, 108, 109, 116, 117, 124T, 126B, 127, 153L, 154L.

Commercial establishments contributing photos

Albany Sauna and Hot Tubs, Artesian Bath House, Bashford's Hot Mineral Spa, Beverly Hot Springs, Bluebonnet, Box Canyon Lodge, Cottonwood Hot Springs Inn, Desert Reef Beach Club, Desert Shadows Inn, Esalen Institute, Essence of Tranquillity, F. Joseph Smith 153R, Faywood Hot Springs, Finnish Country Sauna and Tubs, Gila Hot Springs Vacation Center 74 RT, 75L, 76, Golden Haven Hot Springs Spa, The Homestead, Indian Springs Resort, Lavender Hill Spa, Le Petit Chateau, Mineral Hot Springs Spa, Morningside Inn, Neptunes Lagoons, Pah Tempe 3LT, Pine Street Inn, Puddingstone Hot Tubs, Raffles Palm Springs Hotel, Salida Hot Springs, Sandpipers Holiday Park, Splash, the Relaxation Spa, Steamboat Springs, Ten Thousand Waves, Terra Cotta Inn, Trimble Hot Springs, Veyo Pool, Vichy Hot Springs Resort and Inn, Wally's Hot Spring Resort, Wheeler Hot Springs, White Sulphur Springs Resort, Wiesbaden Hot Springs, Wilbur Hot Springs, Yampah Spa.

Additional credits:

Rick Epstein for his work on Truth or Consequence

To

Jayson Loam

August 29, 1918 - February 22, 1994

"King of the Hot Springs"

who pursued with passion what he

truly loved to do most and, therefore,

benefited us all.

May you soak in peace.

HOT Springs
& Hot Pools
of the Southwest

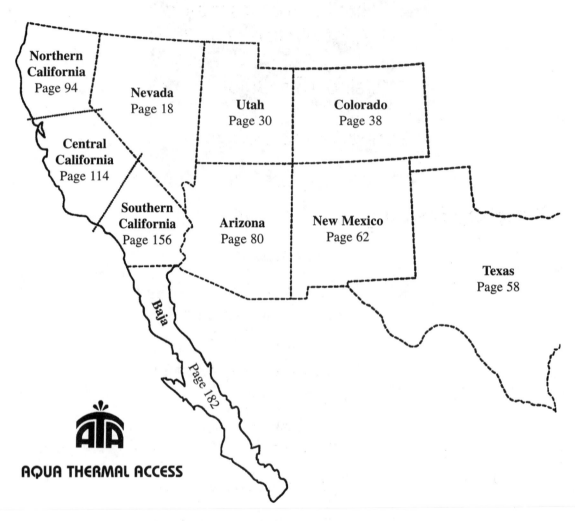

Northern
California
Page 94

Nevada
Page 18

Utah
Page 30

Colorado
Page 38

Central
California
Page 114

Southern
California
Page 156

Arizona
Page 80

New Mexico
Page 62

Texas
Page 58

Baja

Page 182

AQUA THERMAL ACCESS

Companion volume to
Hot Springs and Hot Pools of the Northwest

TABLE OF CONTENTS

INTRODUCTION

By Marjorie Gersh-Young

This book was written with the premise that there is nothing more enjoyable than to soak in a hot spring in ideal conditions. To me this means a beautiful pool with water at 104° cascading in over the rocks out in the middle of the forest at the end of a moderate hike. While definitions of the perfect pool may differ, there does seem to be some standard information that everyone wants to know in order to make an informed choice.

Our hot springs research program started with an analysis of the 1,600 springs listed in the NOAA springs list published by the National Oceanic and Atmospheric Administration. Only seven percent of the listed springs were on public land, accessible without charge, and another fifteen percent were private, commercial enterprises open to the public. Nearly one-third of the locations had temperatures below 90°, so we eliminated them as simply not hot enough. The remaining two-thirds required individual investigation, usually involving personal inspection, which reduced the re NOAA list to a usable twenty-two percent. The unusable seventy-eight percent were often old resorts that had burned down, seeps too small to get into, functioning as cattle troughs, or on posted, private land, making them not usable by the public (NUBP).

As many of you may know, Jayson Loam was the original creator of these hot spring books over fifteen years ago. At that time he did the initial field work and made many decisions as to what information should be included or excluded. Over the years we have refined the format but, without going into an analysis of the chemicals in the water, have maintained the basic premise that soaking in geothermal water does feel good. We have continued to designate hot water at anything above 90° and to include hot wells, treating them the same as hot springs. Rental tub locations, which have now become an integral part of many people's lives, are also included. And, as a special service and option for many of our readers we list several nudist/naturist resorts and parks that welcome visitors with advance reservations. The one thing we do not do is send people onto private property where they can get arrested or shot.

This edition retains these basic criteria while expanding the descriptions, providing more detailed directions, and adding a bit of history whenever possible. I feel sure that the blending of our styles and interests will ensure you, the user, continued enjoyment from the book.

One of the joys of knowing about all of these hot springs was to introduce three of them to a group of our friends when we got together to celebrate my husband's birthday on the East Fork of the Carson River.

REGIONAL CONTRIBUTORS

JUSTINE HILL is a travel writer, photographer, and visual anthropologist who has traveled extensively and has written about and photographed other cultures, travel locations, sacred sites, and the great outdoors.

She currently lives surrounded by nature in Topanga, California, where she has a stock of over 50,000 photos that appear frequently in calendars, posters, magazines, postcards, travel literature, and coffee-table books. For information about her photo collection and related services, contact Justine Hill at PO Box 608, Topanga, CA 90290. 310 455-3409.

ROB WILLIAMS has devoted his life to locating, soaking, and now developing hot springs in remote areas of Baja California. He and his wife's family can be credited with the development of the springs at Guadalupe Canyon.

Whenever Rob can find a dirt road or an old Indian trail, he explores it. Four-wheel drive vehicles are used to reach hidden, remote, and wild canyons filled with palm forests and natural hot springs. Long hikes are rewarded with rejuvenating soaks in natural mineral water. The best time of year to explore these remote, dry wildreness areas is during the winter and spring.

To reserve a place on one of Rob's tours, or to acquire maps and up-to-date information, contact Rob's Baja Tours, PO Box 4003, Balboa, CA 92261. 714 673-2670.

PHIL WILCOX, also known as "the Solar Man," is semi-retired and lives on a remote piece of land in Northern California. He loves to travel often in search of hot springs and has recently been seen in Alaska, Canada, Oregon, Washington, New Mexico, Nevada, and points west. When not traveling, he designs, sells, and installs remote home solar power systems. Send $4.00 for a complete catalog to THE SOLAR MAN, 20560 Morgan Valley Rd., Lower Lake, CA 95457.

And a special thank you to the following:

CAMILLA VAN SICKLE AND BILL PENNINGTON live year round in a small motor home. They travel with the seasons to track down hundreds of remote locations, with an emphasis on hot springs where hiking and camping are permitted in the buff. They have provided details on springs across the United States. All of this information is published in hard copy or on a series of disks that can be ordered from Camilla Van Sickle, NUDISK, PO Box 14418, Sarasota, FL 34230.

HUNTING FOR HOT WATER:
A Bit of History

The cataclysmic folding and faulting of the earth's crust over millions of years, combined with just the right amount of underground water and earth core magma, has produced a hot surface geothermal flow that often goes on for centuries.

Long before the "white man" arrived to "discover" hot springs, the Native American believed that the Great Spirit resided in the center of the earth and that "Big Medicine" fountains were a special gift from The Creator. Even during tribal battles over camping areas or stolen horses, it was customary for the sacred "smoking waters" to be a neutral zone where all could freely be healed of wounds. Back then, hot springs belonged to everyone, and understandably, we would like to believe that nothing has changed.

The Native American tradition of free access to hot springs was initially imitated by the pioneers. However, as soon as mineral water was perceived to have some commercial value, the new settlers' private property laws were invoked at most of the hot spring locations. Histories often include bloody battles with "white men" over hot spring ownership, and there are colorful legends about Indian curses that had dire effects for decades on a whole series of ill-fated owners. After many fierce legal battles, and a few gun battles, some ambitious settlers were able to establish clear legal titles to the properties. Then it was up to the new owners to figure out how to turn their geothermal flow into cash flow.

Pioneering settlers dismissed as superstition the Native American's spiritual explanation of the healing power of a hot spring. However, those settlers did know from experience that it was beneficial to soak their bodies in mineral water, even if they didn't know why or how it worked. Commercial exploitation began when the owner of a private hot spring started charging admission, ending centuries of free access.

The shift from outdoor soaks to indoor soaks began when proper Victorian customers demanded privacy, which required the erection of canvas enclosures around the bathers in the outdoor springs. Then affluent city dwellers, as they became accustomed to indoor plumbing and modern sanitation, were no longer willing to risk immersion in a muddy-edged, squishy-bottom mineral spring, even if they believed that such bathing would be good for their health. Furthermore, they learned to like their urban comforts too much to trek to an outdoor spring in all kinds of weather. Instead, they wanted a civilized method of "taking the waters," and the great spas of Europe provided just the right model for American railroad tycoons and land barons to follow, and to surpass.

Around the turn of the century, American hot spring resorts fully satisfied the combined demands of Victorian prudery, modern sanitation, and indoor comfort by offering separate men's and women's bathhouses with private individual porcelain tubs, marble shower rooms, and central heating. Scientific mineral analysis of the geothermal water was part of every resort merchandising program, which included flamboyant claims of miraculous cures and glowing testimonials from medical doctors. Their promotion material also featured additional social amenities, such as luxurious suites, sumptuous restaurants, and grand ballrooms.

To fulfill her grandfather's dream of having baths on the property he owned during the Arizona gold rush, June Potter bought back the property and has opened *Potter's Aztec Baths* as a bed and breakfast—with soaking pools.

In recent decades, patronage of these resorts has declined, and many have closed down because the traditional medical claims were outlawed and modern medical plans refuse to reimburse anyone for a mineral water "treatment." A few of the larger resorts have managed to survive by adding new facilities such as golf courses, conference and exhibition spaces, fitness centers, and beauty salons. The smaller hot spring establishments have responded to modern demand by installing larger (six persons or more) communal soaking tubs and family-size soaking pools in private spaces for rent by the hour. Most locations continue to offer men's and women's bathhouse facilities in addition to the new communal pools, but most have discontinued the use of cast iron, one-person bath tubs.

Benton Hot Springs in Central California was a thriving town in the 1860s when the silver mines were going strong. Above is one of the original buildings that still remain. It is closed inside, but you can buy gas and soda out front. When the current owners decided to reopen the springs, they followed an old California tradition and used redwood tubs.

In addition to the privately owned hot spring facilities, there are several dozen locations that are owned and operated by federal, state, county, or city agencies. States, counties, and cities usually staff and operate their own geothermal installations. Locations in US National Forests and National Parks are usually operated under contract by privately owned companies. The nature and quality of the mineral water facilities offered at these publicly owned, privately operated hot spring locations varies widely.

Although natural mineral water (from a spring or well) is required for a truly authentic traditional "therapeutic soak," there is a new generation of dedicated soakers who will not patronize a motel unless it has a hot pool. They know full well that the pool is filled with gas-heated tap water and treated with chlorine, but it is almost as good as the real thing and a lot more convenient. We chose to include in our hunt for hot water those locations that offer private-space hot tubs for rent by the hour.

According to California legend, the historic redwood tub was invented by a Santa Barbara group who often visited Big Caliente Hot Springs. One evening a member of the group wished out loud that they could have their delicious outdoor communal soaks without having to endure the long dusty trips to and from the springs. Another member of the group suggested that a large redwood wine cask might be used as an alternate soaking pool in the city. It was worth a try, and it was a success. Over time, other refugees from the long Big Caliente drive began to build their own group soaking pools from wine casks, and the communal hot tub era was born.

USING THIS GUIDE

The primary tool in this guide is the KEY MAP, which is provided for each state or geographical subdivision. The KEY MAP INDEX on the outside back cover tells the page number where each of the KEY MAPS can be found. Each KEY MAP includes significant cities and highways, but please note that it is designed to be used with a standard highway map.

Within every KEY MAP, each location has been assigned a number that is printed next to the identifying circle or square. On the pages following the KEY MAP you will find the descriptions of each location listed in numerical order.

The Master Alphabetical Index of Mineral Water Locations is printed at the end of the book and gives the page number on which each location description will be found. If you know the specific hot spring name, this alphabetical index is the place to start.

The following section describes the quick-read symbols that are used on the KEY MAPS and in the location descriptions.

● **Non-Commercial Mineral Water Locations**

On the key maps and in each hot spring listing, a solid round dot is used to indicate a non-commercial hot spring, or hot well, where no fee is required and pools are generally created by the rearranging of rocks or by using easily available material. At a few remote locations, you may be asked for a donation to help the work of a nonprofit organization that has a contract with the Forest Service to protect and maintain the spring.

The first paragraph of each listing is intended to convey the general appearance, atmosphere, and surroundings of the location, including the altitude, which can greatly affect the weather conditions. The phrase "open all year" does not mean that all roads and trails are kept open regardless of snowfalls or fire seasons. Rather, it means that there are no seasonally closed gates or doors, as at some commercial resorts. Where there is a particular problem we try to note it.

The second paragraph describes the source and temperature of the mineral water and then conveys the manner in which that water is transported or guided to a usable soaking pool. "Volunteer-built pool" usually implies some crude combination of at-hand material such as logs, rocks, and sand. If the situation requires that the pool water temperature be controlled, the method for such control is described.

River-edge and creek-edge pools are vulnerable to complete washouts during high runoff months, so often volunteers have to start from scratch every year. Whether bathing suits are optional or not is indicated. There is also a mention of handicap accessibility.

The third paragraph identifies the facilities and services available on the premises or nearby and states the approximate distance to other facilities and services.

If needed, there is a final paragraph of directions, which should be used in connection with a standard highway map, a National Forest map if applicable, or any local area map.

This small pool up on the hillside at *Buckeye Hot Springs* overlooks the main pools down along the river.

■ Commercial Mineral Water Locations

On the key maps in this book and in the hot springs listings, a solid square is used to indicate a mineral water commercial location. A phone number and address are provided for the purpose of obtaining rates, additional information, and reservations.

The first paragraph of each listing is intended to convey the size, general appearance, atmosphere, and surroundings of the location. "Open all year" does not imply that the facility is open twenty-four hours of every day, only that it does not have a "closed" season.

The second paragraph of each listing focuses on the water facilities available at the location. It describes the origin and temperature of the mineral water, the means of transporting that water, the quantity, type, and location of tubs and pools, the control of soaking water temperatures, and the chemical treatment used, if any.

In all states, health department standards require a minimum treatment of public pool water with chlorine, bromine, or the equivalent. A few fortunate locations are able to meet these standards by operating their smaller mineral water pools on a continuous flow-through basis, thereby eliminating the need for chemical treatment. Many other locations meet these standards by draining and refilling tubs and pools after each use or after the end of each business day.

There actually are a few commercial locations where rare geothermal conditions (and health department rules) make it possible to soak in a natural sand-bottom hot spring open to the sky.

At those hot springs resorts that are being run as a business, bathing suits are normally required in public spaces. A few locations have a policy of clothing optional in the pools and sometimes everywhere on the grounds. Handicap accessibility is mentioned for those locations that provide it.

The third paragraph of a commercial hot spring listing briefly mentions the principal facilities and services offered, plus approximate distances to other nearby services and the names of credit cards accepted, if any. This information is intended to advise you if overnight accommodations, RV hookups, restaurants, health clubs, beauty salons, etc., are available on the premises, but it does not attempt to assign any form of quality rating to those amenities. There is no such thing as a typical hot spring resort and no such thing as typical accommodations at such a resort. Don't make assumptions; phone and ask questions.

☐ Tubs Using Gas-heated Tap Water or Well Water

Listings of rent-a-tub locations, indicated by a hollow square, begin with an overall impression of the premises and with the general location, usually within a city area. This is followed by a description of the private spaces, tubs, and pools, water treatment methods, and water temperature policies. Generally, unless stated otherwise, clothing is optional in private spaces and required elsewhere. Facilities and services available on the premises are described. Credit cards accepted, if any, are listed. Nearly all locations require reservations, especially during the busy evening hours.

Nudist/naturist resorts that have hot pools are included as a special service to those who prefer to soak in the buff. It is true that most nudist/naturist resorts are not open to the public for drop-in visits, but we wanted to give skinny-dippers at least a few alternatives to the conventional motels/hotels/resorts listed in guide books. Most of the nudist/naturist resorts specifically prohibit bathing suits in their pools and have a policy of clothing optional elsewhere on the grounds. The resorts listed in this book are willing to offer a visitor's pass if you phone ahead and make arrangements.

There are times when it is not possible to enjoy a soak out in the wilderness under the trees. Many in-town spa owners add a bit of ambiance to their tubs by planting flowers and trees on the decks surrounding the pools.

A Word about Nudity

You had best start with the hard fact that any private property owner, county administration, park superintendent, or forest supervisor has the authority to prohibit "public nudity" in a specific area or in a whole park or forest. Whenever the authorities have to deal with repeated complaints about nude bathers at a specific hot spring, it is likely that the area will be posted with NO NUDITY ALLOWED signs, and you could get a citation without further warning.

The vast majority of natural hot springs on public property are not individually posted, but most jurisdictions have some form of general regulation prohibiting public nudity. However, there have been some recent court cases establishing that a person could not be found guilty of indecent exposure if he removed his clothes only after traveling to a remote area where there was no one to be offended.

In light of these court cases, one of the largest national forests has retained its general "nude bathing prohibited" regulation but modified its enforcement procedure to give a nude person an opportunity to put on a bathing suit before a complaint can be filed or a violation notice issued.

In practical terms, this means that a group at an unposted hot spring can mutually agree to be nude. As soon as anyone else arrives and requests that all present put on bathing suits, those who refuse that request risk a citation. If you are in the nude group, all you need from the newcomers is some tolerance. You may be pleasantly surprised at the number of people who are willing to agree to a policy of clothing-optional if, in a friendly manner, you offer them an opportunity to say "Yes."

The farther out in the wilderness you travel, the more likely it is you will find a place to soak nude without offending anyone. Other hot springs, such as *Spence,* pictured above, are not that far out but have a history of being clothing optional.

CARING FOR THE OUTDOORS

This is an enthusiastic testimonial and an invitation to join us in supporting the work of the US Forest Service, the National Park Service, and the several State Park Services. At all of their offices and ranger stations we have always received prompt, courteous service, even when the staff was also busy handling many other daily tasks.

Nearly all usable primitive hot springs are in national forests, and many commercial hot spring resorts are surrounded by a national forest. Even if you will not be camping in one of their excellent campgrounds, we recommend that you obtain official Forest Service maps for all of the areas through which you will be traveling. Maps may be purchased from the Forest Service Regional Offices listed below. To order by mail, phone or write for an order form:

Rocky Mountain Region   303 275-5349
Eastern Wyoming, Colorado
740 Simms St., Lakewood, CO 80401

Intermountain Region   801 625-5352
Southern Idaho, Utah,
Nevada, and Western Wyoming
324 25th St., Ogden, UT 84401

Southwestern Region
Arizona, New Mexico
Federal Bldg. 517 Gold Ave., SW
Albuquerque, NM 87102

Pacific Southwest Region
California, Hawaii
630 Sansome St., San Francisco, CA 94111

When you arrive at a national forest, head for the nearest ranger station and let them know what you would like to do in addition to putting your body in hot mineral water. If you plan to stay in a wilderness area overnight, request information about the procedure for obtaining wilderness permits and camping permits. Discuss your understanding of the dangers of water pollution, including giardia (back country dysentery) with the Forest Service staff. They are good friends as well as competent public servants.

The following material is adapted from a brochure issued by the Forest Service, Southwestern Region, Department of Agriculture.

CAUTION

NATURAL HOT SPRINGS

- Water temperatures vary by site, ranging from warm to very hot . . . 180°F.

- Prolonged immersion may be hazardous to your health and result in hyperthermia (high body temperature).

- Footing around hot springs is often poor. Watch out for broken glass. Don't go barefoot and don't go alone. Please don't litter.

- Elderly persons and those with a history of heart disease, diabetes, high or low blood pressure, or who are pregnant should consult their physician prior to use.

- Never enter hot springs while under the influence of: alcohol, anti-coagulants, antihistamines, vasodilators, hypnotics, narcotics, stimulants, tranquilizers, vasoconstrictors, anti-ulcer or anti-Parkinsonian medicines. Undesirable side effects such as extreme drowsiness may occur.

- Hot springs are naturally occurring phenomena and as such are neither improved nor maintained by the Forest Service.

DO NOT WASH IN STREAMS OR SPRINGS

Pour wash water on the ground away from streams and springs.

Wash yourself, your dishes and your clothes in a container, away from water sources.

Food scraps, tooth paste, even biodegradable soap will pollute streams and springs. Remember, it's your drinking water, too!

Try to pack out trash left by others. Your good example may catch on!

DON'T SHORT CUT TRAILS.

Trails are designed and maintained to prevent erosion.

PACK IT IN — PACK IT OUT

Bring trash bags to carry out all trash that cannot be completely burned.

Cutting across switchbacks and trampling meadows can create a confusing maze of unsightly trails.

Aluminum foil and aluminum lined packages won't burn up in your fire. Compact it and put it in your trash bag.

CAMPFIRES Use gas stoves when possible to conserve dwindliing supplies of firewood.

Use only fallen timber for firewood. Even standing dead trees are part of the beauty of wilderness, and are important to wildlife.

If you need to build a fire, use an existing campfire site if available.

Clear a circle of all burnable materials.

Dig a shallow pit for the fire.

Keep the sod intact.

If you need to clear a new fire site, select a safe spot away from rock ledges that would be blackened by smoke; away from meadows where it would destroy grass and leave a scar; away from dense brush, trees and duff where it would be a fire hazard. Keep fires small.

Never leave a fire unattended.

Put your fire COLD OUT before leaving, by mixing the coals with dirt & water. Feel it with your hand. If it's cold out, cover the ashes in the pit with dirt, replace the sod, and naturalize the disturbed area. Rockfire rings, if needed or used, should be scattered before leaving.

DON'T BURY TRASH!
Animals dig it up.

BURY HUMAN WASTE

When nature calls, select a suitable spot at least 100 feet from open water, campsites and trails. Dig a hole 4 to 6 inches deep. Try to keep the sod intact.

Don't pick flowers, dig up plants or cut branches from live trees. Leave them for others to see and enjoy.

After use, fill in the hole completely burying waste and TP: then tramp in the sod.

NEVADA

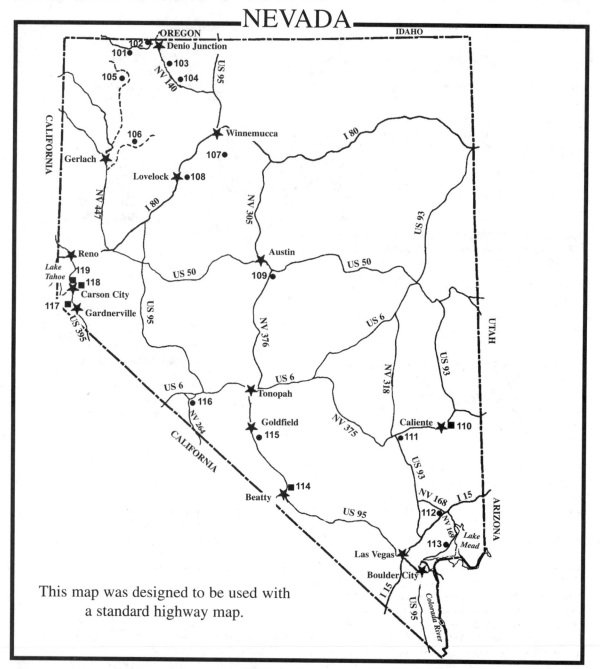

This map was designed to be used with a standard highway map.

MAP SYMBOLS

- ● Non-commercial mineral water pool
- ■ Commercial (fee) mineral water pool
- □ Tap water resorts and rental locations

Paved highway

Unpaved road

Hiking trail

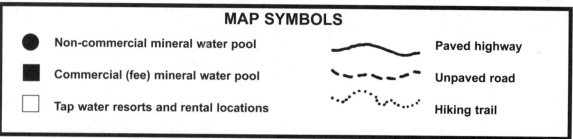

Although the bathhouse is closed at this time, it is still possible to soak in the pond and camp at the spring.

101   VIRGIN VALLEY WARM SPRING

● **In the Sheldon Wildlife Refuge**

A charming, gravel-bottom, warm pond adjacent to a small campground in the high desert foothills near the Nevada-Oregon border. Elevation 5,100 feet. Open all year, subject to snow blockage on road.

Natural mineral water emerges up through the pond bottom (and is piped from other nearby springs) at 89°. The rate of flow maintains pond temperature at approximately 85°, depending on air temperature and wind speed. A new cement pad and ladder into the pond has been installed and the bank between the pond, and the bathhouse has been reinforced. No chemical treatment of the water is necessary. Bathing suits are required.

The old adobe bathhouse is closed at this time. The campground is equipped with chemical toilets. Free camping is available. Services are available 27.5 miles away in Denio.

Directions: On NV 140, 27.5 miles west of Denio Junction and 10 miles east of the Cedarville Road Junction, watch for a road sign to Virgin Valley, Royal Peacock Mine. Go south on the gravel road 2.5 miles to campground.

102   BOG HOT SPRINGS

● **Near the town of Denio**

A large, sand-bottom ditch carrying hot mineral water to an irrigation pond. Located on brush-covered, flat land just below the Nevada-Oregon border. Elevation 4,300 feet. Open all year.

Natural mineral water flows out of several springs at 122°, is gathered into a single man-made channel, and gradually cools as it travels toward the reservoir. A dam with spillway pipe has been built at the point where the temperature is approximately 105°, depending on air temperature and wind speed. Around the dam, brush has been cleared away for easy access and nearby parking, but it is possible to soak in the ditch farther upstream if a warmer water temperature is desired. Clothing optional is probably the custom at this remote location.

There are no services available, but there is an abundance of level space on which overnight parking is not prohibited. It is almost fourteen miles to a restaurant, store, service station, motel, and RV hookups in Denio Junction.

Directions: From Denio Junction, go west on NV 140 for 9.2 miles, turn right and drive north for 4.3 miles on gravel road. Turn left and drive 100 yards to ditch and turn around area.

104   DYKE HOT SPRING

● **South of Denio Junction**

Old porcelain bathtub set in a ravine against the hills on the western side of the Quinn River valley with hills to the west and broad vistas across the valley to the east. Elevation 4,000 feet. Open all year.

A small natural mineral water stream flows out of the hills at 150° and is carried by plastic pipe into the old bathtub. To control the temperature in the tub, remove the hot water pipe and allow the water to cool down. If tub water is dirty, empty tub and refill. Clothing is optional.

Overnight camping is not restricted. All services are thirty-nine miles away in Denio Junction.

Directions: From Denio Junction drive south about 26 miles (9 miles south of road to Howard Hot Spring). Just past mile post 41, turn onto Big Creek Road. (Sign says "Dyfurrena Ranch and Photo Gallery.") Go 7 miles to "T" and turn left onto Woodward Road. Pass ranch on left (2 miles) and take first left (another 2 miles). Park at obvious pull-out and walk a few yards back toward the road and tub, which is hidden in the ravine.

103   HOWARD HOT SPRING

● **South of Denio Junction**

Delightful small soaking pond one mile off Highway 140 on a barren plateau between Denio Junction and Winnemucca with a view of rolling hills on both sides. Elevation 4,200 feet. Open all year; wet weather could make road impassable.

Natural mineral water exits the ground at 135° and flows across the ground. At a spot where the water has cooled to 108°, volunteers have created a log dam and used a green plastic tarp to hold in the water. Clothing is optional.

There are no restrictions against camping at the spring. All services are eighteen miles away in Denio Junction.

Directions: From Denio Junction, head south (toward Winnemucca) on Hwy 140 for 17 miles. Just past mile post 49, turn left on dirt road. Continue 1 mile; take the left fork and then a right fork through a gate, staying on the main road for .25 miles. Spring is visible on the right.

Coming from Winnemucca, turn right just past the sign reading "Denio Junction 20 miles."

Be sure to look for signs for a nearby working ranch offering bed and breakfast if you don't want to camp

105   SOLDIER MEADOW

● **North of the town of Gerlach**

Delightful, deep pond located in the middle of a large meadow with a beautiful view of the surrounding desert and nearby Calico Mountains. Near High Rock Lake in the Black Rock Desert of northwest Nevada. Elevation 4,500 feet. Open all year.

Natural mineral water seeps up through the bottom of this natural sand and stone, five-and-a-half foot pond. The water temperature is approximately 102°. The apparent local custom is clothing optional.

There are no services available, but overnight parking is not prohibited. (Soldier Meadow Ranch near the spring is a private working ranch and bed and breakfast. Do not camp on their property.) It is 62 miles to a service station and mini-mart in Gerlach.

Directions: From Gerlach, take Hwy 34 north and east for 12.2 miles. Turn right on Soldier Meadow Road (mostly good gravel surface) for 50 miles. Bear left toward Summit Lake at first Soldier Meadow sign (Humboldt County Road 217). Turn left one mile at second Soldier Meadow sign. Proceed .2 mile to spring.

Note: There are numerous other hot springs on the road to High Rock Lake, but a four-wheel-drive vehicle is recommended, and the road is rough.

106   TREGO HOT DITCH

● **Northeast of the town of Gerlach**

A hot ditch next to Western Pacific railroad tracks. Located in the Black Rock Desert with a backdrop of the Pahsupp Mountains. Elevation 4,000 feet. Open all year.

Natural mineral water flows out of the ground by the railroad tracks at 107° and cools gradually as it flows toward a small man-made dam. Wooden stairs lead down into the water where the temperature is 104°. Clothing is optional, but pools can be seen from the tracks.

No services are available, but overnight parking is not prohibited. It is 20 miles to a service station and mini-mart in Gerlach.

Directions: From Gerlach, go 3.5 miles south on Route 447. Turn left on gravel county road 48 (no sign). Continue 17 miles and turn left toward railroad radio antenna. Continue 1 mile and turn right at the first fork, left at the second, and right at the third (antenna on left). Take the next left toward the railroad track (pool not visible).

You may have to share the water in this pool with the cows who like to drink out of the stock tanks.

One of the more enjoyable soaking pools to be found out in the middle of this barren desert area.

107   KYLE HOT SPRINGS

● **Near the town of Mill City**

One cement tub and two stock tanks contain high-sulphur content mineral water. Located on a barren mountainside in the East Humboldt Range overlooking a scrub-covered valley. Elevation 4,500 feet. Open all year.

High-sulphur-content mineral water flows out of the ground at over 110°, and hot sulphur dioxide steam comes out of a nearby vent. The water in the ten-foot by ten-foot cement tub is around 110°. The six-foot round galvanized stock tank receives its 104° water via plastic piping. The overflow from this tank goes into a fourteen-foot long, three-and-a-half-foot wide stock tank. Water temperature can be controlled by turning off the pipe at the shut-off valve. Clothing is optional.

There are no services available, but overnight parking is not prohibited. The nearest services are in Winnemucca.

Directions: From Mill City exit 149 on Hwy 80, proceed south on Hwy 400 approximately 16 miles to end of pavement. Turn left at Kyle Hot Springs sign and drive about 10 miles on a mostly good gravel road. Bear left at the fork and proceed toward the white hill with a corral at the bottom. The spring is on top of the knoll; you can drive right to it.

108   SEVEN DEVILS HOT SPRING

● **East of Lovelock**

Delightful, natural stone soaking pool in the barren, very remote, geothermal area at the north end of Dixie Valley. Elevation 5,000 feet. Open all year.

Natural mineral water comes up in several seeps and pools too hot to enter. One spring pool at 114° overflows into the main soaking pool and keeps it at a comfortable 104°. Temperature can be controlled by moving rocks to restrict the flow from the source pool. Clothing is optional.

There are no services on the premises, but overnight parking is not restricted. The nearest services are seventy miles away in Lovelock. Take plenty of food, water, and gasoline with you.

Directions: From Hwy 80 just north of Lovelock take exit 112 and follow Coal Canyon Road up into the foothills for 14 miles. Turn left at Dixie Valley sign and proceed about 42 miles. Pavement eventually ends. Follow all signs to Dixie Valley and Brinkerhoff Seed Ranch. Where the power line crosses the road just before the Seed Ranch, turn right (power pole 2504). Go about 1 mile and turn left after the hill crests. Go to white metal gate. Pools are on the hill by the one lonely tree. The Dixie Valley Geothermal Power Plant is visible to the south.

It would be hard to choose whether to soak in the natural pool or in the stock tank. Why not do both?

109   SPENCER HOT SPRINGS

● **Southeast of the town of Austin**

A group of volunteer-built soaking pools on a knoll with a view of barren hills and snow-capped mountains. Elevation 5,700 feet. Open all year.

Natural mineral water flows out of several springs at 122°, then through a shallow channel down the slope of the knoll. Volunteers have dug a small, three-foot deep, sand-bottom soaking pool next to this channel. The temperature is 104°. A wooden slat deck has been built near the soaking pool. Volunteers have also installed a large metal stock tank downhill for soaking in 107° water. A second stock tank has been installed about one-quarter of a mile to the north where the water is about 112°. Water temperature is controlled by inserting or removing the pipe or hoses carrying the hot water. Clothing optional is the apparent local custom.

There are no services available, but there is a limited amount of level space on which overnight parking is not prohibited. A steel fire pit has been built near the metal soaking tank, and there are several large bins for trash collection. Please do your part to keep this location clean.

Directions: From the intersection of US 50 and NV 376, go 100 yards south on NV 376 and then 5.5 miles southeast on a gravel road. Bear left on a dirt road that leads up to the hot-spring knoll.

110   CALIENTE HOT SPRINGS MOTEL
Box 216   702 726-3777
■ Caliente, NV 89008

Primarily a motel, with some hot-water facilities. Located on the edge of Caliente in beautiful Rainbow Canyon, one hundred and fifty miles north of Las Vegas. Elevation 4,400 feet. Open all year.

Natural mineral water flows from a spring at 115° and is piped to three indoor, family-size, newly retiled soaking pools in which hot mineral water and cold tap water may be mixed as desired by the customer. No chemical treatment is necessary because soaking pools are drained, cleaned, and refilled after each use. Soaking pools may be rented by the public on an hourly basis; free to motel guests.

There are six rooms with kitchenettes and a hydrojet tub using hot mineral water and cold tap water. Major credit cards are accepted. A restaurant, store, and service station are within a few blocks.

111   ASH SPRINGS

● **North of the town of Alamo**

Natural warm-water swimming holes formed in deep channels under ash and cottonwood trees, surrounded by barren desert foothills. Elevation 4,000 feet. Open all year.

Hundreds of gallons per minute of natural mineral water flows out of several springs on Bureau of Land Management (BLM) property and gradually cools as it runs off though clear, large, wide sandy-bottom ditches deep enough to swim in. The water is approximately 92°. A heavy knotted rope hanging from a shade tree gives this pool the feeling of "Ye Olde Swimming Hole." A separate spring feeds a nearby rock,. brick, and cement pool where water temperature measures 98°. In the more secluded areas, clothing optional is the apparent local custom.

Facilities include a picnic area, firepits, trash collection, and level BLM land for parking. No overnight camping. A service station, restaurant, store, campground, and RV park are available in the same commercial area across the highway. Depending upon the current ownership of the resort on the piece of property next to the springs, the resort might be open to the public, or available only to private club members, or closed entirely. Do not enter the private land until you are sure you are not trespassing.

Directions to BLM land pools: From Las Vegas, drive 90 miles north on US 93 to Alamo. Continue four miles on US 93 to Ash Springs Resort on the right (east) side of the highway. Continue north beyond the end of the resort property fence and turn right on a narrow dirt road for 100 yards to the camping/campfire area and adjoining soaking pools.

Native guppies live in the water and nip at your body while you swim or soak. Posted signs ask that you not introduce any other type of fish into the water. Volunteers help to keep the place free of trash. Please do your part.

This ditch used to deliver the hot water to the now closed resort. Locals are keeping the ditches clean and have carved out soaking pools in areas of cooler water.

A delightful desert oasis with an abundance of water and a place to picnic.

112   WARM SPRINGS

● **East of Tonopah**

A hot, sandy-bottom ditch pool formed in a channel that originally fed a large outdoor swimming pool surrounded by barren, nearly treeless high desert. Elevation 1,800 feet. Open all year.

Natural mineral water at more than 120° emerges from the ground with a cloud of steamy vapors and flows down a well-maintained trench with white calcium deposits on both sides (volunteers keep it clean). Just before the water flows through a wide pipe under the road, the channel has been dammed and widened to form a two-foot pool where water temperature measures 110°. When the water emerges on the south side of US 6, the foot-deep channel measures 106-108° and gradually cools as it follows NV 375 for nearly a mile before disappearing into the terrain. Bathing suits are suggested since the pools are right along the road, even though traffic is sparse.

No services are available. There is still a phone booth at the now closed Warm Springs Bar.

Directions: Warm Springs is on US 6, 50 miles east of Tonopah, 160 miles from Bishop, CA, and 190 miles northwest of Las Vegas NV.

113   ROGERS WARM SPRING

● **Near the town of Overton**

A refreshing warm pond and shady picnic oasis on the barren north shore of Lake Mead in the Lake Mead National Recreation Area. Elevation 1,600 feet. Open all year.

Natural mineral water at approximately 90° flows directly up through a gravel bottom into a 100-foot-diameter pool at a sufficient rate to maintain the entire three-foot-deep pool at approximately 80°. Hundreds of gallons per minute flow over a cement and rock spillway in a series of small waterfalls. Bathing suits would be advisable at this location in the daytime.

There are no services available, and overnight parking (after 10 PM) is prohibited. It is eight and one-half miles to a store, restaurant, and service station in Overton, and five miles to a campground.

Directions: From the intersection of US 93 and NV 147 in the city of Henderson, go northeast on Lake Mead Drive. At the intersection with Northshore Road (NV 169), follow Northshore Road northeast toward Overton. Rogers Warm Spring is 4 miles beyond the Echo Bay Marina turnoff.

Alternate Directions: When approaching from the north, take the I-15 exit Logandale/Overton. Turn east on NV 169 to "Lake Mead National Recreation Area" and continue south for 27 miles to the Rogers Spring sign.

114 BAILEY'S HOT SPRINGS
Box 387   702 553-2395
■   **Beatty, NV 89003**

Primarily an RV park with three large, indoor, hot mineral water soaking pools. Located in the high desert country just east of Death Valley National Monument. Elevation 2,900 feet. Open all year.

Natural mineral water emerges from several artesian wells at 110° and bubbles up through the gravel bottoms of three immaculate, indoor soaking pools that used to be railroad water reservoirs. Flow rates are controlled to maintain different temperatures in the three pools, approximately 101°, 105°, and 108°. The rate of flow-through is sufficient to eliminate the need for chemical treatment of the water. Bathing suits are optional in the private-space pools. Pool use is included in the overnight RV fee, and pools are available on a day-use basis to tent campers and the general public for a small fee.

Facilities include tree-shaded full hookup RV spaces with picnic area and barbeque pits, showers, restroom, and a lawn for tent camping. No credit cards are accepted. It is six miles to a store, cafe, and service station.

Directions: From the only traffic signal in Beatty, go 5.5 miles north on US 95. Watch for the large sign on the east side of the road.

115 SILVER PEAK (ALKALAI) HOT SPRING

●   **Near the town of Goldfield**

Two brick-lined soaking pools at the edge of a salt flat in the remains of an abandoned turn-of-the-century hot springs resort, now used as a local party spot. Elevation 5,000 feet, Open all year.

Natural mineral water flows out of the ground through a flow pipe at 120°. On one edge of the source spring, volunteers have used bricks to build two large (four-six person) soaking pools in which the temperature is controlled by diverting or admitting hot water as desired. Wooden steps lead to the pools, and pieces of old carpet are around for sitting or sunning. Some people claim to enjoy the soak more when they close their eyes to block out the party trash. The apparent local custom is clothing optional.

There are no services on the premises, but there is plenty of level ground on which overnight parking is not prohibited. It is eleven miles to a store, service station, and motel in Goldfield.

Directions: From the town of Goldfield (27 miles south of Tonopah) drive north on US 95 for 4 miles and look for a sign to "Alkalai/Silver Peak" on the west side of the highway. Turn west and drive 6.8 miles on a rough paved road to a power substation. A large abandoned swimming pool is near the road, just past the power station. Follow the channel 50 feet up the hill toward the station to the soaking pools. This area can be very muddy after rain or snow.

116   FISH LAKE HOT WELL

● **Near the town of Dyer**

A cement-lined soaking pool on the edge of a barren desert wash in Fish Lake Valley, approximately half-way between Reno and Las Vegas. Winter is most beautiful, with snow-capped peaks encircling the valley. Elevation 4,800 feet. Open all year.

Natural mineral water emerges from a well casing at 105° and at a rate of more than fifty gallons per minute. The well was discovered in the 1880s when ranchers were drilling for oil. The well casing is surrounded by a six-foot by six-foot cement sump that maintains a water depth of four feet above a gravel bottom. From there it flows into a large, 102° cement soaking pool that can easily hold ten to twelve people. A three-foot wide cement deck surrounds the pool, with cinderblock and wooden benches on three sides. Overflow goes into a large man-made swimming hole stocked with a variety of large goldfish and where water temperature measures 95°. Then the water flows into a second pond at 85° and into a third cooler pool. Posted signs say no nude bathing, but the custom seems to be clothing optional at your own discretion, depending on the people present. The pool is handicap accessible with assistance.

There is an abundance of level space for overnight parking. Facilities include a fenced-off area around the tub and pools, metal barbeque stands, campfire rings, and trash receptacles. Signs about not trashing or vandalizing the area reflect the feeling that this is now a heavily used party and camping site. Please help keep it clean.

Directions: From the junction of NV 264 and NV 773, go 5.7 miles south on NV 264 to a gravel road on the east side of the highway. Follow this for 7 miles to a fork, then bear left for .1 mile to the springs. The gravel road is subject to flash-flood damage and should not be attempted at night.

Source maps: USGS *Davis Mountain* and *Rhyolite Ridge* (well not shown on map).

The area around the pools used to feel remote but has been "improved" over the past few years by Esmeralda County to provide recreation for residents and visitors. Unfortunately these improvements seem to have created severe problems—to the point that there are other signs posted warning that the pools will be destroyed if the vandalism does not stop.

117   WALLEY'S HOT SPRING RESORT
PO Box 26   702 782-8155
2001 Foothill Rd.
■ **Genoa, NV 89411**

Elegantly restored 1862 spa and luxury hotel located twelve miles east of Lake Tahoe at the foot of the Sierra Nevada Mountains. Elevation 4,700 feet. Open all year.

Natural mineral water flows from several wells at temperatures up to 160° and is then piped to the bathhouse and to six outdoor cement pools (two with jets) where the temperatures are maintained from 96-104°. The cement swimming pool uses bromine-treated creek water and averages 80°. Bathing suits are required in the outdoor pools.

Bed and breakfast is available in historic cottage accommodations. The main building is a two-story health club with separate men's and women's sections each containing a sauna, steambath and weight training equipment. Massage is also available in each section. Facilities include dining rooms and bars. Visa, MasterCard, and American Express are accepted. It is seven miles to a store, service station, and RV hookups. Phone for rates and reservations.

In 1862 an elegant spa and hotel was built on this exact location, adjacent to the Pony Express route and the Emigrant Trail. Over the generations, Walley's has hosted many notable figures, including President Grant, Mark Twain, Clark Gable, and Ida Lupino.

118   CARSON HOT SPRINGS
1500 Hot Springs Rd.
                          702 882-9863
■   Carson City, NV 89701

Older hot springs plunge with swimming pool and nine large private rooms, each containing a sunken tub large enough for eight persons. Located in the northeast outskirts of Carson City. Elevation 4,300 feet. Open all year.

Natural mineral water flows out of the ground at 126°. Air spray and evaporative cooling are used to lower this water temperature when pools are drained and refilled during each day. No chemical or city water is added. The outdoor swimming pool temperature is maintained at 98° in the summer and 102° in the winter. Individual room pool temperatures can be controlled as desired, from 95-110°. Bathing suits are required in the swimming pool, optional in the private rooms.

Massage, restaurant, and no-hookup RV parking are available on the premises. Visa and MasterCard are accepted. It is one mile to a store and service station.

Directions: From US 395 at the north end of Carson City, go east on Hot Springs Road 1 mile to plunge.

119   BOWERS MANSION
4005 US 395 North   702 849-1825
■   Carson City, NV 89704

A Washoe County Park with extensive picnic, playground, and parking facilities, in addition to a large modern swimming pool. Elevation 5,100 feet. Park open all year; pools open Memorial Day to Labor Day.

Natural mineral water pumped from wells at 116° is combined with cold well water as needed. The swimming pool and children's wading pool are maintained at 80°. Both pools are treated with bromine. Bathing suits are required. There is a charge for using the facilities.

There are no services available on the premises. Tours of the mansion are conducted from Mother's Day to the end of October. It is four miles to a restaurant, motel, service station, and RV hookups in Carson City.

Directions: Go 10 miles north of Carson City on US 395. Watch for signs and turn west on side road 1.5 miles to location.

If you are in this area during the summer months, follow your tour of the historic Bowers Mansion with a cooling soak in the natural mineral water pool.

UTAH

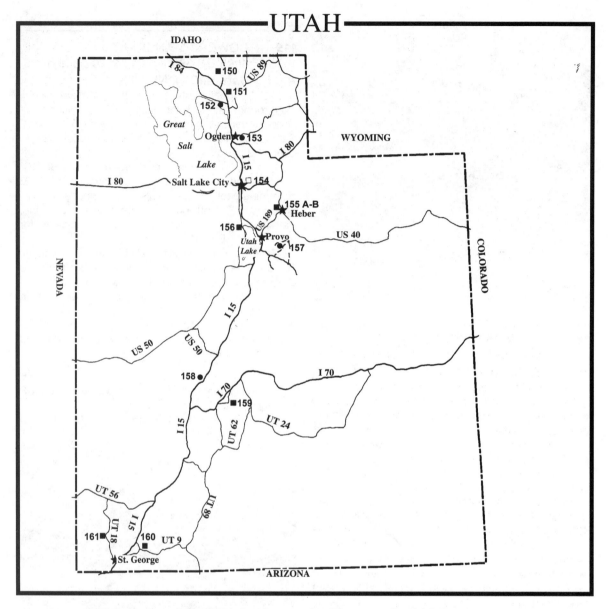

This map was designed to be used with a standard highway map.

MAP SYMBOLS

● Non-commercial mineral water pool

■ Commercial (fee) mineral water pool

□ Tap water resorts and rental locations

〜 Paved highway

╌ Unpaved road

⋯ Hiking trail

While the hot spring has been a commercial venture since 1901, previously it served as a wintering spot for Native Americans and, later, for the Chinese and Japanese who helped build the nearby railroad.

150   BELMONT SPRINGS
Box 36   **801 458-3200**
■   **Fielding, UT 84311**

Modern, commercial plunge with RV park and golf course in a large northern Utah valley. Elevation 4,300 feet. Open April through October; scuba park open during winter.

Natural mineral water flows out of artesian wells at 125° and is piped to four outdoor pools, all of which are treated at night with minimal chlorine that burns off by daytime. The large swimming pool is maintained at 93°, a hot-tub soaking pool at 106°, and two hot-tub hydrojet pools at approximately 106°. Bathing suits are required.

Locker rooms, two picnic areas, golf course, overnight parking, RV hookups, a scuba diving park, and a tropical fish farm are available on the premises. A cafe, store, service station, and motel are available within ten miles. Scuba instructors and classes are welcome. No credit cards are accepted.

Directions: From the town of Plymouth (exit 394) on I-15, go one mile south and watch for resort sign.

151   CRYSTAL HOT SPRINGS
8215 North Hwy 38   801 547-0772
■   **Honeyville, UT 84314**

Small, historical resort featuring one of the world's largest side-by-side hot and cold springs. The property includes spacious, tree-shaded lawns for picnics and camping. Elevation 4,700 feet. Open all year.

Natural mineral water flows out of a spring at 135° and is piped to three outdoor hydrojet pools that are maintained at 102°, 104°, and 106° on a flow-through basis requiring no chemical treatment. A large outdoor soaking pool of natural mineral water is maintained at 100° with a minimum of chlorine treatment. Similar water is used in the catch-pool at the bottom of two large waterslides. There is also an Olympic-size swimming pool that uses cold spring water, is drained and filled weekly, and requires a minimum of chlorine treatment. Bathing suits are required.

Locker rooms, snack bar, overnight camping and RV hookups are available on the premises. It is four blocks to a store and fifteen miles to a motel. Major credit cards are accepted.

Directions: From I-15, take the Honeyville exit. Go one mile east on UT 240 to UT 38, then 2.5 miles north to the resort on the west side of the highway.

Ogden Hot Springs is often crowded during the weekends due to its proximity to town. Help keep it clean.

152   STINKY SPRINGS

● **West of the town of Brigham City**

A small, partly vandalized, cement-block bathhouse alongside a highway in the flat country north of the Great Salt Lake. Elevation 4,000 feet. Open all year.

Natural mineral water flows out of a spring at 118°, through a culvert under the highway, and into three cement soaking pits in the abandoned building. Temperature within each pool is controlled by diverting the hot-water flow as desired. In recent years volunteers have kept the surrounding party trash to a minimum, but the water does have a sulfur-dioxide smell. The apparent local custom is clothing optional within the building.

There are no services available on the premises.

Directions: From I-15, take the Golden Spike exit, then go 9 miles west through Corinne on UT 83. The building is on the south side of the road shortly before you reach Little Mountain, a rocky hill on the north side of the road.

153   OGDEN HOT SPRINGS

● **East of the city of Ogden**

Small, primitive hot spring at the river's edge, located in a beautiful river gorge in Ogden Canyon. Elevation 4,800 feet. Open all year, subject to annual flooding.

Natural mineral water flows out of a spring at 130° and through a pipe and hoses to a volunteer-built, rock-and-mud pool at 107°. The water continues flowing into a rock-and-cement-bottomed pool at 101°. The sides have been built up to prevent the entrance of river water. The temperature is controlled by diverting the hoses when desired. The apparent local custom is clothing optional, even though the highway is visible.

There are no services available on the premises.

Directions: Exit I-15 in Ogden at SR 39 (12th St.) and go east 4.9 miles to the mouth of Ogden Canyon. Park on either side of the road just after passing under suspended water pipe. Short trail downstream to spring starts at mile 9 green marker. (If pulling a trailer, go 1 mile farther upstream to a turnaround and come back to park.)

154   WASATCH SPA
3955 S. State St.   801 264-TUBS

□   Salt Lake City, UT 84107

Basic rent-a-tub establishment, plus spa sales and service, on a main street in southern Salt Lake City.

Private-space hot pools using bromine-treated tap water are for rent to the public by the hour. Four indoor, fiberglass, hydrojet pools are maintained at temperatures ranging from 102-104°. Major credit cards are accepted. Phone for rates, reservations, and directions.

155A THE HOMESTEAD
700 N. Homestead Rd.
800 327-7220
■ Midway, UT 84049

Upscale, historic, destination resort specializing in leisure vacations and group meetings, with extensive access to summer and winter sports and recreation. Elevation 5,600 feet. Open all year.

Natural mineral water flows from a tufa-cone spring at 92°. The water temperature is boosted, and the water is piped to one small outdoor soaking pool that averages 100° and is not treated with chemicals. All other pools use chlorine-treated tap water. The large outdoor swimming pool is maintained at 85°, the indoor hydrojet pool at 102°, and the indoor lap pool at 90°. There is also a dry sauna available. Pool use is available to registered guests only. Bathing suits are required.

Locker rooms, dining rooms, an eighteen-hole championship golf course, hotel rooms, suites, and bed and breakfast are available on the premises. It is two miles to a store, service station, and RV hookups. Major credit cards are accepted.

Directions: From Heber City on US 189, go west on UT 113 to the town of Midway and follow signs to the resort.

155B MOUNTAIN SPAA RESORT
800 North 200 East   801 654-0807
801 654-0721
■ Midway, UT 84049

Historic resort located in beautiful Heber Valley, one mile from Wasatch Mountain State Park. Elevation 5,700 feet. Open daily from Memorial Day to Labor Day and during April, May, September, and October, weather permitting.

Natural mineral water flows from cone-shaped tufa craters at 110° and is piped to two pools. The outdoor swimming pool, with kiddie slide and large deck area, is maintained at 90-95°. The indoor swimming pool is built inside a large crater, maintains a temperature of 95-100°. Both pools are drained twice weekly, disinfected, and refilled.

Guest house, cabins, soda fountain, snack bar, game room, locker rooms, lawn and picnic area, overnight camping, and RV hookups are available on the premises. Banquet room and pavilion facilities available for large groups. Visa and MasterCard are accepted.

Directions: From Heber City on US 189, go west on UT 113 to the town of Midway. Turn north on River Road, go .7 mile to 600 North in Midway, and follow signs to the resort.

The building in the background houses the swimming pool, which is built in a large natural crater.

156 SARATOGA RESORT
Saratoga Rd. at Utah Lake
801 768-8206
■ **Lehi, UT 84043**

Lakeside recreation resort with picnic grounds, rides, and boat-launching facilities. Elevation 4,200 feet. Open May to September.

Natural mineral water is pumped out of a well at 120° and is piped to four outdoor pools, all of which are treated with chlorine. One large hydrojet pool is maintained at 100°. The swimming pool, diving pool, and waterslide catch pool are maintained at 75-80°. Bathing suits are required.

Locker rooms, snack bar, overnight camping, and RV hookups are available on the premises. There are also several amusement park rides. No credit cards are accepted.

Directions: From the town of Lehi on I-15, go west on UT 73 and follow signs to resort.

157 DIAMOND FORK HOT SPRINGS
(also known as Fifth Water Canyon)

● **Spanish Fork, UT (South of Provo)**

Three volunteer-built rock pools in a beautiful canyon at the end of an easy hike, with flowing creek and large waterfall. Elevation 5,800 feet. Open all year subject to snow.

Natural mineral water flows out of the ground at 125° and depending how rocks have been moved along the creek, combines with creek water to cool the higher pool to a comfortable temperature. The lower pool receives the overflow from the upper pool and is slightly cooler. The third pool is across the creek and is quite hot when the creek is low, but it cools some when creek water is high and flows over into pool. The apparent local custom is clothing optional.

There are no services available on the premises, but overnight camping is not prohibited at the trailhead and at the many pull-out spots along the creek. It is fifteen minutes to a mini-mart in Spanish Fork.

Directions: From the junction of SR 89 and SR 6 (off I-15 south of Provo), proceed south on SR 6 for 6.2 miles. Turn left on paved road (Diamond Fork) and drive exactly 10 miles (passing many nice camping sites) to trailhead parking area. Cross bridge and start up trail. Stay straight and do not turn right over the second bridge. Cross the bridge over the creek. After 1 mile, proceed another 1.5 miles slightly uphill on a well-maintained trail along Fifth Water Canyon to the spring and waterfall.

● **South of Provo, near Meadow**

Delightful large rock pool with ample sitting room on underwater stone ledges. Located in the pasture lands of Utah with unobstructed views of the Pahvant Mountain Range. Elevation 4,800 feet. Open all year.

Natural mineral water flows up through the bottom of a beautifully clear, room-sized pool at 100°. Several heavy ropes across the pool allow you to remain on the surface while viewing the clear, deep portions of the pool. The apparent local custom is clothing optional.

There are no facilities on the premises, but overnight parking is not prohibited. It is six miles to a store in Meadow.

Directions: From I-15 (south of Provo) take exit 158 at Meadow. Turn east under freeway and continue 1.6 miles. Turn right on gravel road and continue west over freeway. Cross two cattle guards at 5 miles on gravel road. Turn left into parking area. Spring is about 200 yards south.

Diamond Fork Hot Springs is indeed the jewel in Utah's crown. The best hot spring in the state, it offers three hot soaking pools and a spectacular waterfall.

159 MYSTIC HOT SPRINGS OF MONROE

575 East First North   801 527-4014

■ Monroe, UT 84754

RV park with restaurant, swimming pool, and campground set aboutwith razzleberry bushes, and a hillside soaking pool overlooking a green agricultural valley. Elevation 5,500 feet. Open all year.

Natural mineral water flows out of a spring at 168°, cooling as it flows across the mountains into a soaking pool where the temperature ranges from 100-105°. The water then flows on to the natural tropical fish ponds. Bathing suits are required.

Biking and hiking trails, store, picnic area, camping, full RV hookups, tepees, and a sweat lodge are available on the premises. It is a short walk to the large and colorful Red Hill Spring, the natural warm water caves, and the adjoining tropical fish pond. A service station is within four blocks. No credit cards are accepted.

Directions: From the town of Richfield on I-70, go 6 miles south on US 89, then 3 miles on UT 118 to the town of Monroe. Follow signs to the resort.

160 PAH TEMPE HOT SPRINGS RESORT

825 North 800 East   801 635-2879

Fax   801 635-2353

■ Hurricane, UT 84737

Located in the spectacular Virgin River Canyon, eighteen miles from St. George and twenty miles southwest of Zion National Park. Elevation 3,000 feet. Open all year; reservations required.

Natural mineral water flows up from the earth and out a canyon wall into two primitive, sandy-bottom soaking pools at approximately 105°. Much of the time there are also natural pools in the river. (Rebuilding of some of the riverbank soaking pools is taking place following the 1992 earthquake.) There is one shaded, outdoor swimming pool that averages 94° and does not require chemical treatment. Bathing suits are required; alcohol and tobacco are prohibited.

A bed and breakfast with four charming rooms, shared bathroom, and a central dining facility is available, as are two cabins with private baths. Accommodations for large groups are located nearby. A vegetarian breakfast is served daily. Reiki and yoga classes are offered with advance, pre-paid reservations. Visa and MasterCard and approved checks are accepted.

Directions: From St. George: Take I-15 to exit 16 (Zion National Park, the Grand Canyon). This ramp will merge into UT 9. Continue on UT 9 through the town of Hurricane and turn right onto Enchanted Way located just before a large bridge spanning the Virgin River. Follow the paved, winding road down to the gate.

From Zion National Park: Stay on UT 9 through the town of LaVerkin. Turn left onto Enchanted Way and follow the directions as above.

Note: Because of some significant man-caused damage to the aquifer, the resort owners must limit the number of people per day. Advanced reservations are required. Please call for update and reservations.

A swimming pool and two sandy-bottom pools are currently available for your use at *Pah Tempe Hot Springs*. Pools located along the river, such as the one pictured below, are in the process of slowly being rebuilt. They were damaged both by the earthquake and by man-made destruction when the county water district blasted the area and ruptured the hot springs, disturbing the flow.

161　VEYO POOL
287 East Veyo Resort Rd.
801 574-2300

■　**Veyo, UT 84782**

Completely remodeled, spacious plunge and picnic park with a small running stream. Elevation 4,600 feet. Open end of March to Labor Day.

Natural mineral water flows out of an artesian well at a temperature of 98° and flows over a rock waterfall into the newly redone outdoor swimming pool that is chlorinated and maintains a temperature of 85°. Bathing suits are required.

Locker rooms, snack bar, restaurant with live dancing Friday and Saturday night on the patio in the back, camping sites, a volleyball court, and a picnic area are available on the premises. It is one mile to a store and service station, eight miles to overnight camping and RV hookups, and twelve miles to a motel. No credit cards are accepted. Call to reserve camp sites and picnic areas.

Directions: From the city of St. George on I-15, go 19 miles north on UT 18 to the town of Veyo and follow signs to the resort.

Extensive renovations at *Veyo Hot Springs* include a beautiful waterfall in the rocky backdrop behind the swimming pool. The pool has become so popular it is suggested that you reserve your picnic spot and camping area during the summer's crowded weekends.

COLORADO

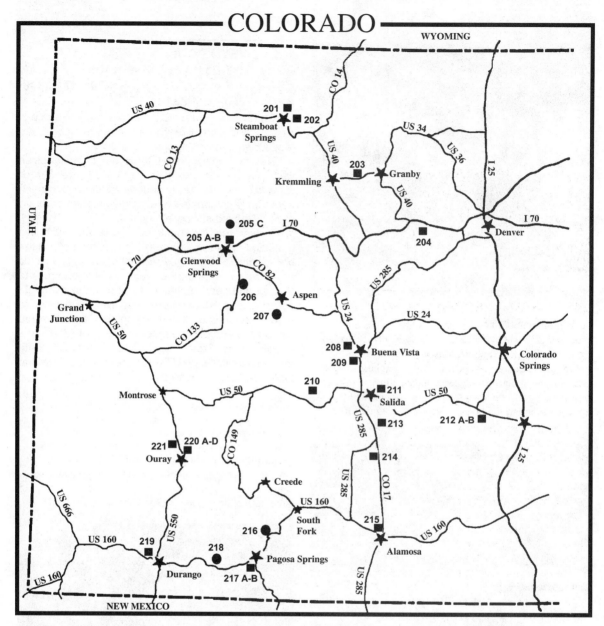

This map was designed to be used with a standard highway map.

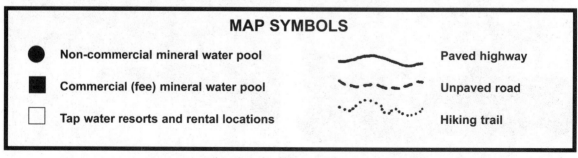

MAP SYMBOLS

- ● Non-commercial mineral water pool
- ■ Commercial (fee) mineral water pool
- □ Tap water resorts and rental locations

- Paved highway
- Unpaved road
- Hiking trail

201   STRAWBERRY PARK HOT SPRINGS

PO Box 77332   970 879-0342
■   **Steamboat Springs, CO 80477**

A unique hot spring that manages to retain a maximum of primitive naturalness while improving the services for a variety of hot-spring enthusiasts. Elevation 7,500 feet. Open all year.

Natural mineral water flows out of many hillside fissures at 146° and cools successively as it is channeled into a series of creek-bank, rock-and-masonry pools where it is combined with creek water to provide a range of soaking temperatures (from 100-105° in the upper pool down to 85° in the lower pool). Continuous flow-through in all pools eliminates the need for chemical treatment. Bathing suits are required during the day (10 AM until dark); optional at night. Handicap access with assistance.

Cabins, overnight camping, and catered private parties are available on the premises. Projected for 1996 is a private pool and changing area, remodeling of four camping cabins, and a small meeting area for rustic retreats and seminars. Massage is also available. A bathhouse provides showers for overnight guests, and cold drinks can be purchased.It is seven miles to all other services. No credit cards are accepted.

Directions: From US 40 in the town of Steamboat Springs, go north on 7th St. and follow signs 7 miles to location at the end of County Road 36. The steep grades are not recommended for trailers. Four-wheel drive or tire chains are required on all vehicles during the winter season. Phone for hours, rates, reservations, and transportation from Steamboat Springs. Note: It is well worth the expense of the shuttle during the winter months, as the roads are narrow and very slippery, resulting in accidents and possible closure of the road during the winter.

Wherever you choose to soak, the water is wonderful, the views are great, and the whole place is a treat to visit.

202 STEAMBOAT SPRINGS HEALTH AND RECREATION
PO Box 1211   **970 879-1828**
■ **Steamboat Springs, CO 80477**

Large community plunge, hot pool, water slide, and sauna near the city center. Elevation 6,700 feet. Open all year.

Natural mineral water flows out of a spring at 103° and is piped to five pools that are treated with bromine and ozone. The soaking pool is maintained at a temperature of 101°, the water slide pick-up pool at 90°, and the large lap pool at 80°. Two large outdoor hydrojet pools are maintained at 102°. Bathing suits are required. Pools are handicap accessible.

Facilities include locker rooms, saunas, snack bar, weight room, cardiovascular equipment and tennis courts. Exercise classes, massage, and child care are available on the premises. It is three blocks to a cafe, store, service station, and motel and two miles to overnight camping and RV hookups. Visa and MasterCard are accepted.

Location: On the north side of US 40, at the east edge of the city of Steamboat Springs.

203　HOT SULPHUR SPRINGS

■ PO Box 275　　　　970 725-3306
Hot Sulphur Springs, CO 80451

Older resort located on US 40, which winds through the Rocky Mountains. Elevation 7,600 feet. Open in summer.

Natural mineral water flows out of a spring at 115° and is piped to a variety of pools. The outdoor swimming pool is treated with chlorine and maintained around 80°. Two outdoor soaking pools are maintained at 100-108° on a flow-through basis that eliminates the need for chemical treatment. There are two indoor pools in private spaces that rent by the hour, and there are two indoor pools in separate men's and women's bathhouses. Temperatures in these pools are 110°. Bathing suits are required.

Dressing rooms, motel rooms, and a picnic area are available on the premises. A free campground on the river is located adjacent to the property. It is three blocks to a cafe, store, and service station, and seventeen miles to RV hookups. No credit cards are accepted.

Directions: From US 40 in the town of Hot Sulphur Springs, follow signs north across the bridge to the resort.

The outdoor pools with the water flowing in over the cliffs are the special treat at *Hot Sulphur Springs*.

Imagine a tropical setting in the middle of Colorado! This large dome with all its greenery also contains the pool, providing year-round swimming enjoymment.

204　INDIAN SPRINGS RESORT

■ PO Box 1300　　　　303 623-2050
Idaho Springs, CO 80452

Popular historic resort just off I-70 in the Arapaho National Forest. Elevation 7,300 feet. Open all year.

Natural mineral water flows out of three underground springs at 124°. Within the men's cave are three walk-in soaking pools ranging in temperature from 104-112°. Within the women's cave are four similar pools. There are four private-space soaking pools outdoors and eleven private-space tubs indoors That are large enough for couples or families. Temperatures are approximately 104°. All of the above pools operate on a flow-through basis; a minimum of bromine is added. A minimum of bromine is also used in the large, landscaped indoor pool, which is maintained at 96° in the winter and 90° in the summer. Bathing suits are required in the swimming pool and prohibited in the caves.

Mud baths, locker rooms, massage, dining room, hotel rooms, overnight camping, and RV hookups are available on the premises. It is five blocks to a store and service station. Visa and MasterCard are accepted.

Directions: From I-70, take the Idaho Springs exit to the business district, then follow signs south on Soda Springs Road to resort.

A complete destination resort close to major winter ski resorts and summer mountain recreation. As a bonus you get to soak in the world's largest outdoor hot springs pool.

205 A   GLENWOOD HOT SPRINGS LODGE AND POOL

PO Box 308   970 945-6571
■   Glenwood Springs, CO 81601

A very large commercial resort, called by many "the grandaddy of them all," near the center of town on the north bank of the Colorado River. Elevation 5,700 feet. Open all year.

Natural mineral water flows out of the spring at 122°. The water is cooled by heat exchangers and supplies four pools. Three of these are treated with chlorine. The 104° therapy pool uses pure untreated spring water that turns over the entire pool contents every hour. The one-hundred-foot-long outdoor soaking pool has eight bubble jet therapy chairs. The two-block-long (405 foot) swimming pool is maintained at a temperature of 90° in summer and 93° in winter. It has a sand/charcoal filtration system that turns the entire pool over four times per day. Water is further purified by a high-tech ozonator system for water clarity. The water slide catch-pool is 85°, and the summer-only kiddie pool is kept at 92°. A private athletic club is available for walk-ins and includes a water jet indoor therapy pool maintained at 102° and treated with bromine. The club also has a steam room, sauna, weight room, and four racquetball courts. Bathing suits are required everywhere. The entire facility is handicap accessible.

Changing facilities, rental swimsuits and towels, a restaurant, sport shop, miniature golf course, massage, and a 107-room lodge are available on the premises. It is one block to a store and service stations and two miles to overnight camping and RV hookups. All major credit cards are accepted.

42

205 B   YAMPAH SPA AND VAPOR CAVES
709 E. 6th   `   970 945-0667
■   Glenwood Springs, CO 81601

Natural underground geothermal steam baths located in historic, natural vapor caves whose use dates back to the time of the Ute Indians. Elevation 5,700. Open all year.

Natural mineral water creates vapor that emerges at 125° within three caves. All caves are coed, and bathing suits are required. There are also two private-space hydrojet pools filled with tap water, treated with chlorine, and maintained at 104°.

Changing facilities, massage, and a full range of health and beauty treatments including facials, herbal wraps, body scrubs, body mud, and massage are available on the premises. It is three blocks to a cafe, store, service station and motel and five miles to overnight camping and RV hookups. Visa and MasterCard are accepted.

205 C   SOUTH CANYON SPRINGS

●   West of Glenwood Springs

A primitive, city-owned geothermal springs with a long history of controversy involving nudity and dynamiting of volunteer-built pools. Located in a narrow wooded canyon leading south off of the Colorado River. Elevation 5,200 feet. Open all year.

Natural mineral water flows out of the ground at 118° cooling to approximately 107° as it flows into four rock-and-sand pools, two on the creek and two up the hillside across from the creek. The area is not currently fenced or posted, and there is no recent pattern of harassment. The local custom is clothing optional.

There are no services on the premises but overnight parking is not prohibited.

Directions: From Glenwood Springs take I-70 to the South Canyon exit 111, cross the Colorado River, cross the railroad tracks, and go up canyon .6 mile. Park along the west bank at a pull-out. Trail starts at north end of pull-out and goes through woods for about 100 yards (take left fork at the Y) to the creek. The first pool is directly across the creek by a small waterfall; the larger and best pool is up the hill behind the first pool.

At this time the pools seem to be open and well cared for. There have been threats to close them down, so check in town before heading out there.

If you try to get to *Penny Hot Springs* after the spring rains, you will be disappointed since they will be underwater.

206   PENNY HOT SPRINGS

● **North of the town of Redstone**

Primitive, riverbank hot spring seasonally flooded by high water. Elevation 8,000 feet. Open all year (subject to flooding).

Natural mineral water flows out of a spring at 133° and drops directly into the Crystal River. In between annual high-water washouts, volunteers build rock-and-sand pools in which hot mineral water and cold river water can be mixed to a comfortable temperature. Because the location is close to the highway, bathing suits are strongly recommended.

There are no services on the premises. All services are within three miles in the historic mining town of Redstone.

Directions: From Glenwood Springs, as you head toward Redstone, on the east side of CO 133 .8 mile south of mile marker 56, there is a small parking area on the east side of the highway next to the river. A short, obvious trail goes down to the pools, visible from the embankment.

207   CONUNDRUM HOT SPRINGS

● **South of the town of Aspen**

Two primitive pools surrounded by spectacular Rocky Mountain scenery midway between Aspen and Ashcroft in a designated Wilderness Area of the White River National Forest. Elevation 11,200 feet. Open all year.

Natural mineral water flows out of a spring at 100° into two volunteer-built, three-to-four-feet deep, rock-and-sand pools right off a very popular trail. The spring may be crowded. A long rugged climb will not necessarily give you quiet solitude. The local custom is clothing optional.

There are no services on the premises. It is a nine mile, gentle hike from the trailhead and five miles of rough road to a campsite. It is twenty miles to all other services.

This is a rewarding but hazardous location. Be sure to obtain directions, instructions, and information about current trail conditions at a White River National Forest ranger station before attempting the trip.

208   COTTONWOOD HOT SPRINGS INN
18999 County Rd. 306 719 395-6434
800 241-4119
■   Buena Vista, CO 81211

A small, relaxing country inn in a natural eco-system nestled in a high mountain valley, surrounded by the San Isabel National Forest in the highest mountain range in the continental US. Close to summer and winter recreation. Elevation 8,550 feet. Open all year (345 days of sunshine).

Odorless natural mineral water flows out of a well at 187° and is gravity fed into the entire facility, feeding three beautiful, natural, rock-lined soaking pools, each cabin's individual private tub, and three outdoor private hydropools (adult only, clothing optional) at 102-110°. All pools, including a cold plunge, operate on a flow-through basis that requires no chemical treatment. The mineral water is so pure that it is used as tap water throughout the resort. Bathing suits are optional within the fenced private spaces. All pools are available to the public as well as to registered guests. This is a drug and alcohol-free environment.

Twelve rooms with private baths are located on the second floor of the main lodge. There are three rustic, creekside cabins, each with an individual trough-type hot tub, and one three-bedroom cottage with a private tub on its own deck. (Three-day minimum stay is required in cabins and cottage during high season.) Camping tepees are also available. There are no TVs or phones in any of the rooms. Available for your enjoyment are the community room, library, and kitchen. The community room is also available for group meetings, seminars, workshops, reunions, and special events. Meals can be arranged for groups, or the kitchen can be leased for your use. Major credit cards are accepted. It is five and one-half miles to all other services. Phone or write for rates and reservations.

Directions: From US 24 in Buena Vista, go west 5.5 miles on CO 306, the road to Cottonwood Pass. Watch for resort signs on the right side of the road.

Surrounded by the highest mountain range in the continental US, unlimited recreational activitiesare available in the area, such as hiking, fishing, mountain climbing, horseback riding, skiing, golfing, sightseeing, ghost towns, and some first-class water for white water rafting and kayaking.

210   WAUNITA HOT SPRINGS RANCH
8007 County Road 887
970 641-1266
■   Gunnison, CO 81230

American-plan guest ranch surrounded by Gunnison National Forest. Elevation 9,000 feet. Open all year.

Natural mineral water flows out of several springs at 175° and is piped to a swimming pool and to geo-thermal heating units in the buildings. The swimming pool is maintained at 95° and operates on a flow-through basis, so only a minimum of chlorine treatment is needed. Pool use is reserved for registered guests, with a minimum stay of six days by prior reservation only. Bathing suits are required. Limited handicap accessibility.

Guest-ranch services, including rooms, meals, saddle horses, and fishing, are available on the premises. It is fifteen miles to a store, service station, and overnight camping and twenty-eight miles to RV hookups. No credit cards are accepted.

Directions: From the town of Gunnison, go 19 miles east on US 50, then follow signs 8 miles north to the ranch.

209   MOUNT PRINCETON HOT SPRINGS
County Road 162   719 395-2361
■   Nathrop, CO 81236

Large, modern resort between Leadville and Salida, surrounded by San Isabel National Forest. Elevation 8,500 feet. Open all year.

Natural mineral water flows out of a spring at 132°. Odorless and tasteless, this water is used in all pipes. Three outdoor swimming pools, one Olympic-size, are maintained at temperatures between 85-95° and are treated with chlorine. All pools are available to the public as well as to registered guests. There are several natural spots down in Chalk Creek. Bathing suits are required.

Locker rooms, restaurant, hotel rooms, picnic area, saddle horses, fishing, and hiking are available on the premises. Skiing and river rafting are close by. A conference center/party room is available for large groups. It is five miles to all other services. Visa and MasterCard are accepted.

Directions: From US 285 in the town of Nathrop, go west 5 miles on CO 162 to resort.

211 SALIDA HOT SPRINGS
410 West Rainbow Blvd.
719 539-6738

■ **Salida, CO 81201**

Modernized, indoor municipal plunge, hot baths, park, and playground. Elevation 7,000 feet. Open all year.

Natural mineral water flows out of Poncha Springs at 200° and is piped six miles to Salida. The large indoor swimming pool is maintained at a temperature of 100-104°, the lap pool is maintained at 90-92°, and a shallow baby pool is 96°. All pools are treated with chlorine. There are six private indoor soaking pools that are drained and refilled after each use and in which the water temperature is controlled by the customer. An extensive warm-water recreational program for people afflicted with arthritis is being offered. Bathing suits are required everywhere except in private soaking pools.

Locker rooms are available on the premises. It is less than five blocks to all other services. No credit cards are accepted.

Directions: From the junction of US 50 and US 285, go 6 miles east on US 50. Look for signs on the north side of the street.

Visible behind the hot waterfall at *Desert Reef* is the steam from the artesian well that keeps this beautiful tub filled at just the right temperature all year round. The sandy part of the beach consists of a regulation-size volleyball court to the left of the pool.

212 A DESERT REEF BEACH CLUB
PO Box 503   719 784-6134

■ **Penrose, CO 81240**

A small, remote, recreation club located east of Florence, Colorado. The club has grown up around a geothermal well in the desert foothills south of Colorado Springs. Elevation 5,200 feet. Open all year on Wednesday, Thursday, Saturday, and Sunday, 10 AM to 10 PM.

Natural mineral water flows out of an artesian well at 130° and is piped to a dramatic large pool where the water flows in over a waterfall on a flow-through basis so that no chemical treatment of the water is necessary. Flow rate is adjusted to maintain pool temperature within a comfortable range for soaking through all seasons. Bathing suits are optional.

There is a landscaped lawn area for sunning and picnicking, and cold drinks are available on the premises. A large greenhouse in which plants are raised is also used as a meeting room, shelter, and massage studio. Therapeutic massage and Trager are offered. Regulation size sand volleyball court and horseshoe pits are provided for your enjoyment.

Visa and MasterCard are accepted. It is two miles to all other services. As this is a membership facility, it is necessary to phone during business hours for information on guest passes, rates, and directions.

212 B THE WELL
Hwy 50 at Penrose   719 372-9250
                          800 898 WELL

■   **Penrose, CO 81240**

Large, hot mineral water swimming/soaking pool recently reopened after being abandoned for years. Located in high desert country between two mountain ranges in a broad valley called the Banana Belt of Colorado, with sunshine 350 days a year. Just west of Pueblo and Colorado Springs. Elevation 5,200 feet. Open all year (except Thanksgiving and Christmas); closed Tuesdays and Wednesdays.

Artesian well water at 108° emerges from a depth of 2,000 feet and flows through a pipe at 325 gallons per minute, showering into a large, oval-shaped, seventy-foot diameter cement pool. Pool temperature is maintained at approximately 98-100° in winter and 94° in summer and is controlled by the amount of aeration. No chemicals are added to the water, which remains clear due to CO_2 that bubbles into it. The pool is drained and cleaned once a week. Clothing or no clothing is entirely optional.

Facilities include overnight RV and tent sites (no hookups), laundromat, modern bathhouse, cabana building with soft drink machine, volleyball, and horseshoes. Future plans include cabins, sauna, and bed and breakfasts. Massage is available. No cameras or radios are allowed, and no glass of any kind in the pool area. Facilities are handicap accessible with assistance. Nonmembers are welcome to use the facilities as well as members, who receive discounted day-use and overnight fees. It is one and one-half miles to a motel, restaurant, gas, and market in Penrose.

Directions: From the junction of US 50 and CO 115 (36 miles southwest of Colorado Springs, 27 miles west of Pueblo), drive west for 1 mile to the second highway crossover. The Well is at the only lamppost streetlight on the south side of the street.

The rate of water flow is so great that no chemicals are ever needed in this large cement pool, which has recently been reopened—luckily for all of you looking for a fun place to soak.

213 VALLEY VIEW HOT SPRINGS
PO Box 175   719 256-4315

■ **Villa Grove, CO 81155**

Unique combination of clothing-optional primitive hot springs and primitive camping facilities on the west slope of the Sangre De Cristo Mountains. Elevation 8,700 feet. Open all year.

Natural mineral water flows out of several springs at temperatures ranging from 85-96°. All pools are supplied on a flow-through basis so that no chemical treatment is needed. The main outdoor cement swimming pool is maintained at 85°. The outdoor soaking pool is built right over a spring, so the water flowing up through the gravel bottom maintains a temperature of 96° in the pool. The small gravel-bottom upper pool is also built right over a spring, and the pool temperature varies from 80-105° depending on the volume of snow melt. There is also a small soaking pool at 83° inside the wood-fired sauna building. The waterfall pool is maintained at 96°. Clothing is optional everywhere on the extensive grounds.

Rustic cabins and tent spaces are available on the premises. It is twelve miles to all other services. Visa and MasterCard are accepted.

Note: This is primarily a membership facility, with the premises reserved for members and their guests on holidays and weekends. The public is welcome to visit during the week. Write or phone first for full information.

Directions: From the junction of US 285 and CO 17 near Mineral Hot Springs, take the gravel road CR-GG due east 7 miles to the location.

A must stop for any of you hot spring enthusiasts who like to be "barefoot all over." A variety of pools and accommodations are here for you to enjoy.

You can watch the sun set or the moon rise over the Sangre De Cristo Mountains from any of the glassed-in pools (right and above) at *Mineral Hot Springs Spa.*

214 MINERAL HOT SPRINGS SPA
28640 CR 58 EE   719 256-4328
■ **Moffat, CO 81143**

A newly renovated bathhouse at an historic resort, located in the north end of the San Luis Valley in southern Colorado, with spectacular views of the sunsets and moonrises of the Sangre De Cristo Mountains. Elevation 7,747 feet. Open all year for day use.

Natural mineral water flows from two main springs at temperatures ranging from 90-140°, providing three outdoor soaking pools with sufficient flow through to require no chemical treatment and to keep water at optimal temperatures according to seasonal conditions. The tower pool, under the old water tower, is five feet deep. All pools are tiled and protected by glassed-in decks, providing wonderful views. The bathhouse includes private individual tubs with controllable temperatures. Bathing suits required in public areas.

Men's and women's lockers, a sauna, massage, wraps and spa treatment, a shop, snack foods and beverages, a gallery of local artisans, gardens, and picnic area are all available on the grounds. A separate pool and deck area is available for groups and private parties. Overnight facilities are planned for the future, and several small rural inns and bed and breakfasts are within a half-hour drive. Credit cards are accepted. It is six miles to all other services.

Location: On Colorado 17 1 mile south of the junction with US 285, 50 miles north of Alamosa, and 30 miles south of Salida.

215 SPLASHLAND HOT SPRINGS
Box 972   719 589-6307(summer)
719 589-5772 (off season)
■ **Alamosa, CO 81101**

Large, rural, community-owned plunge in the center of a wide, high valley. Elevation 7,500 feet. Open Memorial Day through Labor Day.

Natural mineral water flows out of a spring at 106° and is piped to a large outdoor swimming pool that maintains a temperature of approximately 94° and to a wading pool for toddlers. The water is treated with chlorine. Bathing suits are required.

Locker rooms, suit and towel rentals, and a snack bar are available on the premises. It is one mile to a cafe, store, and service station and two miles to all other services. No credit cards are accepted.

Location: On CO 17, 1 mile north of Alamosa.

216 RAINBOW (WOLF CREEK PASS) HOT SPRINGS

● **Northeast of the town of Pagosa Springs**

A primitive riverside hot spring at the end of a very rugged five-mile hike in the Weminuche Wilderness, northwest of CO 160. Elevation 9,000 feet, with a 1,000-foot elevation gain from the trailhead. Open all year (subject to flooding). Hard to reach during winter (this is avalanche country).

Natural mineral water flows out of a spring under a rock, cascades down the side of a bluff leaving a rainbow-colored pattern formed by the minerals, and fills two shallow, eight-to-ten person, rock-log-and-mud pools at the east edge of the San Juan River. A high rate of geothermal flow maintains a temperature of more than 100° in these pools. A third sandy-bottom, twelve-inch-deep pool is approximately one-hundred yards up river. Water at 106° bubbles up through the bottom into this rock-and-mud pool. This pool is useable only during the low water season of July and August. Clothing is optional.

There are no services available except pack-in camping areas scattered along the trail. Two national forest campgrounds are located one and one-half to two miles before the trailhead. Three miles before the trailhead is a trailer park with hookups, showers, propane, cabins, outfitters for horse rides, fishing, and snowmobile tours. It is seventeen miles from the trailhead to all other services in Pagosa Springs.

Directions: From the eastern end of Pagosa Springs, at the junction of CO 160 and CO 84, drive northeast on CO 160 for 14 miles to a national forest sign for West Fork Road, Trailhead, FS 648. Turn left (north) and drive 3 miles, past two national forest campgrounds to a parking area and trailhead, following signs for Rainbow Trail. The trail begins with a short steep climb up a 4WD road through Born Lake Ranch. Stay on the trail; you are on private property. After passing a sign saying "Hot Springs 4 miles," bear left when the trail forks. Cross the first of three bridges over the creek after passing a sign for "Weminuche Wilderness." When the trail forks after the third bridge, take the left fork up a very steep trail. Rainbow Trail is marked by red-painted horizontal steel bars extending from trees. At the junction with Beaver Creek Trail, continue on Rainbow Trail. It is approximately 1 mile from here to the springs. After crossing several small rivulets, the trail ascends to a large clearing with fallen logs and campfire rings.

The hot springs are just below to the left at river level and are visible at the foot of a rocky bluff. There is no official trail down to the pools.

To reach the pool upriver, continue on the trail through the camping area and down into a meadow where the trail is at river level. The pool is across the river from a seep in the rocks and can be reached by rock-hopping during low water.

Note: Allow three to four hours for the hike in, and about half that time to hike out. Weather changes very rapidly in this area. It is a good idea to check with the San Juan National Forest, Pagosa Ranger District, 970 264-2268.

Source map: *San Juan National Forest.*

A soak in either pool would feel great after the long hike to get here. You can plan on camping in the area.

The overflow from all the pools spills over the ledges or through channels in the multicolored mineral terraces to a large, warm fishpond in the center of the pool area.

217 A PAGOSA SPRINGS POOL
(THE SPA MOTEL)
PO Box 37   **970 264-5910**
■   **Pagosa Springs, CO 81147**

Older motel with swimming pool (dating back to 1938) and bathhouse with modern hot tubs. Located across the San Juan River from downtown Pagosa Springs. Elevation 7,100 feet. Open all year.

Natural mineral water is pumped from a well at 130° and piped to the swimming pool and bathhouse. The outdoor swimming pool is maintained at 95° in winter and 88° in summer. Two indoor soaking pools in separate men's and women's sections are maintained at 108°. The outdoor hot tubs are maintained at 110°. All pools have continuous flowthrough, so no chemical treatment is necessary. Each of the two bathhouse sections also has its own steambath. The outdoor pools are handicap accessible. Bathing suits are required in the outdoor pools. In winter the facilities are free to motel guests and open for a fee to the general public.

Rooms, RV spaces, locker rooms, and horse stalls are available on the premises. It is less than three blocks to all other services. Visa, American Express, and MasterCard are accepted.

Directions: In Pagosa Springs on US 160, turn south at the one traffic light in town. One-half block west of the high school, cross the bridge and watch for the motel and pool on your left.

217 B THE SPRING INN
PO Box 1799   **970 264-4168**
                     800 225-0934
■   **Pagosa Springs, CO 81147**

Nicely refurbished inn with ten riverside mineralwater pools across the river from downtown Pagosa Springs. Elevation 7,100 feet. Open all year.

Natural mineral water flows out of a spring at 155° and is piped to ten cement pools of varying sizes and temperatures from 95-112°, all about three feet deep and sculpted into the gently sloping hillside overlooking the San Juan River. A submerged wooden walkway with a rope handrail leads you through a large, warm fishpond in the center of the pool area to the different pools. All pools have continuous flowthrough, so no chemical treatment is necessary. Two of the pools are handicap accessible. Bathing suits are required.

Facilities include motel rooms, three massage rooms, a Zen bookstore, exercise gym, sundecks with lounge chairs, and a hike and ski shop. Showers with dressing rooms, and lockers are available for day use. All other services are within three blocks. Major credit cards are accepted.

Directions: From the one traffic light in downtown Pagosa Springs turn south over the bridge across the San Juan River. The Inn is on the right, just past the Visitor Information Center. Phone for rates and reservations.

218 PIEDRA RIVER HOT SPRING

● **West of Pagosa Springs**

A series of shallow primitive pools in a beautiful mountain setting at the end of a moderately rugged two-mile hike in the San Juan National Forest. Elevation 7,400 feet. Open all year, subject to flooding, mud, and snow.

Natural mineral water at about 110° flows up from the bottom of several ankle-deep, volunteer-built, rock-and-mud pools on the east bank of the Piedra River, each pool large enough for one or two people lying down. Within fifty yards along the east riverbank are additional pools, rocky and often filled with mud that need to be scooped out before you can soak. Being at river level, the springs and pools may be submerged during high water. When necessary, air cooling can be supplemented by adding cold river water. The local custom is clothing optional.

No services are available on the premises. There is primitive pack-in camping in the surrounding national forest. It is approximately seven miles to a campground, cabins, and outfitters for pack trips at the junction of US 160 and FS 622. Three miles east of this junction, at Chimney Rock, are a cafe, gas, laundry, and store.

Directions: From US 160, 21 miles west of Pagosa Springs, 40 miles east of Durango, and just east of the Piedra River, turn north onto First Fork Rd., FS 622, marked with a national forest access sign. Follow FS 622, a one-lane dirt road (can be muddy) for 6.7 miles to a marked intersection with Sheep Creek Trail (left) and Monument Park Rd. (right). Turn left and park at the clearing and Sheep Creek trailhead. Hike down the steep, rocky trail for

approximately 1 mile to where it widens into a meadow with a dilapidated steel cable bridge over the river. Do not cross the bridge; instead turn right and follow the trail north along the river for approximately 1 mile. The trail, which has been above the river, crosses tiny Coffee Creek, then drops down to a clearing at river level with fallen trees and logs. A sign posted on a tree points to "Hot Springs," to which someone has added "along the river."

Note: The ascent back up to the parking area is fairly strenuous along the steep, rocky trail.

Source map: *San Juan National Forest* (springs not shown).

Be sure to bring a shovel with you as these river-level pools often fill up with mud. After you've dug out the pool, you get your reward—a nice hot soak.

The original buildings at *Trimble Hot Springs* go back over one hundred years. Unfortunately, they all burned down. Fortunately, they have been replaced by beautifully cared-for gardens and pools of varying shapes and temperatures, all with year-round magnificent views of the La Plata Mountains.

219   TRIMBLE HOT SPRINGS
6475 County Road 203
970 247-0111

■   **Durango, CO 81301**

Restored historic resort in the scenic Animas River Valley, below the La Plata Mountains. Elevation 6,500 feet. Open all year.

Natural mineral water flows out of a spring at 120° and is piped to three outdoor pools where it is treated with ozone. The Olympic-size swimming pool is maintained at 82°, one of the hydrojet pools is maintained at 100-102°, and the other is maintained at 108-110°. Bathing suits are required.

Facilities include dressing rooms, a workshop and party room great for private parties and wedding receptions, a fitness studio, snack bar, picnic area, and a fully equipped apartment. Massage, physical therapy, aqua aerobics, and yoga classes are available on the premises. It is two miles to a bed and breakfast inn and six miles to all other services. Visa and MasterCard are accepted.

Directions: From the city of Durango, go 7 miles north on US 550, then west 100 yards on Trimble Lane to the springs.

220 A OURAY HOT SPRINGS
PO Box 468   **970 325-4638**
■ **Ouray, CO 81427**

Large, city-owned swimming pool and visitor information complex. Elevation 7,800 feet. Open all year.

Natural mineral water flows out of a spring at 150° and is cooled with city tap water as needed to supply three large outdoor pools. The shallow soaking pool is maintained at 100°; the deep swimming and diving pool is maintained at 80°; and the therapy pool is maintained at 105°. All pools have continuous flow-through with a filtration system, so no chemical treatment is needed. There are rails at the pools and the guards are able to help anyone who might need assistance. Bathing suits are required.

Locker rooms, snack house, fitness center, and swim shop with suit rentals are available on the premises. All other services are within six blocks. Visa and MasterCard are accepted.

Location: The entire complex is easily visible on the west side of US 550 in the town of Ouray.

220 B WIESBADEN HOT SPRINGS SPA & LODGINGS
625 5th St.   **970 325-4347**
PO Box 349 (mailing address)
■ **Ouray, CO 81427**

Charming mountain resort built to complement the spectacular canyon area of Uncompahgre National Forest. Geothermally heated. Elevation 7,700 feet. Open all year.

Natural mineral water flows from three springs at temperatures ranging from 108-130°. All pools operate on a flow-through basis, requiring no chemical treatment. The outdoor swimming pool ranges from 99° to 102°. The soaking pool in the natural vapor cave is maintained at 109-110°, a challenge well worth meeting. The soaking pool in the sauna is maintained at 108°. Bathing suits are required.

A 105° flow-through soaking pool is supplied by a hot-spring waterfall in a private area called "The Lorelei." In this beautifully landscaped space, which may be rented by the hour, suits are optional.

Geothermal heat is used to warm the individually decorated rooms, some with fireplaces and some with kitchens. European mud wraps, aromatherapy wraps, facials, massage, acupressure, reflexology, and a float tank are available on the premises. It is two blocks to a restaurant, store, shops, and service station and eight blocks to overnight camping and RV hookups. Visa and MasterCard are accepted.

Location: Located on the corner of 6th Ave. and 5th St. in the town of Ouray, 2 blocks east of Main Street (US 550). Follow signs.

Four outdoor hot tubs with incredible views make this a great place to stay, summer or winter.

220 C BOX CANYON LODGE AND HOT SPRINGS
45 3rd Ave. **970 325-4981**
■ **Ouray, CO 81427**

Modern lodge at the base of mountains in a quiet off-highway location adjacent to the Box Canyon Falls and the Uncompahgre River. Elevation 7,800 feet. Open all year.

Natural mineral water flows out of a spring at 140° and is piped to four outdoor continuous flow-through redwood tubs requiring no chemical treatment. The four hydrojet tubs are situated on redwood decks that are terraced up the mountainside behind the lodge, offering spectacular views of the city and surrounding mountains. Temperatures in the tubs range from 103-107°. Use of the tubs is reserved for registered guests and bathing suits are required. Major credit cards are accepted.

Several geothermal springs, varying in temperature from 138-156°, are located on the property, and the water is used to heat all lodge rooms as well as to heat shower water.

Location: Two blocks west of US 550 on 3rd Ave.

220 D BEST WESTERN TWIN PEAKS MOTEL
125 3rd Ave. **970 325-4427**
■ **Ouray, CO 81427**

Modern, major hotel in a picturesque mountain town. Elevation 7,700 ft. Open April through October.

Natural mineral water flows out of a spring at 156° and is piped to two pools. The outdoor swimming pool is maintained at 82°, the outdoor waterfall soaking tub at 106°, and the indoor soaking pool at 104°. Pools are reserved for the use of registered guests. There are railings on the pools. Bathing suits are required. Major credit cards are accepted.

Location: One block west of US 550 on 3rd Ave.

In addition to these two outdoor pools, one for soaking and one for swimming, there is also an indoor soaking pool. All the pools use natural mineral water.

221 ORVIS HOT SPRINGS
1585 County Rd. #3　970 626-5324
■ **Ridgway, CO 81432**

Small and charming rustic lodge with multiple geothermal pools, located in a wide mountain valley. Elevation 7,000 feet. Open all year.

Mineral water flows from several springs at temperatures ranging from 112-127° and is piped to a variety of tubs and pools, all of which operate on a flow-through basis requiring no chemical treatment. All pools are available to the public for day use as well as to registered guests.

There are four private rooms with tiled soaking pools that have a water temperature of 102-108° and are drained and cleaned every day. Immediately adjoining the sauna building is one outside soaking pool built of stone, which has a water temperature of more than 110°. There is one large, cement, indoor soaking pool (three feet deep, twenty-five feet in diameter) that has a temperature of 101°. There is also one large, excavated soaking pond (six feet deep, thirty feet in diameter) that has hot mineral water continuously flowing in from the bottom and the sides. This enlarged natural hot-spring maintains a year-round temperature of 103-105°. Clothing is optional in all pools except the twenty-five-foot indoor soaking pool.

Facilities include six lodge rooms which share two baths. Room rates include unlimited use of sauna and pool facilities. Massage therapy available by appointment. Visa and MasterCard are accepted. It is less than two miles to the town of Ridgway and all other services. Phone for rates, hours, reservations, and directions.

This indoor soaking pool, originally built in the 1920s, is the only pool where bathing suits are required.

TEXAS

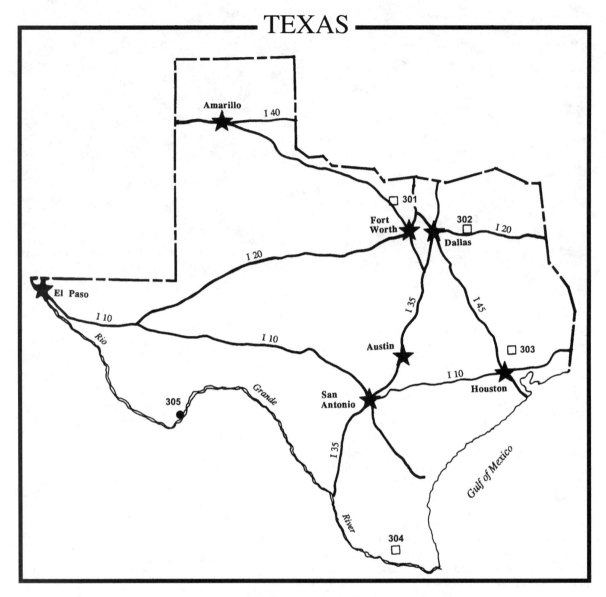

This map was designed to be used with a standard highway map.

MAP SYMBOLS

⬤ Non-commercial mineral water pool

⬛ Commercial (fee) mineral water pool

☐ Tap water resorts and rental locations

〜 Paved highway

- - - Unpaved road

· · · Hiking trail

301 BLUEBONNET
Rte. 1, Box 146   817 627-2313
☐   Alvord, TX 76225

Modern nudist resort on sixty-six acres of rolling hills, four miles north of Decatur in North Central Texas. Elevation 1,100 feet. Open all year.

The indoor whirlpool spa is filled with gas-heated well water, treated with chlorine, and maintained at 103°. The outdoor swimming pool, surrounded by two large sundecks, is filled with solar-heated well water, treated with chlorine, and maintained at 80°. Clothing is prohibited in spa, pool, and sauna and is optional elsewhere.

Facilities include cabins, trailers, tenting spaces, RV hook-ups, tenting spaces, clubhouse, sauna, and volleyball, tennis, and shuffleboard courts. Visa, MasterCard and American Express are accepted. It is four miles to all other services.

Note: This is a membership organization not open to the public for drop-in visits, but interested visitors may be issued a guest pass by prior arrangement. Telephone or write for information and directions.

302 PONDAROSA RANCH
PO Box 133   903 873-3311
☐   Wills Point, TX 75169

Modern, residential nature park and health resort on sixty rolling acres, fifty-five miles east of Dallas. Elevation 2,000 feet. Open all year.

The outdoor hydrospa is filled with gas-heated well and tap water, treated with chlorine, and maintained at 102°. The outdoor swimming pool is filled with unheated well and tap water and treated with chlorine. Clothing is prohibited in the spa, pool, and sauna and is optional elsewhere.

Other facilities include rental trailers, RV hook-ups, tenting spaces, a clubhouse, and volleyball, horseshoe and shuffleboard courts, plus a full service restaurant during the summer season. Visa and MasterCard are accepted. It is eight miles to all other services.

Note: This is a membership organization, but it is open to the public for drop-in visits. No reservations are required except for the rental trailers. Telephone or write for further information.

303   LIVE OAK RESORT, INC.
　　　Rte. 1, Box 916　　　409 878-2216
☐　　Washington, TX 77880

A well-maintained, family nudist park with seventeen acres of mowed lawn, interspersed with shade-providing oak trees, nestled in rolling farm country near Houston. Elevation 525 feet. Open all year.

Gas-heated well water, chlorine-treated, is used in an outdoor hydropool maintained at 104°. The Olympic-size swimming pool using similar water is unheated but averages over 80° between June and September. Clothing is optional on the first visit, except in the pools, where it is prohibited at all times.

Cabins, camping, and RV hookups are available on the premises. Other facilities include a lighted, sand volleyball court, a clubhouse with pool table and ping pong, and a snack bar open on weekends only during the summer months. A children's playground is also available. It is four miles to a store and service station. Major credit cards are accepted.

Note: This is a membership organization not open to the public for drop-in visits, but a guest pass may be issued by prior arrangement. Resort rules prohibit guns, drugs, and erotic behavior. Phone for more information and directions.

304   SANDPIPERS HOLIDAY PARK, INC.
　　　Rte. 7, Box 309　　　210 383-7589
☐　　Edinburg, TX 78539

North America's southernmost nudist park located on twenty-one acres, seven miles north of Edinburg and twenty miles north of Mexico. Elevation 100 feet. Open all year.

The outdoor hydrojet spa is filled with gas-heated well water, treated with chlorine, and maintained at 103°. The outdoor Olympic-size swimming pool is filled with unheated well water in the summer and is gas-heated in the winter to maintain 85°. Clothing is prohibited in the spa and pool, optional elsewhere.

Facilities include rental units, tenting spaces, RV hook-ups, clubhouse, volleyball and shuffleboard courts, and two lighted tennis courts. Meals are served on weekends. Visa and MasterCard are accepted. It is one mile to all other services.

Note: This is a membership organization not open to the public for drop-in visits, but prospective members and guests may be issued a guest pass by prior arrangement. Telephone or write for information.

305 BOQUILLAS (LANGFORD) HOT SPRING

● **Near the town of Lajitas, Texas**

Historic masonry hot pool in the ruins of an old resort on the banks of the Rio Grande River. Located near the Rio Grande Village Campground in Big Bend National Park. Elevation 1,800 feet. Open all year.

Natural mineral water flows out of the ground at 105° into a large, shallow soaking pool a few feet above river level. Bathing suits are advisable in the daytime.

There are no services on the premises. It is six miles to a store, service station, overnight camping, and RV hookups and twenty-eight miles to a motel and restaurant.

Directions: From Big Bend National Park Headquarters, drive 16 miles toward Rio Grand Village Campground. Turn right at Hot Springs sign, then drive 2 miles on dirt road to the end and walk .25 miles downriver to hot spring.

Source map: *Big Bend National Park.*

The only natural mineral water hot springs in Texas. I wonder if they had as much fun at the old resort as everyone seems to be having in the ruins.

NEW MEXICO

COLORADO

US 64 · US 64 · US 285 · US 64

402 A-B

401 ■ ★ Taos

US 666 · NM 44 · I 25

403 A-B
404 A-B · NM 4 · □ 405 · 406 ★ Las Vegas
Santa · ★

ARIZONA

I 40 · US 285 · US 84

Albuquerque ★ · I 40

I 25 · Grande River · US 60

TEXAS

US 60 · US 60

413 · NM 12 · US 60 · US 380 · US 285

US 180 · Rio

412 A-B · 411 · 410 A-B
409 ■ · NM 35 · US 70
Silver City ★ · NM 152 · 407 A-F
Truth or Consequences ★

NM 90 · 408 ● · I 25

I 110 · US 180 · ★ Deming · I 110

MEXICO · **TEXAS**

This map was designed to be used with a standard highway map.

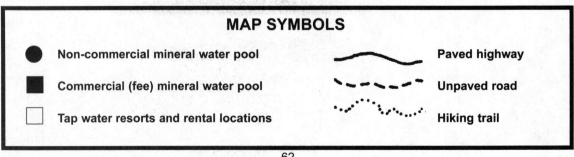

MAP SYMBOLS

● Non-commercial mineral water pool   —— Paved highway

■ Commercial (fee) mineral water pool   - - - Unpaved road

□ Tap water resorts and rental locations   ···· Hiking trail

401 OJO CALIENTE RESORT
Box 468   505 583-2233
■ **Ojo Caliente, NM**

One of the oldest health resorts in north America, located in the foothills of Carson National Forest, forty-six miles north of Santa Fe. The old adobe hotel was built in the early 1900s, but the tubs are new. Elevation 6,300 feet. Open all year.

Natural mineral water flows out of five different springs with different temperatures and mineral contents. An outdoor, sandy-bottom, iron mineral-water soaking pool is directly over the source of the spring, with a pool temperature up to 105°. An indoor soda pool has piped in water measuring up to 104°. The sun beating on the roof creates a natural steam room, and a sign inside says "Quiet Zone." Taps are available at both pools for a drink of the healing mineral water. The outdoor swimming pool and spa contain traces of arsenic with cold water added to maintain a temperature in the pool of 85° year round and 106° in the spa. The iron and soda pools have continual flow-through and are drained three to four times a week requiring no chemicals. The swimming pool and spa are treated with chlorine.

The private tubs in the men's bathhouse, large enough for two people, can also be used coed. The women's bathhouse is for women only. Water temperatures can be adjusted by adding cold water. One tub is handicap accessible, as are all the pools. Bathing suits are required in all the pools, except in the bathhouses.

Massage, sweat wrap, herbal wraps, salt glows, and herbal facials are offered. Towels and bathing suits can be rented. The bathhouses have showers, lockers, and dressing areas. Also available is a dining room, lodging in the adobe hotel or cottages, a gift shop, RV hookups, and horseback trail rides. Major credit cards are accepted.

Directions: From Santa Fe go, 46 miles north on US 285. Watch for signs.

Each of the pools at the resort has its own specific concentration of minerals. In order to have time to soak in all of them, you might want to consider staying in the old adobe hotel built in the early 1900s.

These bathers have interrupted their soak to look at a moose across the river, said by some to be the first one ever seen in New Mexico. The high water that made this pool inaccessible until July may have brought the moose out of the highlands to look for food in previously unexplored territory.

402 A   BLACK ROCK HOT SPRINGS

● **West of the town of Arroyo Hondo**

Two mud-bottom rock pools located on the west bank of the Rio Grande Gorge, just a few feet above river level. Elevation 6,500 feet. Open all year; pools may not be open until summer, and the road is subject to flooding.

Natural mineral water flows up through the bottom of the inland pool, maintaining the pool temperature at 97° except when high water in the river floods the pool. The adjacent pool, closer to the river, is much cooler due to more mixing with river water. The apparent local custom is clothing optional.

There are no services available except pit toilets near the John Dunn Bridge. This is also the staging area for kayaking and float trips down the river. It is three miles to a store, cafe, service station, etc., and nine miles to RV hookups. Note: Unpaved roads may become impassable during wet weather.

Directions: From NM522 in Arroyo Hondo, take either County Rd. B-002 at Herb's Lounge and Mini-Mart just north of the river or County Rd. B-005 just south of the river. At .2 mile they join. Continue for .7 mile to where the pavement ends. Bear left over a tiny bridge. At 1. mile bear right, and you'll pass a B&B on the left .1 mile farther on. You are now on a two-lane gravel road above the south bank of the Arroyo Hondo River. At .5 mile past the B&B, cross a bridge over the tiny creek and bear right. (The very rough road to the left heads toward Stagecoach [Manby] Hot Springs.) Drive for 1 mile, cross another bridge over the river, and .1 mile farther cross the John Dunn bridge, a steel bridge over the Rio Grande where the Arroyo merges. Just past the bridge are pit toilets and a swimming beach to the right. To get to the hot springs, turn left after the bridge and head uphill. Park at the flat clearing in the horseshoe of the turn and walk straight ahead on a path that leads down to the pools near the river, approximately .25 mile (a 5- to 10-minute walk).

402 B   STAGECOACH (MANBY)
HOT SPRINGS

• **Southwest of the town of Arroyo Hondo**

Three shallow, sandy-bottom rock pools at river's edge, near the ruins of a bathhouse that was an old stagecoach stop on the east bank of the Rio Grande Gorge. Elevation 6,500 feet. Open all year; subject to road flooding.

Natural mineral water flows out of the ground at 97° directly into the one-foot deep rock pools, which are large enough for three to four people. The lower pool is only slightly above low water in the river, so the temperature depends on the amount of cold water seeping in. Two larger, shallow 80° pools are a few feet away near a sandy beach. The apparent local custom is clothing optional.

There are no services on the premises, but overnight camping is not prohibited on the sandy beach. Overnight parking is also not prohibited in the flat parking clearing and surrounding areas at the top of the trail. It is nine miles to a store and service station. Note: Unpaved roads may become impassable during wet weather.

Directions: The suggested route begins at the blinking light (a landmark from which locals give directions) north of Taos and south of Arroyo Hondo where NM 64 heads west toward the Rio Grande Bridge and the Taos Municipal Airport. Follow NM 64 from the blinking light for 4.2 miles (.3 mile west of the airport). Turn right (north) onto an unpaved, graded two-lane road that has a posted speed limit of 20 mph. Drive for 4.5 miles to a fork and bear left onto a badly rutted road. Go .3 mile to a large parking clearing. A wide path leads down from the southwest end of the parking clearing to the springs. Although the trail goes down from the ridge to river level, it is very gradual and not strenuous (a 15- to 20-minute walk).

Source maps: USGS *Arroyo Hondo.*

The bather above is leaning against the remains of an old bathhouse along the stagecoach route. Just south of the springs, remains of rocky walls are visible where a bridge used to span the river on the route. The old stagecoach road can be seen from the parking clearing. Look across the gorge for a route that cuts diagonally in switchbacks down to the river. Small stones decorate the edge of the retaining wall.

You can soak, shower, or relax in any season in the many pools here at *Spence Hot Spring*. This is a very special place with its many pools and beautiful water. There has been some discussion about closing the pools because of inappropriate behavior—please do your part to make sure this doesn't happen.

403 A   SPENCE HOT SPRING
(see map)
- **North of the town of Jemez Springs**

A unique group of several sandy-bottom pools on a steep hillside with a spectacular view of surrounding mountains. Located in the Santa Fe National Forest on the east side of the Jemez River. Elevation 6,000 feet. Open all year.

Natural mineral water at 109° flows up through the sandy bottom into a rock-bordered pool large enough for ten people. There is a pipe for draining and cleaning. A series of pipes and waterfalls leads to the pools just below, which have gradually cooler temperatures.

Two other groups of rock-and-mud pools are further uphill. The first is a shallow, one-foot deep sandy-bottom pool between huge boulders with the 100° water source inside a cave. Air temperature and wind affect the temperature in this shallow pool. There is also a pipe here for draining and cleaning. Hike uphill for fifty feet, cross a clearing, then follow the runoff around some large boulders uphill and to the left of the five lower pools.

The third pool is about two hundred feet straight uphill from the lower pools. Hike across the clearing and continue uphill, following the runoff. This primitive knee-deep, squishy bottom, sand-and-rock pool is large enough for two to three people. The water source which flows out between the rock measures 109°. The apparent local custom is clothing optional.

There are no services available. It is 1.5 miles north of the parking area to a store, gas, restaurant and lodge in La Cueva at the intersection of NM 4 and NM 126, five miles to a campground, seven miles to an AYH youth hostel, and seventeen miles to RV hookups.

Directions: From the town of Jemez Springs, go 7 miles north on NM 4 to a large parking area on the east side of the highway 2 miles past "Battleship Picnic Area." From the town of Los Alamos, drive west on NM 501 to the intersection in La Cueva with NM 126 and NM 4. Then go south on NM 4 for 1.5 miles to the large parking area on the east side of the road. From the parking area, a rocky clearing is visible across the river to the northeast. The trail begins at the south end of the parking pull out. A sturdy wooden footbridge across the Jemez River replaces a log crossing. The trail continues up a steep slope to the springs. The parking pull out is posted "No parking after 10 PM." During snow and rain, the slope can become very slippery.

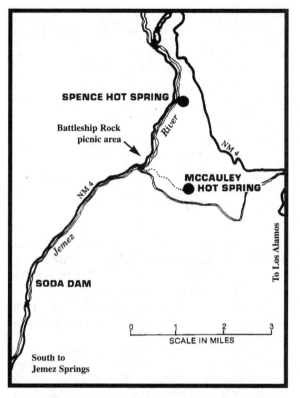

SPENCE HOT SPRING

Battleship Rock
picnic area

River

NM 4

NM 4

MCCAULEY
HOT SPRING

Jemez

To Los Alamos

SODA DAM

0   1   2   3
SCALE IN MILES

South to
Jemez Springs

403 B   MCCAULEY HOT SPRING

(see map)

● **North of the town of Jemez Springs**

Very large, shallow, warm pool whose water flows into several deeper primitive pools in a gorgeous mountain clearing. Elevation 7,300 feet. Open approximately mid-April through October due to rain, mud, and snow conditions.

Natural mineral water flows out of the ground at 92° into a small, three- to four-person rock-and-log pool and directly into an adjacent two-foot-deep pond, forty feet in diameter. Pool temperature measures between 85-90°, depending on air and wind conditions. A second, rock-and-log pool, three feet deep, is approximately fifty feet downhill in the creekbed run-off where water cascades into two separate places in the pool. From here it falls down to another pool, four- to five-feet deep where the temperature is a degree or two cooler. The apparent local custom is clothing optional.

There are no services on the premises, except level areas for pack-in camping. However, the guppies and neon tetras that live in the pool will entertain you by nibbling on your body hair. It is 3.5 miles to a store, gas, restaurant, and lodge in La Cueva at the intersection of NM 4 and NM 126, five miles to a campground and AYH youth hostel, and seventeen miles to RV hookups.

Directions: From the ranger station at the north end of Jemez Springs, go 4 miles north on NM 4 to Battleship Rock picnic area, which is open 6AM to 10PM only. A day-use fee is charged. Starting from the firepit gazebo in the picnic area, follow FS trail 137, called East Fork trail. Just past the gazebo,the trail immediately forks. Follow the right fork along the river. Stay on the main trail (despite many spurs) that gradually ascends in switchbacks. Hike approximately two miles until you hear the gurgling creek ,which is runoff from the warm spring. A large clearing with campfire rings is off to the right just before you reach the pond. This trail is moderately strenuous, especially at this altitude.

404 B JEMEZ SPRINGS BATH HOUSE
Box 105   505 829-3303
■   **Jemez Springs, NM 87205**

An older, traditional bathhouse located in the park on the main street of Jemez Springs. Elevation 6,200 feet. Open all year.

Natural mineral water flows out of a city-owned springs at 155-158° and is piped to a cooling tank and then to the bathhouse. There are eight private rooms, each containing a one-person bathtub, and a private outdoor cedar tub available to groups of up to six. Cool and hot mineral water are mixed to provide the desired water temperature. Tubs are drained and refilled after each use, so no chemical treatment of the water is necessary. Clothing is optional.

Massage, reflexology wraps, and a fully equipped fitness room are available on the premise, as is a store selling local crafts, beauty supplies, cold drinks, and pastries. Major credit cards are accepted. It is one block to a store, restaurants, and service station. Phone for rates, reservations, and directions.

404 A BODHI MANDA ZEN CENTER
MOTEL AND HOT SPRINGS
Box 8   505 829-3854
■   **Jemez Springs, NM 87205**

A four-unit motel a few minutes stroll away from primitive, riverbank hot pools. Operated by the Bodhi Manda Zen Center and located in the town of Jemez Springs. Elevation 6,300 feet. Closed between September and December 15 for retreats.

Natural mineral water flows out of the ground at 169°, then into four rock-and-sand soaking pools where natural cooling results in varying temperatures. Bathing suits are required. Pools are reserved for motel guests only. No drop-ins, please.

It is one block to a store and cafe and seven miles to a service station. Phone ahead for current information, rates, and reservations.

405 TEN THOUSAND WAVES
PO Box 10103   **505 988-1047**
(Reservations) 505 982-9304

☐   **Santa Fe, NM 87504**

An intriguing blend of American technology and Japanese hot-tub traditions offers a range of soaking possibilities and the newly built Houses of the Moon, four handcrafted Japanese guest suites. Located three and one-half miles up Ski Basin Road with breathtaking mountain views.

Eight privately enclosed outdoor tubs and one indoor tub with two balconies are available. Four of the nine tubs include a sauna, and one includes a steam room. A communal wood tub and sauna large enough for twenty-five people and a separate women's pebble-bottom tub with sauna are also available. The tubs use gas-heated well water and a purification method of ultraviolet light, ozone, and hydrogen peroxide and are maintained at a temperature of 104-106°. Bathing suits are optional in all tubs. Handicap accessible.

Kimonos, sandals, soap, shampoo, and hair dryers are provided. Private lockers are available in both the men's and women's dressing rooms. A juice and snack bar is on the premises. Various other treatments offered include massage, herbal wraps, salt glows, watsu (in-water massage), East Indian cleansing treatments, and facials. Visa, MasterCard, and Discover Card are accepted. Phone for rates, reservations, and directions.

The winding pathways, lined in the evenings with twinkling lanterns, lead you to the nine uniquely decorated pools, two of which are shown above.

406   MONTEZUMA HOT SPRINGS

● **Northwest of the town of Las Vegas**

The once-abandoned ruins of a major turn-of-the-century hot-springs resort bathhouse. Located just across the Gallinas River on the property of the lavish Victorian "Montezuma's Castle," now Armand Hammer's United World College. Elevation 6,450 feet. Open all year.

Natural mineral water flows out of several artesian springs at 94-113° into three clusters of concrete soaking pools of various sizes and depths up to six feet, resulting in a wide range of temperature choices. Continuous flow-through (fifteen gallons per minute) eliminates the need for chemical treatment of the water. Volunteers are fastidious about keeping the pools clean, draining and scrubbing them every two weeks. One cluster of pools (the hottest) has been newly redesigned, sculpted, and landscaped into the hillside; a second group of two pools is near a coffin-looking concrete block; the third sit near the old bathhouse. The whole area around the pools can be very wet and marshy. The pools are just steps from the road. Bathing suits are required.

There are no services available on the premises. It is six miles to a store, cafe, service station, etc., in Las Vegas.

Directions: From I-25 take exit 65W in Las Vegas, cross over I-25, turn right on Business 25 to Mills Ave. Turn left on Mills for 1.5 miles to Hot Springs Rd., marked with a sign to Montezuma and United World College. Turn right (this is NM 65) for 5 miles until you see the castle on the hill. A sign along the right side of the road along the metal guard rail indicates "Hot Springs Baths." Park along the shoulder of the road. Several openings in the fence lead to railroad-tie steps down to the pools. The five indoor pools are now fenced and closed. The outdoor pools are open to the public year-round at no charge.

Note: These pools are on the grounds of the college. Officials request that you keep the area clean, respect the bathing suit requirement, and keep noise levels down. Please do your part so that the college will continue to allow the pools to remain open to the public.

A special thank you to those volunteers who have rebuilt these pools and who keep them clean.

TRUTH OR CONSEQUENCES

The hot springs at Truth or Consequences produce two and one-half million gallons of water per day, have the largest mineral-water table in the Southwest, and boast the highest mineral content of any springs in the United States.

These were the sacred springs of the Apaches, and Geronimo speaks of spending a peaceful year in the area. Artifacts indicate high usage by the earlier Mimbres Indians. The springs were known to the Spanish as Ojo Caliente de Las Polomas, Hot Springs of the Doves. The crystal clear water is also good for drinking (no unpleasant odor or taste). The town itself sits on the banks of the Rio Grande, just below Elephant Butte, the largest fresh-water lake in the region, offering boating, sailing, and some of the best bass fishing around.

There has recently been an upsurge of interest in this area, and many commercial establishments are being renovated and enlarged. If you haven't visited this area in a while, you will be pleasantly surprised to find that while the area has retained its uniqueness, it can also offer such amenities as golf courses, a museum, restaurants, and many small shops.

407 A ARTESIAN BATH HOUSE AND TRAILER PARK
312 Marr   505 894-2684
■ **Truth or Consequences, NM 87901**

Five single-size and three family-size ceramic tubs at an average water temperature of 108°,.are available for rent by the hour. Tubs are refilled for each use so no chemicals are necessary. Each room contains a bench and cold shower.

RV hookups, tenant laundry, and public showers are available on the premises, plus massage by appointment. No credit cards are accepted.

407 B CHARLES MOTEL AND BATH HOUSE
701 Broadway   505 894-7154
■ **Truth or Consequences, NM 87901**

Individual baths are cleaned and refilled for each bather, eliminating the need for chemicals. While the hot water comes in at temperatures between 108-111°, cold water is available to cool the water. Following the soak, the bather can be wrapped in a sheen and then a wool blanket by the bath attendants.

Twenty apartment-style motel units are available for rent nightly or weekly. A complete fitness center offering personalized weight training, cardiovascular training, and nutritional counseling is on the premises. Massage therapists are also available.

Note: Plans are in progress for the addition of a larger family pool, roof-top communal tubs for sunbathers, and a general upgrade of the facilities. Phone for status of construction.

407 C FIREWATER LODGE
309 Broadway   505 894-3405
■ **Truth or Consequences, NM 87901**

New owners are involved in a complete renovation of this older adobe villa. Baths with water temperatures between 108-111° are available in large private rooms.

Motel rooms are currently available for short-term or long-term stays.

Note: Building will continue with the addition of an outdoor family-size pool. A restaurant will also be added so that bed and breakfast can be offered. Phone for status of construction.

407 D INDIAN SPRINGS NATURAL FLOWING POOLS, WATER HOLE #1

218 Austin St.   505 894-2018

■ Truth or Consequences, NM 87901

Motel units, some with kitchenettes.

407 E MARSHALL HOT SPRINGS

311 Marr   505 894-9286

■ Truth or Consequences, NM 87901

Three restored six-foot by six-foot by four-foot deep pools, each with a gravel bottom and direct flow-through of unchlorinated hot mineral water. Temperatures range from 106-112°. Each tub is in a private room with benches to rest on and colorful Mimbres Petroglyphs decorating the walls. Mineral water is available to drink.

407 F RIVERBEND HOT SPRINGS
(affiliated with Hosteling International)

100 Austin   505 894-6183

■ Truth or Consequences, NM 87901

Three outdoor soaking tubs on a deck overlooking the Rio Grande with a view of Turtleback Mountain. Elevation 4,300 feet. Open all year.

Natural mineral water at 114° is pumped up from a well and cools as it flows through pipes to the soaking tubs. A three-foot deep, five- by seventeen-foot former bait tank is divided into three tubs, each one a degree or two cooler than the first with temperatures ranging form 104-107°. The pools, which are nicknamed "Hot Minnow Baths," are filled twice daily, morning and evening, for registered guests who may use them free of charge. The pools are drained after each use, so no chemical treatment is necessary. Non-guests may rent the tubs for private use during the day. Bathing suits are required. Two outdoor private tubs with private decks and lanai enclosures where suits will be optional are being planned.

Men's and women's dormitories with a shared kitchen, two private units with kitchenettes that will sleep four to six persons, tepee camping, and a pontoon houseboat are available. Laundry, cold drinks, barbecue, merchant discounts, and morning bakery goods for dormitory guests are offered. Also available are canoeing, hiking, swimming, and host tours. All other services are within five blocks.

Directions: Coming from the north, take exit 79 off I-25. Drive 2.5 miles to the only traffic light and turn left at Third St. Turn left for 1 block, then right on Cedar. Drive five blocks to the hot springs just south of the park along the river. From the south on I-25 take exit 75 through downtown for 2.5 miles, turn right at the First Baptist Church for 1 block, and turn left for 1 block to the springs.

408   FAYWOOD HOT SPRINGS
165 Highway 61   505 536-9663
HC 71 Box 1240
■   **Faywood, NM 88034**

Halfway between Deming and Silver City, next to City of Rocks State Park, lies a true desert oasis with large trees and parklike surroundings. Newly renovated, Faywood offers a clothing optional public soaking pool as well as a separate soaking pool that requires bathing suits. Elevation 5,000 feet. Open all year.

Natural mineral water flows from the top of a tufa dome at 130° downhill into several stone soaking pools in a naturally beautiful desert setting. The water cools to comfortable temperatures around 104°. There are both clothing-only and clothing-optional areas. Several private pools and tubs are also available. The water is pure enough to be used for drinking.

A picnic area, changing rooms, tent spaces, and an RV park with power, water, and a dump station are available. Beautiful vistas and walking trails are on the premises. Massage is also available. Lodging and a cafe are planned for the near future. (Phone for the status of construction.) It is fifteen miles to a store.

Directions: From Deming, take 180 north for 24 miles, turn right (east) on Highway 61, and go about 2 miles from the intersection of 180 and 61. A sign and entrance are on your left. From Silver City, take 180 south about 25 miles, turn left on Highway 61, and proceed about 2 miles from the intersection.

The pool in the photo above is in an area set aside for those who are comfortable wearing bathing suits. The private space below, along with other pools, is available for those who prefer to soak without a suit. Whatever you prefer, this is a wonderful place to camp and hike, and the mineral-water quality is among the best.

409   GILA HOT SPRINGS VACATION CENTER

Gila Hot Springs, Rte. 11 505 536-9551
■ Silver City, NM 88061

An all-year vacation center providing multiple services located in the middle of the Gila National Forest. Elevation 5,000 feet. Open all year.

Doc Campbell's Post offers a country store with groceries, snack bar, ice, gas, fishing and hunting licenses, supplies, gifts, laundromat, showers, and most important, knowledgeable advice about the area. Arrangements can be made for wilderness pack trips, fishing and hunting trips, youth group trips, drop camps, and pack stock for backpackers. Reservations for lodging are also made here. Credit cards are accepted at the store.

Lodging includes a spacious apartment with kitchenette, and a completely furnished trailer all using natural hot springs water for drinking, showers, and baths. The RV park has hot and cold taps at all hookups. Hot springs water can be hooked up to your trailer, or you can use the RV Park showers and hot tub. Picnic pavilion offers grill and fire ring, plus a children's playground.

● River Campground

Shady, primitive area with natural hot pools beside the river. Natural mineral water flowing at 150° from the springs on the east bank of the Gila River, is piped to the riverside camping area. The first pool is quite hot at 110° and greenish-orange with algae. The other two pools cool to 105° as the water is air cooled in these shallow pools. All that is provided are water spigots with safe drinking water, rest rooms, and trash cans. The bathing suit issue seems to be decided by those who are camping there, although official policy is bathing suits required. Located right off of NM 15, the main road into the area. Watch for signs on your right (before you get to the store). There is a small fee.

Note: Allow two hours for the forty-four mile drive from Silver City along scenic route NM 15, a two-lane mountain road which twists and winds through the Gila National Forest.

Primitive soaking pools and a primitive campground have a special appeal, convincing you that you are really out in the wilderness. Actually, you are within a short distance of supplies at Doc Campbell's Post and some wonderful Indian ruins at the Gila Cliff Dwellings.

As these pools are only one-half mile from the trailhead, they are a convenient stop on some of the horseback trips in the area.

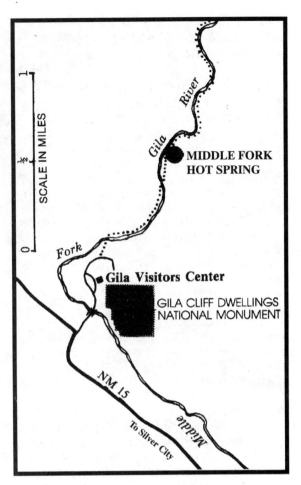

410 A   MIDDLE FORK (LIGHTFEATHER) HOT SPRING

(see map)

● **North of the Gila Visitors Center**

A series of shallow rock-and-sand soaking pools on the Middle Fork of the Gila River, one-half mile from the Gila Visitors Center and the Indian Cliff dwellings. Elevation 5,800 feet. Open all year, subject to high water in the river, which must be forded twice each way.

Natural mineral water flows out of the spring on the east side of the canyon at 130°, directly into several shallow pools next to the river, where the water gradually cools as it flows through the pools. Bathing suits are advisable during the daytime.

All services are back at the Gila Hot Springs Vacation Center.

Directions: To reach the trailhead, go to the far end of the visitor center parking lot and turn right. There is a special parking area for hikers, up the hill on the left. Walk down the road past the gate to the bottom of the hill. The main trail (157) continues toward the canyon, crossing the river almost immediately. The springs are on the east (right) side of the canyon after the second crossing. The water is almost always very coldand often deep. Check at the ranger station before starting out.

Note: Allow two hours for the forty-four mile drive from Silver City along scenic route NM 15, a two-lane mountain road that twists and winds through the Gila National Forest.

410 B   HOUSE LOG CANYON (JORDAN) HOT SPRINGS

● **Northwest of the Gila Visitors Center**

Remote, unimproved hot springs on a tree- and fern-covered hillside in the Gila Wilderness, where the canyon meets the Middle Fork of the Gila River. Elevation 6,200 feet. Accessible only during low water in the river.

Natural mineral water flows out of several springs at 92° and cascades directly into a log- and rock-dammed pool large enough to hold ten people. The apparent local custom is clothing optional.

All services are back at the Gila Hot Springs Vacation Center. Check with the very knowledgeable people here about trails, etc., as they have hiked this area for years. Make sure you have sufficient supplies for whatever trip you take.

Directions: To begin the 8-mile hike, park at the Middle Fork trailhead (trail 157). Follow the trail past the locked gate and straight upstream into the canyon. The trail follows the river for six miles until it junctions with the trail from Little Bear Canyon. There should be 14 more crossings (about 2 miles) before you reach the hot springs on the northeast side of the canyon. Look for a marshy area with hot water seeps. A mile farther up the Middle Fork beyond Big Bear Canyon, are more warm springs called The Meadows, at the mouth of Indian Creek Canyon.

Note: A wilderness permit is required before entering this area. While obtaining your permit from the ranger at the Gila Visitors Center, check on the adequacy of your provisions and on the level of the water in the river.

Source maps: *Gila National Forest*. USGS *Woodland Park*. (Springs not shown on either map.)

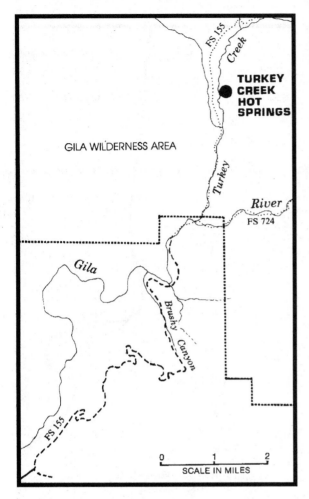

411   TURKEY CREEK HOT SPRINGS
(see map)

● **North of the town of Gila**

Several truly primitive hot springs accessible only via a challenging and rewarding hike into the Gila Wilderness. Elevation 5,200 feet. Not accessible during high water in the Gila River.

Natural mineral water (approximately 160°) flows out of many rock fractures along the bottom of Turkey Creek Canyon and combines with creek water in several volunteer-built soaking pools. Temperatures are regulated by controlling the relative amounts of hot and cold water entering a pool. Be careful, as many of these pools are quite hot. The apparent local custom is clothing optional.

There are no services available, but there are a limited number of overnight camping spots near the hot springs. Visitors have done an excellent job of packing out all their trash; please do your part to maintain this tradition. All services are seventeen miles away.

Directions: Starting at the end of the 4WD road, Wilderness Trail FS 724 crosses the Gila River several times before reaching Wilderness Trail FS 155, which starts up Turkey Creek Canyon. Approximately 2 miles from the trail junction, FS 155 begins to climb a ridge separating Turkey Creek from Skeleton Canyon. Do not follow FS 155 onto that ridge. (If you encounter switchbacks you've gone the wrong way.) Instead, stay to the right in the bottom of Turkey Creek Canyon, even though there is often no visible trail. Another half-mile will bring you to the first of the springs.

Source maps: *Gila National Forest. Gila Wilderness and Black Range Primitive Area.* USGS *Canyon Hill.* (Note: Springs are not shown.)

Directions and impressions from Shara Biggs and Steve Hereema, who hiked into this remote area to take the photo above right: After a short walk on what is left of a road that has been washed away, cross the Gila River. Follow the road and cross the river two more times. Then cross Turkey Creek to reach the junction with trail FS 155. Follow this trail, which disappears in the rocky river bed at times. Approximately 2 miles later there are campsites near the trail. This is a good place to camp. To reach the springs, follow the trail until you notice a faint trail leading to the right. Take this trail, which will cross a dry creek bed and continue walking upstream for .50 mile. This part of the hike is very rugged and can be slow going. Be prepared and able to cross the creek several times, climb over boulders, and crawl through a cave.

412 A   SAN FRANCISCO HOT SPRINGS
—LOWER

(see map)

● **South of the town of Pleasanton**

Several primitive hot springs along the east bank of the San Francisco River in the Gila National Forest. Elevation 4,600 feet. Open all year.

Natural mineral water flows out of the ground at 110° into a series of volunteer-built, rock-and-mud, riverbank pools. The parking area for this popular site is only ten yards away, so the Forest Service has posted a "nudity prohibited" sign, but clothing optional seems to be the local custom when there are no rangers around. However, people have been fined.

There are no services available. Primitive camping is permitted for up to seven days on the river side of the parking area, which is Forest Service land. Overnight camping is not permitted on the inland side under the trees, which is private property. Campers have done an excellent job of respecting the pristine beauty of the area and packing out trash. There is also Forest Service trash collection once per week. It is five miles to a store, cafe, and service station and twelve miles to RV hookups.

Directions: On US 180, 2 miles south of Pleasanton, watch for Forest Service sign with a pair of binoculars indicating viewing site. (When approaching from the south, the signs will be on the left, 1.3 miles after crossing the S. Dugway Canyon bridge.) Turn onto the gravel road and travel 1.3 miles to the parking area. The pools are down along the river's edge. This road crosses two creek beds and can be muddy after rain or snow.

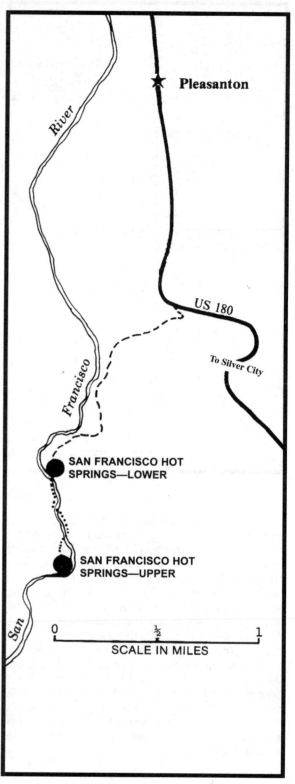

Pleasanton

River

US 180

To Silver City

Francisco

SAN FRANCISCO HOT
SPRINGS—LOWER

SAN FRANCISCO HOT
SPRINGS—UPPER

San

0   ½   1

SCALE IN MILES

412 B SAN FRANCISCO (BUBBLES) HOT SPRING—UPPER

(see map)

● **South of the town of Pleasanton**

A series of very enjoyable soaking pools requiring fording the river from Lower San Francisco Hot Springs. Elevation 4,600 feet. Open all year; during high water, fording the river is very dangerous.

Several years ago a major flood scoured out a fifty- by one-hundred-foot pool under a spectacular cliff, deposited a giant sand bar in front of the pool, and dropped the normal river flow into a channel one hundred yards away. Natural mineral water now flows up through the sandy pool bottom at 106°, maintaining the entire five-foot-deep pool at 96-102°, depending on air temperature. The pool even skims and cleans itself by flowing out over a small volunteer-built dam. Other nearby geothermal water outflows feed a series of small volunteer-built pools that maintain a temperature of 106°. The apparent local custom is clothing optional.

Primitive tent camping is permitted for up to seven days on the flat area near the pool. It is five miles back across the river to a store, cafe, and service station in Pleasanton and twelve miles to RV hookups.

Directions: From the parking area at San Francisco Hot Springs, hike downstream approximately .5 mile, crossing the river three times.

Source map: USGS *Wilson Mountain*.

413 FRISCO BOX HOT SPRING

● **East of the town of Luna**

Shallow, concrete soaking pool with spectacular views, located in a scenic canyon at the end of a rough road and a rugged but beautiful one and one-half mile trail. Elevation 6,800 feet. Open all year, subject to high water.

Natural mineral water flows out of a spring at 100° and is piped to a four-foot by eight-foot by twenty-inch-deep concrete box located above river level. The apparent local custom is clothing optional.

There are no services available on the premises. There is a walk-in camping area just north across the river from the hot spring. Overnight parking is permitted on level land just east of the private property gate. It is ten miles to groceries and gasoline and twenty miles to all other services.

Directions: Start at the Luna Ranger Station to obtain current information on weather conditions, river level, and a Gila National Forest Map. From US 180 in Luna, drive north on FS 19 (signed Bill Knight Gap Road) and turn east on FS 210 (signed Frisco Box Road) to a private property gate. Pass through the gate, carefully closing it after you, and continue east until this very rough road becomes impassable. Park and hike an additional 1.5 miles east, fording the river six or more times. On the south bank, look for a pipe and sign for Frisco Box Spring. Follow a well-worn, slightly uphill path 75 yards to the concrete box.

ARIZONA

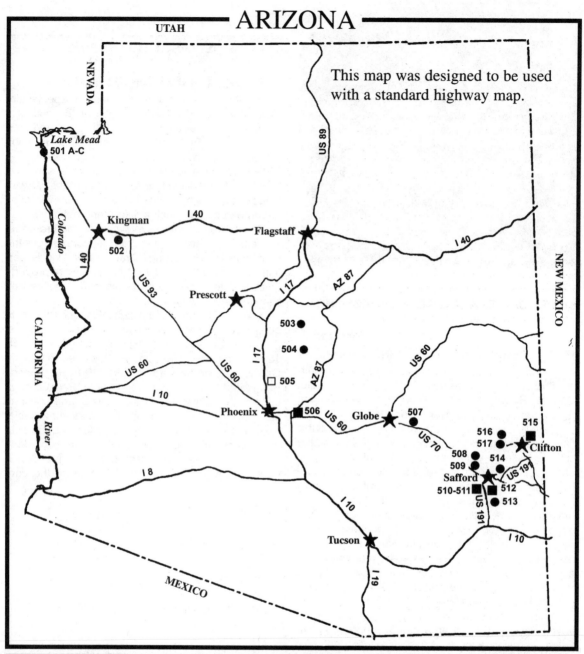

UTAH

NEVADA

This map was designed to be used with a standard highway map.

Lake Mead
501 A-C

Colorado

CALIFORNIA

US 89

Kingman
502

I 40

Flagstaff

I 40

NEW MEXICO

US 93

I 17

Prescott

AZ 87

503

504

US 60

US 60

I 17

505

AZ 87

US 60

River

I 10

Phoenix

506

US 60

Globe

507

515

516

517

Clifton

US 70

508

509

514

US 191

Safford

510-511

512

513

I 8

US 191

I 10

Tucson

I 10

I 19

MEXICO

MAP SYMBOLS

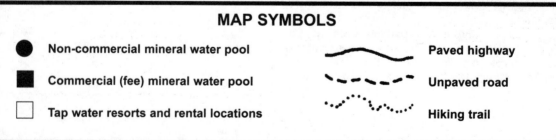

●   Non-commercial mineral water pool

■   Commercial (fee) mineral water pool

☐   Tap water resorts and rental locations

〜   Paved highway

- - -   Unpaved road

····   Hiking trail

HOT SPRINGS OF THE LOWER COLORADO

Over many centuries, flash floods have carved hundreds of spectacular canyons that lead into the Colorado River. In three of these canyons, downstream from Hoover Dam, natural mineral water flows out of rocky sidewalls at temperatures up to 125°, then gradually cools as it tumbles over a series of waterfalls between sandy-bottom pools. The water is sparkling clear, with no odor and a pleasant taste. In all three of these canyons, volunteers continue to build rock-and-sand soaking pools, even though most of them are washed away every year by the floods. Elevation 800 feet. You can reach these pools all year; however, the extreme heat during the summer months may make this area unpleasant. It is also highly recommended that you check at Willow Beach regarding floods and high water during the rainy season.

Land routes to these springs range from the difficult to the impossible. Most visitors rent an outboard-powered boat at the Willow Beach Marina, which is located at mile marker 52, eight miles downriver from Arizona (Ringbolt) Hot Springs. Willow Beach also has a ramp for launching your own boat, gas for boats, and a store for supplies. There are no overnight facilities at Willow Beach. It is twenty miles to all services in Boulder City, Nevada. The access road to Willow Beach connects with US 93, thirteen miles south of Hoover Dam on the Arizona side of the river.

Rafters and kayakers can obtain a special permit from the Lake Mead National Recreation Area to put in just below Hoover Dam, float to the various hot springs, and take out at Willow Beach.

The National Park Service maintains pit toilets at the entrances to Gold Strike and Arizona.

Note: The amount of water being released from Hoover Dam is controlled by the Bureau of Reclamation and may change from hour to hour, substantially affecting the water level in the river. Therefore, it is important that you secure your boat or raft in a manner that will withstand such changes.

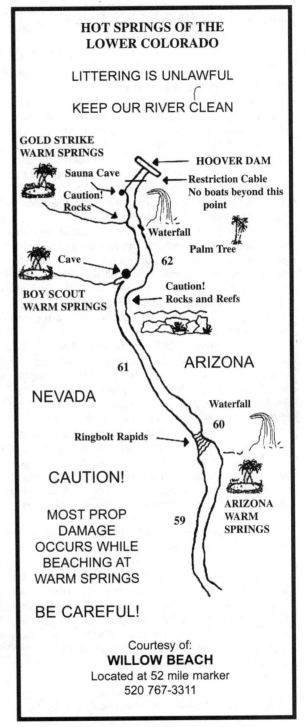

HOT SPRINGS OF THE LOWER COLORADO

LITTERING IS UNLAWFUL

KEEP OUR RIVER CLEAN

GOLD STRIKE WARM SPRINGS

Sauna Cave

Caution! Rocks

HOOVER DAM

Restriction Cable No boats beyond this point

Waterfall

Palm Tree

Cave

62

BOY SCOUT WARM SPRINGS

Caution! Rocks and Reefs

ARIZONA

61

NEVADA

Waterfall

60

Ringbolt Rapids

CAUTION!

MOST PROP DAMAGE OCCURS WHILE BEACHING AT WARM SPRINGS

59

ARIZONA WARM SPRINGS

BE CAREFUL!

Courtesy of:
WILLOW BEACH
Located at 52 mile marker
520 767-3311

501 A   ARIZONA (RINGBOLT) HOT SPRINGS

(see map)

- **Near Hoover Dam**

This is the most popular of the three hot springs because it is closest to Willow Beach and downstream from the turbulent water of Ringbolt Rapids. It is one-eighth mile downriver from mile marker 60, and two small warning buoys can be seen on a large submerged rock near the beach at the bottom of this canyon. There is no visible stream at the beach because the hot water disappears into the sand a hundred yards before reaching the river.

The long narrow canyon has beautiful rock formations and a few sections that require some scrambling ability. As you head upstream, you will often be walking in the streambed as well as climbing over sharp rocks, so be prepared with appropriate footwear. Barefoot is definitely not recommended. There is a ranger-installed metal ladder at the one major waterfall.

Source springs in the upper canyon flow at 106°, and volunteers have built a series of sandbag or rock-and-sand soaking pools, each with a slightly lower temperature than the one above. The geothermal water is cooled down to approximately 95° by the time it flows over the twenty-five-foot waterfall.

There is a large amount of camping space in the lower canyon and on a dry sandy plateau just south of the canyon mouth. When you enter the canyon from the river, bear left when the trail splits inland from the beach. A pit toilet is near the camping area. This is the only spring along the river that has a practical overland route.

Hiking directions: From Hoover Dam, drive southeast on US 93 to mile post 4.2 and a dirt parking area on your right, at the head of White Rock Canyon. Follow this canyon downhill, through the wash, to the river. Then follow the edge of the river .25 miles south to the lower end of Ringbolt Hot Springs canyon and hike upstream to the springs. Distance 2.9 miles, with an 800-foot elevation change. The trail is rated moderately strenuous, so allow at least 2.5 hours one way. Watch for Bighorn sheep.

The pool shown at right is located in the stream before you reach the hot shower and the ladder that leads you to another wonderful soaking pool at the top. If you walk through the pool at the top, you will come out on top of the rocks and have a wonderful, panoramic view.

501 B   GOLD STRIKE HOT SPRINGS
(see map)

● **Near Hoover Dam**

The beach at the bottom of this canyon is within sight of the warning cable stretched across the river just below the dam. One hundred yards up the canyon from the beach, natural mineral water flows out of cliff seeps at 109° into a series of volunteer-built soaking pools.

As you head farther up the canyon, you will often be walking in the stream bed as well as climbing over sharp rocks, so be prepared with appropriate footwear. Barefoot is definitely not recommended.

The canyon includes several beautiful waterfalls, which can be bypassed only with some strenuous scrambling along smooth rock walls. Near the bottom of the first large falls is a sandy-bottom pool with a water temperature of 100°.

From the river, the landmark for this canyon is a pit toilet on the sandy area at the wide canyon mouth. In the river near the canyon mouth, there are some large underwater rocks that cause rapids. There are also large rocks in the shallow water close to shore, making it difficult to navigate into this canyon entrance. Space for overnight camping at the beach is very limited. If you do choose to camp, set up at the far inland edge of the sand, or the changing river levels may flood your site.

Note: Hiking overland to this spring is not recommended. It is extremely difficult and dangerous.

501 C   BOY SCOUT HOT SPRINGS
(see map)

● **Near Hoover Dam**

A large cave, shaped like a human ear, can be seen on the west riverbank just upstream (north) from this canyon, whose entrance is protected by a land spit that blocks visibility from the south. When coming from the north, look for the bend in the river on the left past mile marker 62. Ahead of you is a layered rock formation. The canyon entrance and small beach sit in front of you before the river veers left. Landing on the gently sloping sandy beach is easy, but a sudden drop in river level could leave your boat many yards from the water.

The wide sand-and-gravel canyon mouth has a trickle of 70° water and plenty of camping space for a group. As you head upstream, the canyon narrows. You will often be walking in the streambed as well as climbing over sharp rocks, so be prepared with appropriate footwear. Barefoot is definitely not recommended. Remains of previously constructed cement dams and pipes are visible as you walk upstream into the canyon. There are several pools and waterfalls with temperatures up to 104° in the narrow upper canyon. The apparent local custom is clothing optional.

Note: There is no safe overland hiking trail to this hot spring.

502   KAISER WARM SPRINGS

- ### Southeast of Kingman
  ### Between Wikieup and Nothing

A primitive rock-and-mud pool in a beautiful serene desert canyon with nearby cold creek pools. A fairly easy mile-and-a-half walk with minor elevation change. Elevation 2,400 feet. Open all year, but recommended only October through April due to extreme summer heat. This area is also prone to flash floods.

Natural mineral water at about 100° bubbles up through the sandy creekbed where Warm Spring Canyon meets Burro Creek. The six- to-eight-person, volunteer-built pool is approximately eighteen inches deep. Runoff flows through openings in the rock-and-mud wall into the creek. To ensure a great soak, take along a stiff brush to remove the algae that forms on the rocks. Fifty yards further down the canyon cold Burro Creek emerges, surrounded by large flat pink and purple sandstone boulders that are ideal for sunning. Clothing is optional.

There are no facilities at the springs. There is plenty of BLM land along US 93 where overnight parking is not prohibited. Park well of the highway. Pack-in camping is also possible on BLM land in the canyon. It is seven miles from the trailhead to Burro Creek Campground, which has restrooms and RV dump, but no hookups. All other services are eleven miles from the trailhead in Wikieup. Fourteen miles south of the trailhead Nothing, Arizona has gas, AAA garage and towing, and the "T'Aint Much Store."

Note: The warm springs are located on private land, on a registered mine claim, surrounded by public BLM land. We have heard of no objection to using the springs, but please do not trespass on the private portion of Burro Creek, which is approximately one mile south of the springs.

Directions: From Kingman drive 60 miles southeast on US 93, also I-40. After Wikieup, watch for mile markers. At .1 miles past mile marker 135, look for a gated dirt road just before the impressive Kaiser Canyon Bridge. This rocky road is the Trailhead. As this is a very dangerous stretch of US 93, park well off the highway.

To reach the pool, take the rough rocky "trailhead" just north of the bridge (close the gate). The creekbed is visible just ahead. Hike down to the sandy creekbed, then walk along the fairly level canyon floor for approximately 1.5 miles (30 minutes) until the canyon bends sharply to the left in a 90-degree angle. Within 100 yards after veering left you will see warm seeps in the sandy canyon floor. Just ahead on the left is the soaking pool. Continue another 100 yards to reach the cold pools in Burro Creek. With a 4WD you can follow a jeep trail that leads down to the springs from Cholla Rd., the third dirt road north of the bridge.

Source map: USGS *Kaiser Spring.*

503   VERDE HOT SPRINGS

● **Near the town of Camp Verde**

Small, cement soaking pools, all that remains of an historic resort which burned down years ago, that are decorated with artwork and historic paintings, including one of the springs resort as it appeared in its heyday. Located on the west bank of the Verde River in a beautiful, high desert canyon. Elevation 2,800 feet. Open all year, subject to river level and bad-weather road hazards.

Natural mineral water flows out of several river-bank springs at 104° and into a small, indoor, cement soaking pool. A larger, outdoor cement pool is built over another spring and averages 98°. Twenty feet below, at low-water level, are several more springs that feed volunteer-built, rock-and-sand pools. Fifty feet upstream from the large cement pool is a 104° pool in a riverbank cave. The apparent local custom is clothing optional. Conscientious visitors have done a superb job of packing out all trash. Please respect this tradition.

There are no services available on the premises, and it is more than twenty miles to the nearest store, service station, and market. Parking and camping are permitted only in a Forest Service campground one mile south of the Childs Power Plant. Therefore, it is a one and one-half mile hike to the river ford at Verde Hot Springs. Check at the ranger station in Camp Verde regarding road conditions and river level before attempting to reach this site.

Directions: From the north end of the campground look for a sign marked "River Crossing for Hot Springs, 1 mile." Follow this trail north, across a wooden bridge at the power plant and along the river until it heads inland up a hill for a short jog to a two-lane, dirt jeep road marked "hot springs road." Follow this road until you see a trail down to the river on your left marked with stone pilings. The hot springs are across the river, visible from the jeep road. Look for palm trees across the river and a stone wall along the riverbank. Depending on the river level, it may be necessary to ford the river twice, first to an island and then to the springs.

Note: These directions keep you on public land. Any attempts to cross fences puts you in real danger of entering private property and getting shot.

Source maps: *Coconino National Forest*. USGS *Verde Hot Springs*.

When the Verde River level is high after heavy rains or spring runoff, this is about as close to the springs as you can get. Be sure to check at the ranger station before attempting to cross the river.

504   SHEEP BRIDGE HOT SPRING

●   **Southeast of Prescott**

Fiberglass tub on a ledge above the Verde River, surrounded on three sides by a dense growth of bulrushes. Elevation 1,400 feet. Open all year; be aware of flooded roads.

Natural mineral water flows out of a spring at 99° and is piped to a fiberglass tub close to the river. Other natural pools may be found, depending on water level, below the tub. The apparent local custom is clothing optional.

There are no services available on the premises. A level camping area is seventy-five yards upstream. It is fifty miles to all other services in Black Canyon City.

Directions: It is possible to reach this spring via a very difficult 4WD route from Carefree. However, the following is the recommended route: From I-17 north of Black Canyon City, take the Bloody Basin off-ramp and drive southeast on FS 269 for 37 miles. This road crosses several streambeds that are usually dry. The first 16 miles to Summit (elevation 4,500 ft.) is a good gravel road. The remaining 21 miles is a poor dirt road, but it is passable by a high-clearance 2WD vehicle. From a parking area at the bridge, walk 75 yards upstream to the soaking tubs.

To locate the campground, drive .3 mile back up from the bridge and look on the north side of the road for the remains of a building foundation. A steep path (4WD only!) leads 150 yards down to a level camping area by the river. The soaking tub is 75 yards downstream from this area.

Source maps: *Mazatzal Wilderness, Tonto National Forest*; USGS quads, *Brooklyn Park, Bloody Basin, Chalk Mountain*.

Sheep Bridge Hot Spring: The thick bullrushes surrounding the tub provide a nice screen for the tub and possibly some shade during the hot summer months.

---

505   SHANGRI LA II RESORT
       Box 4343 New River Rte.

                        602 465-5959

☐   Phoenix, AZ 85027

Naturist resort being upgraded and enlarged by new owners. Located in a scenic high desert valley twenty-five miles north of Phoenix. Elevation 2,000 feet. Open all year.

Gas-heated well water, chlorine treated, is used in all pools. A large, shaded, fiberglass hot pool is maintained at 104°. The adjoining swimming pool averages 75-80°. Bathing suits are prohibited in both pools. Many areas are handicap accessible.

Facilities include a large clubhouse, volleyball court, tennis courts, and sauna. Lodge rooms, camping spaces, cottages, and RV hookups are available.

Visa and MasterCard are accepted. It is five miles to a restaurant and seven miles to a store and service station.

Note: Because it is a membership club, Shangri La II is not open to the public on a drop-in basis. However, a limited number of guest passes may be issued to qualified visitors. Write or telephone well in advance to make arrangements to visit.

Hot water comes up from the river bottom both upstream and downstream in the San Carlos River. Just look for the green algae to find the warm spots.

506 BUCKHORN MINERAL WELLS
5900 East Main St. 602 832-1111
■ **Mesa, AZ 85205**

An historic, older motel-spa still offers many traditional hot-mineral-water treatment services. Elevation 1,200 feet. Open all year.

Natural mineral water is pumped from two wells at 130 and 140° and is then run through a cooling tower. Facilities include separate men's and women's departments, each containing 12 small, individual rooms with cement tubs. A whirlpool pump is mounted on the side of each tub. The temperature of the tub water may be varied by controlling the proportions of hot and cold water admitted. Tubs are drained, cleaned, and refilled after each use so that no chemical treatment is required.

Massage, sweat-wrap therapy and motel rooms are available on the premises with an adjoining cafe and small shopping center. Other stores and restaurants are located across the street. Service stations and RV spaces are available within one-half mile.

No credit cards are accepted. Phone for rates, reservations, and directions.

507 SAN CARLOS WARM SPRINGS

● **East of Globe**

A series of pools in the slow-flowing San Carlos River on the San Carlos Apache Reservation. Located in a tree-covered canyon with an abundance of wildlife. A permit is an absolute requirement. Elevation 3,500 feet. Open all year; pools may be under water during high runoff.

Natural mineral water bubbles up from several spots in the bottom of the river at temperatures between 85-95°. Warm spots are to be found both upstream and downstream, but most are above the ford in the river. You can also follow the trail of green algae to where the warm spots are. Clothing optional would be all right during low use times but suits seem to be the order of the day on weekends and holidays.

There are three campgrounds on the reservation (make arrangements at the Recreation Department). All other services are 20 miles away in Globe.

Directions: From Globe, take AZ 70 and go 20 miles east to the San Carlos Recreation and Wildlife Department, where you must stop and buy a permit. From the headquarters, continue east 3.5 miles to Hwy 8. Turn left (north) and continue 15 miles. Turn left on an unmarked gravel road (Indian Hwy 3). Go 3.5 miles to where the road ends at the river. It is possible during low water for 4WD vehicles to cross the river and explore the other side.

508   WATSON WASH HOT WELL

● **Northwest of the town of Thatcher**

Stone tub with foot bath surrounded by willows in a primitive setting. Elevation 3,000 feet. Open all year, subject to flash floods.

Natural mineral water flows out of a well casing at 102° and directly into a volunteer-built stone tub large enough for six or eight people. The overflow creates a foot bath that should be used to remove the surrounding sand before getting into the tub. The tub can be drained and refilled, and locals seem to do a good job keeping it clean. Since this area is also used as a party spot, be prepared to pack out more trash than you packed in. Even though "No swim suits" is carved in the cement, clothing optional is the apparent local custom only in the evening or during the week. The rest of the time, it seems best to rely on the preference of those soaking first.

There are no services available on the premises. The BLM land around the well allows for fourteen days of free camping. Undeveloped picnic sites are available along the road. It is six miles to a store, cafe, service station and other services.

Directions: From US 70 at the west end of Thatcher, go north on Reay Lane 3.2 miles to the "Y" intersection, which is Safford-Bryce Road. Turn left and drive .25 miles to the first wash across the road. Turn right and drive up the unimproved wash bottom .5 miles to the hot tub, going left at the first "Y" and right at the second. Most portions of the road are rough gravel, with some areas of hard-packed earth and a few sandy spots, all of which are passable in a standard passenger vehicle, except during or just after heavy rains.

The two different faces of *Watson Wash Hot Well*: a busy time with families and clothing, and a quiet time where you get to soak without a suit. You never know what you will find. However, if you camp nearby, you will probably experience both.

Since the city has taken over the cleanup of this area and keeps it patrolled, *Thatcher Hot Well* is once again a pleasant place to soak.

509　THATCHER HOT WELL

● **North of the town of Thatcher**

A substantial flow of hot mineral water out of the Gila River bank and a well casing just outside of town. Elevation 2,900 feet. Open all year, subject to flash floods.

Natural mineral water flows out of a large well casing at 112°, then runs across mud flats toward the current channel occupied by the Gila River. Volunteers dig shallow soaking pools in the mud adjoining the flow of 112° water, controlling the pool water temperature by limiting the amount of hot water admitted. Bring your own shovel; the volunteer-built pools are very temporary due to frequent flooding. It is possible to drive within five yards of the hot well, so bathing suits are advisable in the daytime. The area is now patrolled and cleaned by the city.

There are no services available on the premises. It is one mile to a store, cafe, service station and other services in Thatcher.

Directions: From US 70 in Thatcher, drive north on First Avenue for .6 mile to the end of the pavement. Continue another .6 on the hard packed dirt road to the river bed and the hot well.

510　ESSENCE OF TRANQUILITY
6074 S. Lebanon Loop　520 428-9312
■　Safford, AZ 85546

A series of soaking tubs, medicine wheel, and sweat lodge surrounded by mesquite, eucalyptus, palm trees, and salt cedars. Elevation 3,000 feet. Open all year.

Natural mineral water from a 1,531-foot artesian well flows over rocks and waterfall into three indoor private tubs surrounded by greenery. The tubs are drained after each use and require no chemical treatment. The first tile bathing tub is three and one-half- by three and one-half- by three-feet and is kept at a temperature of 108°. Pools two and three are eight-feet square, four and one-half feet deep, made of rock and cement, maintained at 106° and 104° respectively, and reached by going down six steps that allows for hot showers over the rocks. The fourth tub is outdoors behind a lattice enclosure, is kept at 104°, and is the only pool where suits are required.

Primitive campsites, tepee rentals, and RV hookups are available by reservation. Massage, sinus, and reflexology treatments are available by appointment. No credit cards accepted.

Directions: Starting in Safford at the intersection of US 70 and US 191, go south 6 miles on US 191. Turn right at Lebanon Rd. and follow road around a 90-degree curve onto Lebanon Loop. Continue .25 miles further. Establishment is on the right.

Roper Lake State Park: Very few other state parks anywhere can offer a hot, natural, mineral water soak.

511 KACHINA MINERAL SPRINGS SPA
Route 2, Box 987   520 428-7212
■   **Safford, AZ 85546**

Therapy-oriented bathhouse located in the suburbs south of Safford. Elevation 3,000 feet. Open all year.

Natural mineral water flows out of an artesian well at 108° and is piped into private-room soaking tubs. There are six large, tiled, sunken tubs. They are drained, cleaned, and refilled after each customer so that no chemical treatment is necessary. Two large soaking pools, a hot one at 104°, and a cold one, large enough for eight to ten people are also available. A free hot-pool soak comes with each therapy service, but private-pool use may also be rented. No credit cards are accepted. Phone for rates and reservations.

Directions: From the intersection of US 70 and US 191 in Safford, go 6 miles south on US 191, then turn right on Cactus Rd. for .25 miles.

512 ROPER LAKE STATE PARK
Route 2, Box 712   520 428-6760
■   **Safford, AZ 85546**

A small, neatly constructed outdoor soaking pool in a popular state park surrounded by rolling desert hills. Elevation 3,100 feet. Day-use fee. Open all year, 6 AM to 10 PM.

Geothermal mineral water flows from an artesian well at 99° directly into a stone-and-cement pool large enough for six to eight good friends. The water flows through continuously, so no chemical treatment is needed. There is a fifteen-minute limit when other people are waiting. Bathing suits are required. Access to the tub is ramped, with stairs and a handrail leading into the tub.

Facilities at the state park include camping and RV spaces, rest rooms, changing rooms, day-use picnic ramadas, a swimming beach, two stocked lakes for fishing, a boat ramp, and nature trails. It is 6.5 miles to all other services in Safford.

Directions: From Safford, drive south on US 191 for 6 miles, turn left (east) at the sign for Roper Lake State Park, and continue .5 mile to the park entrance.

513 HOT WELL DUNES

● Southeast of Safford

Two fenced-in soaking pools and one shallow pond surrounded by hundreds of acres of Bureau of Land Management (BLM) desert sand dunes open to, and popular with, off-road vehicles. Elevation 3,450 feet. Open all year, subject to flash floods.

Geothermal mineral water flows out of an artesian well at the rate of 200 gallons per minute and a temperature of 106° into two fenced soaking tubs. Overflow from the tubs spills into an adjoining shallow sand-bottom pool that provides soaking at a lower water temperature. Bathing suits are required.

A few developed tent or RV camp sites, fire grills, trash can, and vault toilets are available on the premises. Two weeks of camping are permitted on the level ground in this desert area, except where indicated right near the tubs. You will need to bring all your own supplies, including water. It is thirty-two miles to all services in Safford.

Directions: There are several access roads to the area but only the following one is recommended for standard passenger vehicles. From Safford, follow US 70 east for 7 miles to the Agricultural Inspection Station for vehicles entering from New Mexico. At .3 miles east of the station, turn right (south) onto an unmarked gravel road (Haekel Rd.). When road forks at 1.5 miles, take left fork. Continue south for 25 miles and turn left at the sign for Hot Well Dunes.

514 BUENA VISTA HOT WELLS

■ East of Safford, North of San Jose

Soaking areas in the bottom of an irrigation canal are shared with the fish, and the people fishing and farming in this rural agricultural area. Elevation 3,000 feet. Open all year.

Hot mineral water flows through open pipeways at temperatures between 130-150° and drops into an irrigation canal. There are no pools per se, and warm areas are found by walking up and down the canal area to a comfortable spot. Since the bottom of the canal is sandy, it is possible to scoop out a soaking pool. Bathing suits are a good idea as there seem to be a fair number of people around.

There are no services at the site. All services can be found about ten miles back in Safford.

Directions: From Safford, drive 7 miles east on US 70 and turn left onto San Jose Rd. After 2 miles, the road splits. Take Buena Vista Rd. to the left about .8 miles and make another left on a dirt road. This road crosses the irrigation ditch, and there is parking to your right. There is also pullout parking right before you cross over the ditch, and a path there leads down into the canal, probably the easiest way to get into the water.

515 POTTER'S AZTEC BATHS
BED AND BREAKFAST
PO Box 8443   520 865-4847

■ Clifton, AZ 85533

Two outdoor fiberglass pools on the grounds of the historic Potter Ranch in high desert country near Copper King Mountain in the mining area of Clifton-Morenci. Elevation 3,700 feet. Open all year.

Natural mineral water at 150° is pumped up from hot seeps along the San Francisco River thirty feet below and into two six-person fiberglass pools on outdoor wooden decks. Pool temperature is controlled at each pool by faucets that admit cold city water for the desired mix. The pools are drained after each use, so no chemical treatment of the water is necessary. Runoff goes into the river below. Pools are available to the general public for a day-use fee, as well as to registered guests at no charge. Management has no policy about bathing suits, so it is up to the mutual consent of those present. The pools and other facilities are handicap accessible with assistance.

Facilities include three bed and breakfast rooms, with several more under renovation. National Forest camping is along the Coronado Trail thirty miles away. All other services are two miles away in Clifton. Credit cards are accepted.

Directions: At the American Legion building in Cllifton, just north of the historic railroad station (now the Chamber of Commerce), turn east toward the steel bridge. Do not cross the bridge, but make an immediate left for .6 mile to the concrete Polly Rosenbaum Bridge. Cross this bridge and bear left along the river for 1.8 miles to the first road down toward the river on the left. The historic mansion is visible when you look down from the edge of the road. The "Potter Ranch" is on the the mailbox. At the foot of the hill bear left to the house.

Note: Primitive seeps along the San Francisco River on the Potter property have been used for years by volunteers who build simple rock-and-mud pools that get washed out and rebuilt every year. The seeps may still be used, but please inquire at Potter's for directions. A recent flood created a twenty-five-foot bank along the river which needs to be protected from foot traffic.

The grandfather of gracious hostess June Potter was one of the first gold miners in this area. June herself was born in this house and has been in the process of restoring it and the pools into a bed and breakfast since 1992.

516 GILLARD HOT SPRINGS

● **Near the town of Clifton**

Remote hot springs along the Gila River in the Black Hills area of southeastern Arizona's Greenlee County. Located at the end of a six-mile drive on unpaved roads and a short walk through a sandy wash. Elevation 3,500 feet. Open all year, subject to road washouts due to heavy rain.

Natural mineral water seeps up from underground at over 180° along the northeast bank of the Gila River. Following each year's high water and spring runoff, the primitive rock-and-mud pools must be redug. Water temperature is controlled by mixing in cold river water. Due to the slow rate of flow, it may take some patience to achieve the proper soaking temperature. The apparent local custom is clothing optional.

There are no facilities on the premises, but there is plenty of BLM land where camping is permitted. There are areas for car camping along Old Safford Road near the Gila River. North of the bridge, a road heads down to the river where you can park under the trees.

Directions: Drive 35 miles northeast of Safford, AZ on US 70 and US 191 to Three Way (where Hwys 191, 75, and 78 meet). Or, from US 70 in Lordsburg, NM, drive 55 miles northwest through Duncan to the Apache ranger station at Three Way. From Three Way, continue north toward Clifton on US 191 for 5.5 miles. When the divided highway ends, make an immediate left (west) on Black Hills, Back Country Byway (also called Old Safford Rd.). Drive 2.1 miles to a primitive dirt road on the right with a sign to Gillard Hot Springs. Turn right onto this unmaintained road for 1 mile to a three-way intersection. Follow the middle fork for .3 mile to a sandy wash. Unless you have a 4WD, you may want to park near here rather than attempt to cross the deep sandy wash. At 4 miles in, the road ends in a wash where it is blocked by a fence. Park and follow the wash and blocked road to the river. The seeps are on the northeast bank right near the end of the road.

Source map: USGS *Apache-Sitgreaves National Forests* (springs not shown).

517 EAGLE CREEK HOT SPRING

● **Near the town of Morenci**

Natural hot water pool in a small grotto in remote high desert country reached by a hike along Eagle Creek, which involves six river crossings. Elevation 4,000 feet. Open all year, subject to river flooding.

Natural mineral water at 104° fills a small five-foot grotto thirty inches high and big enough for two people (or four very good friends). It is located on a hillside in a side canyon off Eagle Creek. Several other hot water seeps and small trickling waterfalls in the area range up to 109°, but volunteers could possibly create some nice soaking pools. The springs are located on private property. Clothing is optional.

There are no facilities at this remote location except level areas for pack-in camping and car camping on nearby BLM land.

Directions: (See directions for #516 as far as Clifton.) From Clifton, follow US 191 to Morenci. Turn right at the first traffic light in Morenci and go 1.5 miles to a "Y" at Mine Rd. Stay on US 191 another 3 miles to a small cemetery on your right. Opposite the cemetery is Eagle Creek Rd. (unmarked), a wide gravel road with yellow highway markers. Follow this road for 5.3 miles to a power plant at the creek. Unless you have a 4WD, park here. You will cross the river 6 times to get to the springs.

Walk south past the farmhouse just south of the power plant. Or, with a 4WD, cross the river by the power plant and immediately cross again. Past the fifth crossing (seventh if driving) is a swimming hole. Near the next crossing are two swimming holes, one just upstream, the other farther downstream. If driving, park after the eighth crossing and walk across the river just below the downstream swimming hole. Below this swimming hole is Hot Springs Canyon, which is almost free of vegetation.

Hike into the canyon approximately 300 feet to a small stream. Continue another 500 feet to a small trickling 50-foot warm waterfall on your left. Follow the stream up the canyon. After it veers left, you will see a 20-foot waterfall ahead and on the right a smaller stream of warm water flowing from above. Scramble up the hill on a faint path past an old, water-filled mine shaft (timbers rotten, so don't go in). A few yards up hill is the grotto source pool.

When heading back to Eagle Creek follow a faint easterly trail from the grotto to the top of the 50-foot waterfall. The source, a small spring at 109°, has been trampled by cattle but could be formed into a pool. The faint trail gradually descends to Eagle Creek between crossings 5 and 6 (when walking).

NORTHERN CALIFORNIA

This map was designed to be used with a standard highway map.

MAP SYMBOLS

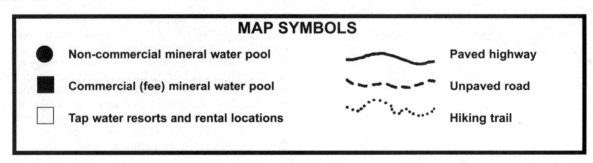

- ● Non-commercial mineral water pool
- ■ Commercial (fee) mineral water pool
- □ Tap water resorts and rental locations
- ⎯⎯⎯ Paved highway
- - - - Unpaved road
- ····· Hiking trail

Both the pools at *Glen Hot Springs* and *Leonard's Hot Springs* have been dug by volunteers in wide portions of the ditches and runoffs where the water has cooled to a comfortable temperature.

601   GLEN HOT SPRINGS
(see map)

● **Near the town of Cedarville**

Undeveloped cluster of hot springs on a barren slope along the east side of Upper Alkali Lake. Elevation 4,600 feet. Open all year.

Natural mineral water flows out of several springs at 150° and cools as it runs toward the lake. Volunteers have built shallow soaking pools where the water has cooled to approximately 100°. The apparent local custom is clothing optional.

No services are available on the premises. There is a limited amount of unmarked open space on which overnight parking is not prohibited. It is ten miles to a service station and all other services.

Source map: *USGS Cedarville*.

602   LEONARD'S HOT SPRING
(see map)

● **Near the town of Cedarville**

Abandoned and deteriorated old resort on a barren slope along the east side of Middle Alkali Lake. Elevation 4,500 feet. Open all year.

Natural mineral water flows out of the ground from several springs at a temperature of 150° and cools as it runs toward the lake. A diversion ditch used to carry this water to the resort, but it now flows through a winding ditch fifty yards southeast of the old swimming pool. Volunteers have built shallow soaking pools in the ditch where the water has cooled to approximately 100°. The apparent local custom is clothing optional.

No services are available on the premises. There is an abundance of unmarked level space on which overnight parking is not prohibited. It is nine miles to a service station and all other services.

Source map: *USGS Cedarville*.

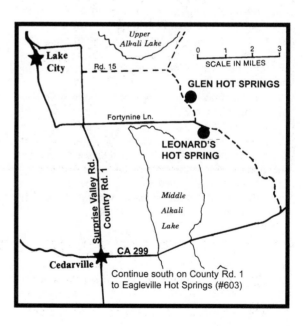

Eagleville Hot Spring provides you with an incredible view whether you are soaking in the redwood hot tub or in the shallow soaking pool.

603   EAGLEVILLE HOT SPRING

● **South of the town of Cedarville**

Shallow, primitive soaking pool and tub with a commanding view of Surprise Valley and surrounding mountains. Elevation 4,600 feet. Open all year.

Natural mineral water flows out of two PVC pipes in the road embankment at 104°. One pipe goes to a volunteer-built rock-and-sand soaking pool, and the other goes to an adjacent five-foot redwood tub. The pools are not visible from the road, so the apparent local custom is clothing optional. Local custom also expects new arrivals to await the departure of those already there.

There are no services available on the premises. It is seven miles to Eagleville and twenty-three miles to Cedarville.

Directions: From Cedarville, on Modoc County Road 1 (Surprise Valley Road), drive south 15 miles to Eagleville. From the post office, drive 7 miles to a slight turnout on the east side of the road and continue 75 yards down the embankment to a dead end. Walk 135 yards north to pool and tub.

604   STEWART MINERAL SPRINGS
4617 Stewart Springs Rd.
800 322-9223

■   Weed, CA 96094

A well-kept rustic retreat available to individuals or groups for special events or seminars. Located on a mountain stream in a green canyon northwest of Mt. Shasta. Elevation 3,900 feet. Open March through November on a reservation basis only.

Natural mineral water is pumped from a well at 40° and is propane heated as needed. There are twelve individual bathtubs and larger tubs in private rooms. Water temperature in each tub is controlled, as desired, by mixing cold and hot mineral water. Tubs are drained and refilled after each use, so no chemical treatment of the water is necessary. Bathing suits are required in public areas.

Facilities include rooms, restaurant (for groups of ten or more), camping spaces, and partial-hookup RV spaces. Massage is available by appointment. A sweat lodge is available for groups. Major credit cards are accepted. It is seven miles to a store, service station, and public bus. Special pickup at the bus depot and at the Weed airport can be arranged.

Directions: Take the Edgewood exit on I-5 north of Weed. Turn north on the west side of I-5 and turn at the first left onto Stewart Springs Rd. Drive 4 miles to the resort at the end of the road.

605 BIG BEND HOT SPRINGS
PO Box 81   916 337-6680
■ **Big Bend, CA 96011**

The remains of an historical resort being improved and operated by a very hospitable, cooperative family group representing Indian, African, Asian, and European backgrounds. Located fifty miles northeast of Redding on the tree-shaded south bank of the Pit River. Elevation 2,000 feet. Open all year.

Natural mineral water from three springs is 180°.

(1) Hot mineral baths. Located on the edge of a plateau thirty feet above the Pit River are three interconnected natural stone/cement pools, each large enough for six persons. Faucet-controlled cold creek water is added to each pool to produce whatever temperature is desired by occupants. Each pool has seating at various depths, and all have a superb view of the river.

(2) Indian Springs. Located about ten feet above the level of the adjacent Pit River, 180° mineral water flows into a series of secluded, shallow pools created by volunteers from riverbed rocks.

Bathing suits are optional in all springs and pools.

Rustic cabins with kitchen facilities, as well as peaceful campsites, are available on the premises. No credit cards are accepted. It is one-quarter mile to a cafe, store, and service station in the small town of Big Bend.

Directions: From I-5 in Redding, go 35 miles east on CA 299. Turn north 17 miles toward the town of Big Bend. Turn left on Hot Springs Road just prior to Big Bend Store and the bridge over the Pit River. Continue .25 miles to the end of the road and check in at the office.

Big Bend Hot Springs is one of those lucky places that can offer a soak in the river (above) and a series of man-made, multi-level pools (below) that affords the soaker a beautiful view of the river from all of the pools.

A whole family can soak in one of the tubs that have a variety of seat heights and where the temperature can be adjusted to everyone's comfort.

Several hot source springs are used to feed the swimming pool at *Drakesbad Guest Ranch* which is located in beautiful Lassen Volcanic National Park.

606   HUNT HOT SPRINGS

● **Near the town of Big Bend**

Delightful rock-and-cement soaking tub and several creek-side rock pools situated on Kosh Creek where it joins the Pit River. Located in a beautiful river valley near Mount Shasta. Elevation 2,000 feet. Open all year; road may not be passable during wet weather.

Natural mineral water flows out of several hillside seeps at 104° and cools on its way through several pools down to Kosh Creek. There is one rock-and-cement pool large enough for four, and a varying number of volunteer-made rock pools. It is a good idea to bring a bucket for the cold creek water to help regulate the pool temperatures. Clothing is optional.

There are no services available on the premises, but there is plenty of wide open space where camping is not restricted. General store, service station, cafe, and ranger station are approximately two miles away in Big Bend.

Directions: From Big Bend store, proceed across Pit River Bridge. About .5 mile, FS 3702 goes off to the right. Continue straight (FS 11) another 100 yards and take the first dirt road to the lefeet Go right at the fork. From this point the road is quite rough for the 1 mile down to its end (just past the Wright Historical Cemetery on your left). Low clearance vehicles may have a problem.

607   DRAKESBAD GUEST RANCH
c/o California Guest Services, Inc.
2150 Main St. #5   916 529-1512
■ **Red Bluff, CA 96080**

A rustic mountain ranch/resort, reservations only, with a mineral-water swimming pool, plus horses and guides for riding and hiking. Located in a superb mountain meadow within the boundaries of Lassen Volcanic National Park. Elevation 5,700 feet. Open first part of June to first part of October.

Natural mineral water flows out of two springs at temperatures between 140-150° and is piped to the pool. The swimming pool is maintained in at 95° during the day and 105° at night by mixing the two hot water flows. Minimal amounts of chlorine are added to control algae growth. One lodge is handicap accessible. Bathing suits are required. The pool is available to registered guests only. No day use is permitted.

Facilities include lodge, rooms, cabins, bungalows, and dining room. Saddle horses and guides are available by the hour. Visa and MasterCard are accepted. It is 17 miles to RV spaces, store, and service station. Telephone for reservations.

Directions: From CA 36 in the town of Chester, take Warner Valley Road northwest 17 miles to the resort, which is at the end of the road. The last 3 miles are dirt/gravel road.

After a hike along the Pacific Crest Trail, a soak at *Terminal Geyser* sounds like just the thing to ease those aching feet.

608   TERMINAL GEYSER HOT SPRINGS

● **Northwest of the town of Chester**

Two volunteer-built soaking pools downstream from an active steam geyser just off the Pacific Crest Trail in Lassen National Park. Elevation 6,000 feet. Open all year, subject to snow closures in winter.

Very hot mineral water erupts from a steam geyser into a stream that cools as it flows down through a gulch into the two volunteer-built rock-and-sand pools. The first pool maintains a temperature of 104°; the second is around 98°. Clothing is optional.

There are no services on the premises, and it is 2.7 miles to the nearest campground. All other services are seventeen miles from the trailhead, in Chester.

Directions: From CA 36 in the town of Chester, take Feather River Drive at fire station to Warner Valley Road. Go northwest 17 miles to the Drakesbad Resort, which is at the end of the road. The last 3 miles are dirt/gravel road. The trailhead starts at the entrance to the resort. It is 2.7 delightful miles on a well-maintained, moderate trail that goes by Boiling Springs Lake. (The trail is mostly up hill going and down hill returning.)

609   WOODY'S FEATHER RIVER HOT SPRINGS
PO Box 7   916 283-4115
● **Twain, CA 95984**

Primarily a fishing and hunting resort, this site does have one small soaking pool on the north bank of the Feather River, where you can also pan for gold. The resort is located in the tree-covered upper Feather River Canyon. Elevation 2,700 feet. Open all year.

Natural mineral water flows directly into one cement, sandy-bottom pool at 90-100°. No chemical treatment is added. Clothing is optional in the pool and in the adjoining river.

Facilities include motel rooms, RV spaces, restaurant, and bar. No credit cards are accepted. It is three miles to a store and fifteen miles to a service station.

Directions: On CA 70, go 4 miles west from the Quincy-Greenville "Y," the junction of Hwy 89 and Hwy 70. Located at mile post 28.

610 SIERRA HOT SPRINGS
PO Box 366   916 994-3773
■ Sierraville, CA 96126

A six-hundred-acre rustic resort with secluded forests, meadows, and streams is being restored and expanded by a nonprofit spiritual community. Public use of the facilities is welcome on a space-available basis. While this is a membership facility, non-resident fees are minimal. Elevation 5,000 feet. Open all year.

Natural mineral water flows out of several springs at temperatures up to 112°. On a wooded slope a variety of tubs at several temperatures use flow-through mineral water without chemical treatment and maintain temperatures ranging from 98-110°. Clothing is optional in all pool areas.

Hotel and lodge rooms, dormitory accommodations, camping spaces, and massage are available on the premises. Also available is a restaurant (check for open times) or facilities to cook your own food. Most major credit cards are accepted. Non-denominational weekly spiritual gatherings are open to everyone. It is two miles to all other services in Sierraville. No pets, alcohol, drugs, or smoking on the property, and no soap may be used in the pools. Phone for rates and reservations.

Directions: From the junction of CA 89 and CA 49 in Sierraville, follow CA 49 north to Lemon Canyon Rd., which runs along the north edge of the airport; then turn right on Campbell Hot Springs Rd., which runs along the east edge of the airport, and continue into the foothills to the main office.

By the time you get to *Sierra Hot Springs,* many of the current tubs will have been totally renovated and new ones built for you to enjoy. A great deal of work will also have been put in updating the lodge and cabins.

611 A   NEPHELE
1169 Ski Run Blvd.   916 544-8130
☐   So. Lake Tahoe, CA 95729

Combination bar, restaurant, and rent-a-tub establishment located between the lake and a ski run.

Three private, enclosed outdoor pools are for rent to the public, and a shower is also available. Using gas-heated tap water and treated with bromine, the pools are maintained at 102°. Bar service (but not food) is available at poolside.

A bar and restaurant are available on the premises. There are dinner-and-soak combination discounts. Visa, MasterCard, and American Express are accepted. Phone for rates, reservations, and directions.

611 B   PINEWOOD LODGE
3818 Hwy 50   916 544-3319
☐   So. Lake Tahoe, CA 95729

Small motel with one separate room containing a hot tub, sauna, and shower. Located on the south side of Hwy 50.

Gas-heated tap water treated with chlorine is used in the redwood tub, and water temperature is maintained at 100°.

Major credit cards are accepted. Phone for rates, reservations, and directions.

611 C   TAHOE HACIENDA MOTEL
3820 Hwy 50   916 541-3805
☐   So. Lake Tahoe, CA 95705

Major motel with a dozen rooms containing hydropools. Located on the south side of Hwy 50.

Gas-heated tap water is used in twelve in-room pools that may be rented for private use overnight or longer. These pools are refilled after each check-out, so no chemical treatment is needed. Temperature is adjustable to individual preference.

The outdoor communal swimming pool (approximately 80°) is open June through September, and the outdoor communal hydropool (approximately 103°) is open all year. Both outdoor pools require chlorination. Bathing suits are required in outdoor pools. Major credit cards are accepted. Phone for rates, reservations, and directions.

611 D   PACIFICA LODGE
931 Park Ave.   916 544-4131
☐   So. Lake Tahoe, CA 95729

Large motel with some special theme rooms containing heart-shaped hydropools. Located a few blocks from the beach and the Nevada state line.

Gas-heated tap water is used in six in-room pools that may be rented overnight or longer for private use. These pools are drained and refilled after each check-out, so no chemical water treatment is necessary.

Two of the rooms with tubs have fireplaces, as do some of the other rooms. A separate Chalet, which will accommodate six, is also available.

The outdoor communal swimming pool is maintained at 80° and uses gas-heated tap water treated with chlorine. All pools are for registered guests only. Major credit cards are accepted. Phone for rates, reservations, and directions.

Sonoma Mission Inn & Spa: The outdoor soaking pool (left), and the swimming pool (above) are filled with hot natural mineral water, as are two other available pools. Treat yourself to any of several spa packages, romantic rooms, and excellent cuisine.

612 SONOMA MISSION INN & SPA
PO Box 1447   707 938-9000
■ Sonoma, CA 95476

Luxuriously restored resort providing multiple beauty and health packages for your benefit and enjoyment in a beautiful, romantic setting. Elevation 100 feet. Open all year.

Mineral water flows out of the source at 135° and is piped to one large outdoor and one large indoor whirlpool tub. Both are lightly treated with bromine and refilled daily. The water is maintained at 102°. The mineral water is also used to fill the two outdoor swimming pools, which are treated lightly with bromine and refilled daily. The large pool is maintained at 82° and the spa pool at 92°. Mineral water showers are also available in the spa.

Beautifully appointed rooms, a gourmet restaurant, a cafe, coed exercise and spa facilities, and tennis courts are available on the premises. In addition, over forty different spa treatments are offered. Call for rates, reservations, directions, and details.

613 AGUA CALIENTE MINERAL SPRINGS
17350 Vailetti Dr.   707 996-6822
■ Sonoma, CA 95476

A summertime plunge and picnic grounds in the middle of the Sonoma Valley. Elevation 100 feet. Open summer months only.

Natural mineral water is pumped from a well at 96° and piped to a swimming pool that averages 86° and to a hydropool that averages 95°. The adjoining diving pool and wading pool, averaging 70°, are filled with unheated tap water; both pools are treated with chlorine and are drained and filled every day. Bathing suits are required.

A seasonal snack bar is available on the premises. No credit cards are accepted. It is less than one mile to a store, service station, and all other services.

Directions: From the city of Sonoma, go 3 miles north on CA 12 and watch for Agua Caliente signs.

614 WHITE SULPHUR SPRINGS RESORT
3100 White Sulphur Springs Rd.
707 963-8588

■ **St. Helena, CA 94574**

Historic, three-hundred-thirty-acre resort surrounded by the beauty of the Napa Valley. Elevation 400 feet. Open all year.

Natural mineral water flows out of several springs at various temperatures up to 95° and is piped to one outdoor soaking pool that operates on flow-through basis requiring no chemical treatment and is maintained at 85-87°. Also available is a twenty-person jet tub filled with chlorine-treated spring water and maintained at an average temperature of 103°. All pools are available to the public for day use, as well as to registered guests. Bathing suits are required.

Extensive hiking trails on the wooded premises extend through forested canyons and fern-lined creeks. Other facilities include a sauna, extensive sunning areas, a new health center that offers massage (indoors and out), and herbal and mud wraps. A special "Mud Adventure," including a vine-covered water spray arbor, invites you to apply a body mask of sulphurated clay; bathing suits are not required in this area for obvious reasons. Overnight accommodations include cottages and inn rooms. Fully equipped meeting rooms and kitchen facilities are available. The redwood grove is a perfect setting for weddings, picnics, or family reunions. Visa and MasterCard are accepted. It is three miles to central St. Helena and all other services.

Directions: From CA 29 in the center of St. Helena, drive 3 miles west on Spring St. to the resort.

Tired of the crowds and traffic as you drive around the wine country? For a delightful change of pace spend time hiking on the beautiful grounds of *White Sulphur Springs Resort*, soaking in their pools, and experiencing an all-over mud body mask.

CALISTOGA SPAS

CALISTOGA, CA 94515

All of the following locations are in or near the charming town of Calistoga, which is on CA 29 in Napa County, adjacent to the Napa Valley wine country, and is a wonderful getaway. These facilities are open all year and stores, restaurants, etc., are available in the town.

Each of the locations has its own hot wells, which are used to supply the water to the soaking and swimming pools. Chlorination of the pools is a state regulation. Soaking tubs in bathhouses are drained and filled after each use so no chemical treatment is necessary. Unless otherwise noted, resorts with pool facilities are available for day use except during peak times and holidays. Bathing suits are required in all public places. Major credit cards are accepted. Phone first for rates, reservations, availability, and details.

Calistoga Spa Hot Springs has several outdoor pools; one with a temperature just right for you.

615 A   CALISTOGA OASIS SPA
1300 Washington St.

■   707 942-2122

Modern spa with facilities for couples and individuals located on the premises of Roman Spa. (See complete listing under Roman Spa.)

615 B   CALISTOGA SPA HOT SPRINGS
1006 Washington St.

■   707 942-6269

Resort motel with separate men's and women's bath areas.offers volcanic ash mud baths, mineral baths, steam baths, blanket wraps, and massage.

Resort has four naturally heated mineral baths: outdoor soaking pool, 100°; outdoor swimming pool, 83°; outdoor wading pool, 90°; and a covered hydropool, 105°. Landscaped area surrounding pools has places to lounge and a refreshment stand. Indoor men's and women's bathhouses each contain four individual tubs, two mud baths, and three steambaths.

All rooms are equipped for light housekeeping. Aerobic classes, workout rooms, and a conference room are available on the premises.

615 C   CALISTOGA VILLAGE INN AND SPA
■   **1880 Lincoln Ave.   707 942-0991**

Offers a wide range of affordable lodging, some with Roman tub or whirlpool in room. Spa offers traditional mud bath, therapeutic massage, salt scrubs, facials, and reflexology.

Spa has an outdoor swimming pool at 80-85°, wading pool at 90-95°, and enclosed hydropool at 100-105°. Indoor men's and women's bathhouses, each contain two hydrotherapy tubs, two mud baths, two steam cabinets, and a sauna.

Facilities include rooms, conference meeting rooms, and an on-site restaurant serving all meals.

615 D   CARLIN COUNTRY COTTAGES
■   **1623 Lake St.   707 942-9102**

Fifteen cottages, seven with a two-person, in-room spa, are decorated with an Irish and Shaker country theme. Pools for registered guests only.

MIneral water outdoor pool is maintained at 90-95° in winter and 85° in summer. Outdoor hydropool is 104°. Cottage pools are controllable to 104°.

Continental breakfast served buffet style; can be taken to the poolside or to your room. Late afternoon refreshments are also provided.

615 E COMFORT INN
■ **1865 Lincoln Ave.**
Lodging 707 942-9400
Spa 707 942-4636

Fifty-four beautifully decorated rooms. Complete spa facilities offered across the street at Calistoga Village Inn and Spa (see above).

Large geothermal outdoor swimming pool is maintained at 85-90°; one whirlpool is 104°. Sauna and steamroom are also available.

Complimentary continental breakfast included with room. Facilities include meeting room and non-smoking and handicap rooms.

615 F DR. WILKINSON'S HOT SPRINGS
■ **1507 Lincoln Ave.** 707 942-6257

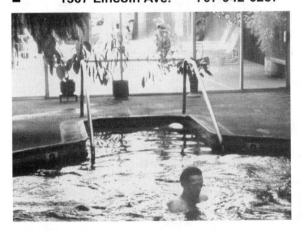

Dr. Wilkinson's is available to registered guests staying at the Hideaway Cottages.

One of the original locations (since 1946) offering massage, mud baths, blanket wraps and skin care.

Two outdoor mineral pools are 82° and 92°; one tropical-foliage indoor mineral pool is 104°. Indoor men's and women's bathhouses each contain four individual tubs, two mud baths, and a steambath.

Contemporary or Victorian style lodgings.

615 G GOLDEN HAVEN HOT SPRINGS SPA AND RESORT
■ **1713 Lake St.** 707 942-6793

One of only two spas in town offering coed mud and mineral baths as well as massage. Spa open to the public, you need not be a guest at the resort.

Enclosed mineral water swimming pool is 80°; covered hydropool is 102°.

Rooms, some with private sauna or hydropool, some with kitchenettes, are available.

615 H HIDEAWAY COTTAGES
■ **1412 Fairway** 707 942-4108

Seventeen cottages for adults only. Spa facilities at Dr. Wilkinson's (see above).

Outdoor swimming pool is 82°, and hydropool, is 104°. Reserved for registered guests; no day use.

Various accommodations include some non-smoking rooms some with kitchens. A conference room for up to twenty-five persons is also available.

615 I INDIAN SPRINGS
■   **1712 Lincoln Ave.   707 942-4913**

California's oldest continuously operating pool and spa offering mud baths, soaking tubs, steam room, massage, and facials. Three active geysers on the premises supply the hot mineral water.

Outdoor, Olympic-size swimming pool is 90-102°, depending on the season. Men's and women's bathhouses, each contain five one-person mud or mineral water soaking tubs and a steam room. Only this spa uses pure volcanic ash, no additives.

Comfortable bungalows have recently been restored. Clay tennis court, shuffleboard, bicycle surreys, croquet, and rose gardens are available on the premises.

Lavender Hill Spa offers complete privacy for singles or couples. The bathhouses are nestled into a terraced garden hillside, and a few steps through the gardens brings you to the main house where massages and facials are offered.

615 J LAVENDER HILL SPA
■   **1015 Foothill Blvd.   707 942-4495**

Two private bathhouses for couples offer a full range of mud and seaweed baths, herbal wraps, aromatherapy, facials, massage, and reflexology. You can also make an appointment to create a personalized perfume just for you.

Hydropool mineral-water tubs includes a choice of herbal essentials to enhance the soak.

615 K   NANCE'S HOT SPRINGS
■   **1614 Lincoln Ave.   707 942-6211**

One of Calistoga's original spas offering mud baths, mineral baths, blanket wraps, and massage.

Indoor hydropool is 103°. Indoor men's and women's bathhouses contain four individual tubs (up to 110°), three mud baths, and two steambaths in each section.

Quality lodgings feature kitchens and rooms for the handicapped. Glider rentals are available at the adjoining airport.

615 L   PINE STREET INN AND EUROSPA
■   **1202 Pine St.   707 942-6829**

Luxurious full-service spa surrounded by poolside gardens with a view of mountains and vineyards.

Outdoor unheated mineral water pool and heated whirlpool are 103-105°. Three gas-heated, tap water hydropools allow customers to control temperatures.

Sixteen nicely decorated rooms are available.

615 M   ROMAN SPA
■   **1300 Washington St. 707 942-4441**

Well-appointed rooms in a garden surrounding with Calistoga Oasis Spa on the premises offering massage, reflexology, acupressure, coed mud and enzyme baths, mineral baths, hydrotherapy massage, herbal blanket wrap, facials, aromatherapy baths, and Japanese enzyme baths. Four mud tubs are 101°, and two single and two double whirlpool allow customers to control temperatures.

Outdoor swimming pool is 92-95°, and hydropool is 104°. Indoor hydropool is 100°.

Some suites, some rooms with kitchens, one room with a private whirlpool,.and non-smoking rooms are available.

615 N   SILVER ROSE INN HOT SPRINGS AND SPA
■   **351 Rosedale Rd.   707 942-9581**

A three-star rating ranks this romantic, upscale resort as one of the best. All the intimacy of a bed and breakfast inn. Hot mineral water supplies all the showers. Spa area offers two massage rooms for couples or a massage in your room. Full range of body and facial treatments, mud and herbal soaks, bodywraps, and hydrotherm massage are also available. Facilities for registered guests only.

Two large outside pools are 80-90°, and two outdoor whirlpools are 102°.

Nine guest rooms are each decorated around a theme. Many rooms offer fireplaces, two-person whirlpool tubs, and private balconies. Breakfast can be enjoyed in the dining area, outside on the terrace, or delivered to your room. Entire inn is non-smoking. Afternoon hospitality hour is included.

This mythical dragon welcomes you to *Harbin Hot Springs*. It serves as a reminder that the cares of the real world are to be left outside.

Rooms are beautifully and comfortably decorated, and a small cottage is just perfect for a romantic getaway. Movies and other evening programs are available. A wide range of massage techniques are offered in the separate massage building. For a special treat, indulge yourself in the Harbin Clay Works and create a therapeutic body mask for yourself. Massage and Watsu training in state-accredited schools is available on the premises. (In fact, a complete Watsu center is currently on the drawing board.) Visa and MasterCard are accepted. It is four miles to a service station in Middletown.

Phone for rates, reservations, and directions.

616   HARBIN HOT SPRINGS
PO Box 782   707 987-2477
■   **Middletown, CA 95461**

Surrounded by 1,100 acres of secluded forest, meadows, and streams, this historical resort is constantly being enlarged by a nonprofit residential community in the spirit of preserving the springs as a place to come for rest and renewal. Located in a rugged foothill canyon south of Clear Lake. Elevation 1,500 feet. Open all year.

Two natural hot mineral water springs (one sulphur, one iron) flow out of the earth at 120°, and the water is piped to an enclosed cement pool that has an average temperature of 110-115°, and an adjoining cement pool, fed by the overflow, that has an average temperature of 95-98°. The heart pool, cold plunge, and swimming pool are filled with pure cold water from the same springs that feed the drinking supply. The temperature of the heart pool is maintained at 95-98°. The temperatures of the cold plunge and the swimming pool depend on the weather. All pools operate on a frequent cleaning and flow-through basis combining sand filters, peroxide and ozone injections, and ultra-violet sterilizers. Clothing is optional everywhere within the grounds except in the front office, in the kitchen and dining room, and on the main roads where public access is allowed.

Facilities include day use of pools, camping, RV spaces, several conference buildings for the many retreats and workshops offered, two small stores, a cafe by the pools, and a restaurant with a wonderful view where vegetarian meals (breakfast and dinner) are optional. All products are organic.

The mood is one of peaceful contemplation in this pool, the most popular one at *Harbin* a special place to come and relax by yourself or to talk quietly with friends.

The large swimming pool at *Harbin Hot Springs*, filled with natural mineral water, leads onto decks and to a small cafe where you can get a bite to eat and enjoy the view of the beautiful surroundings.

The best way to get dressed at *Harbin*—a specialized body mask designed for you at the "Harbin Clay Works."

A study in contrasts: A couple shares a quiet moment in the indoor hot plunge, and a family has a good time outdoors in the heart-shaped hydropool.

A massage on the lawn is often observed by a family of deer who must sense the tranquility.

618   CRABTREE HOT SPRINGS

● **East of the town of Upper Lake**

Natural hot pools adjacent to a creek-fed stream with a cold swimming hole for a quick plunge. Located in a remote, beautiful rock canyon in Mendocino National Forest. Elevation 2,400 feet. Open all year; roads impassable during wet weather.

Natural mineral water flows out of the ground at approximately 106° into three volunteer-built pools. The first pool uses sandbags and rock to keep the cold creek water out and accommodates six to eight persons. The second pool built with rock and cement and located about three feet above the creek-fed swimming hole is just right for two and is drainable. The third pool located at the west end of the swimming hole and built of sandbags and rocks, will accommodate ten to twelve people. Depending on air temperature, water varies between 98-104°.

There are no services on the premises, although overnight camping is not prohibited. It is approximately four miles to Bear Creek Campground (uphill from springs and left at "T"). All other services are twenty miles away in Upper Lake.

Directions: From Hwy 20 in Upper Lake proceed .3 mile east on Main St. Turn right at Second St. and take first left onto Middle Creek Rd. (Ranger station on left at 1 mile.) Turn right at Pitney Lane (1.6 miles), go 2.3 miles, and turn left onto 16N30 (also known as Sam Alley Ridge Rd). Pavement ends and 16N30 becomes 16N01 at High Glade Lookout sign at 9.1 miles. Continue straight and then make a hard right at French Ridge sign (13.2 miles). At 19 miles, turn left at "T" toward Bear Creek. Park .8 miles farther on at the confluence of two creeks. Cross creeks and follow trail about .25 mile downstream to springs. Low clearance vehicles not recommended. Parking is limited and springs are often crowded on long weekends.

Note: As the springs itself is on private property, please make a special effort to keep the area clean.

Source map: *Mendocino National Forest.*

617   WILBUR HOT SPRINGS
3375 Wilbur Springs Rd.   916 473-2306
■ **Williams, CA 95987**

A self-styled "Health Sanctuary" twenty two miles from the nearest town, with an abundance of hot mineral water. The large, multi-temperature soaking pools, sundecks, and restored turn-of-the-century hotel are located in the foothills of the western Sacramento Valley. Elevation 1,350 feet. Open all year.

Natural mineral water flows out of several springs at 140°, through a series of large concrete soaking pools under an A-frame structure, and into an outdoor swimming pool. Soaking pool temperatures are approximately 115°, 105° and 95°, with the swimming pool kept warm in the winter and cool in the summer. The water is not chemically treated. Bathing suits are optional in pool areas only, required elsewhere.

Massage, rooms, dormitory, and communal kitchen are available on the premises. Visa and MasterCard are accepted. It is twenty two miles to a restaurant, store and service station.

Note: Please, no drop-in visitors. Phone first for reservations and confirmation of services or uses.

Directions: From Interstate 5 in Williams, go west on CA 20 to the intersection with CA 16. A few yards west of that intersection, take gravel road heading north and west for approximately 5 miles and follow signs.

Gracious hosts welcome you to these charming, restored accommodations. This cottage, along with two others, were built in 1854. *Vichy* has hosted such famous persons as Mark Twain, Jack London, and Grace Hudson. This historical landmark provides fun and relaxation.

After a walk to the waterfall, take time to bathe in the fizzy, warm, naturally carbonated mineral water—the only place in North America where you can do so.

619   VICHY SPRINGS RESORT AND INN
2605 Vichy Springs Rd.
707 462-9515
FAX 707 462-9516

■   **Ukiah, CA 95842**

Historic, beautifully restored resort in the Ukiah Valley foothills of Mendocino County. Famous for its warm and naturally carbonated mineral water, which is bottled and sold to the public. Guests are invited to explore the 700-acre ranch where wildlife abounds. Elevation 900 feet. Open all year.

Naturally carbonated mineral water flows out of the springs at 90° and through traditional redwood pipes to ten enclosed, two-person concrete soaking tubs. Tubs are drained and filled after each use, so no chemical treatment is necessary. One large, communal soaking tub in which the water is treated with ozone is heated to 104°. The Olympic-size swimming pool contains ozone-treated mineral water maintained at approximately 80° during the summer. All tubs and pools are available to the public for day use and to registered guests at any time.

Facilities include a tree-shaded, four-acre central lawn ringed by country-style cottages and rooms, overnight parking for self-contained RVs, a tree-ringed pond, a running stream, and a thirty-minute hike to a lovely waterfall. Massage and facials and bed and breakfast are available by appointment on the premises. Visa, MasterCard, and American Express are accepted. It is five miles to a campground and three miles to the center of Ukiah.

Phone for brochure, rates, reservations, and directions.

620 ORR HOT SPRINGS
13201 Orr Springs Rd. 707 462-6277
■ Ukiah, CA 95482

A charming, rustic resort being continually improved and offering friendly informality and colorful flower beds. Located on a wooded creek, thirty-five miles inland from the ocean. Elevation 800 feet. Open all year.

Natural mineral water flows out of several springs at 100° and is piped to a swimming pool, an indoor soaking pool, and four bathtubs in private rooms. The swimming pool averages 70°. The indoor tub and outdoor soaking pool are housed in a bathhouse built in 1858. Some of the water is heated to 105° and pumped to an enclosed redwood tub that overflows into an adjoining shallow outdoor soaking pool famed for stargazing. All pools operate on a flow-through basis, so no chemical treatment is added. Clothing is optional everywhere on the grounds, except in the lodge and kitchen.

Facilities include a sauna, communal kitchen, rooms, dormitory, and tent spaces along the creek. Massage is available by reservation. Space is limited, so telephone first for any use of the facilities. No pets are allowed, and there is a strict policy regarding the child-to-adult ratio. Visa and MasterCard are accepted. The entire facility can be rented. It is thirteen miles of steep and winding roads to a restaurant, store, and service station in Ukiah.

Directions: From Route 101 in Ukiah, take the North State Street exit, drive .25 mile north to Orr Springs Road, turn west, and drive 13 miles to the resort.

621 SWEETWATER SPA AND INN
955 Ukiah St. 707 937-4140
□ Mendocino, CA 95460

Rustic rent-a-tub establishment with attractive accommodations featuring natural wood tubs, walls, and decking with hanging greenery. Located in the town of Mendocino.

Pools are for rent to the public and use gas-heated tap water treated with bromine. One private enclosure can be rented by the hour. The water temperature is maintained at 104°, and a sauna is included. One communal hydropool is available at a day-rate charge. The water temperature is maintained at 104°, and a sauna is included.

Special features: Sweetwater has a variety of unique lodging options, including ocean view units, cottages, and romantic water tower rooms. One private suite can be rented by the hour and also by the night, and a sauna is included. One deluxe Oriental room with spa, ocean view, fireplace, and private sun decks offers privacy and romance. Bathing suits are optional everywhere except in the front office. Professional massage offering a wide range of body work is available on the premises. Visa and MasterCard are accepted. Phone for rates, reservations, and directions.

Right outside your garden cottage is your very own private hot tub.

622 (CASPAR) THE GARDEN COTTAGE
45310 Pacifica Dr. 707 964-6456
☐ Caspar, CA 95420

Beautifully furnished cottage with private outdoor hot tub midway between Mendocino and Fort Bragg. Open all year.

Private hot tub using gas-heated well water treated with chlorine is maintained at 104° and, along with a sauna is included in the rental of a cottage for two or the cottage with bedroom for four. Clothing is optional in private spaces.

Facilities include a completely equipped kitchen, VCR, stereo, telephone, and gas and wood heat. No credit cards are accepted. Phone for rates, reservations, and directions.

623 FINNISH COUNTRY SAUNA & TUBS
5th and J St. 707 822-2228
☐ Arcata, CA 95521

A charming pond surrounded by grass-roofed Finnish style saunas, private outdoor hot tubs, and a European-style coffeehouse in a small Northern California coastal town. Elevation 50 feet. Open every day except Christmas.

Tubs are for rent to the public and use gas-heated tap water treated with bromine. There are six private Burmese teak wood hot tubs rented by the half-hour and maintained at 104°. The conical tubs have benches all the way around and jets at three different levels. Clothing is optional in private spaces.

Facilities include two private sauna cabins and Caffe Mokka, a coffeehouse serving espresso and juices with live folk music on the weekends. No credit cards are accepted. Phone for rates, reservations, and directions.

These large wooden tubs have benches all the way around and jets at three different levels.

CENTRAL CALIFORNIA

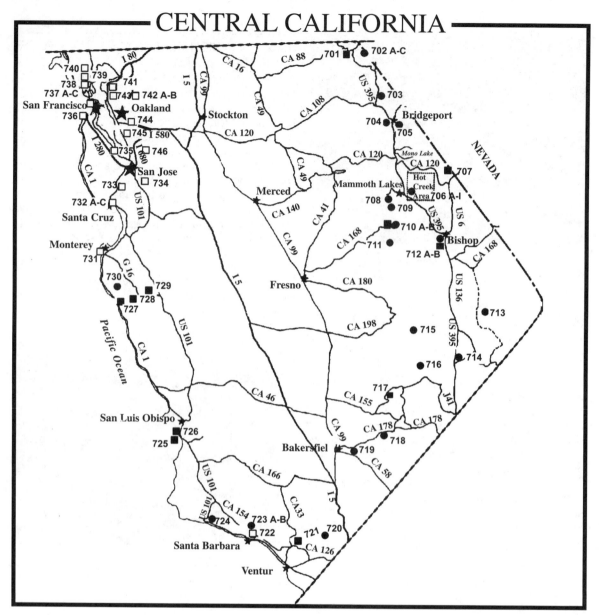

This map was designed to be used with a standard highway map.

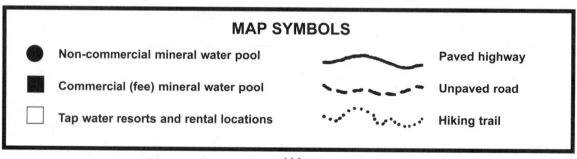

MAP SYMBOLS

● Non-commercial mineral water pool	~ Paved highway
■ Commercial (fee) mineral water pool	- - - Unpaved road
☐ Tap water resorts and rental locations	···· Hiking trail

701   GROVER HOT SPRINGS

     Box 188   916 694-2248
■   Markleeville, CA 96120

Conventional swimming pool and soaking pool next to a major state campground and picnic area, located in a wooded mountain valley. Elevation 6,000 feet. Open all year.

Natural mineral water flows out of several springs at 147° and into a holding pond from which it is piped to the pool area. The soaking pool, using natural mineral water treated with bromine, is maintained at approximately 103°. The swimming pool, using creek water treated with chlorine, is maintained at 70-80°. A heat exchanger is used to simultaneously cool down the mineral water and warm up the creek water. Admission is on a first-come, first-served basis, and the official capacity limit of fifty persons in the hot pool and twenty-five in the cold pool is reached early every day during the summer. Bathing suits are required.

Campground spaces are available by prior reservation, as with all other California state parks. Cross-country skiers are encouraged to camp in the picnic area during the winter and to ski in to use the soaking pool. It is four miles to the nearest restaurant, motel, and service station in Markleeville.

Location: On Alpine County Road E4, 4.5 miles west of Markleeville. Follow the signs.

In summer, as big as this hot soaking pool is, it fills up very quickly. In winter, skiing in lets you soak almost by yourself.

Three wonderful hot springs with beautiful mountain views are to be found along the banks of the East Fork of the Carson River in Toiyabe National Forest. The springs are accessible during the rafting season, approximately May through July, depending on water flow. Elevation 5,000 feet.

There are no services available at any of the hot spring sites. While the apparent local custom at the pools is clothing optional, please be respectful of those people already there. These springs are not shown on any Forest Service or USGS map but are well known to raft trip guides.

While you can navigate this river yourself if you are an experienced kayaker, for a real treat, one- and two-day raft trips (Class 2 rapids) are available through commercial outfitters. We had a wonderful trip with River Adventures and More (RAM), PO Box 5283, Reno, NV 89513, 800 466-RAFT.

702 A   RIVERSIDE HOT SPRING

● **Near the town of Markleeville**

Approximately eight miles downstream from where you put into the water three small pools are visible from the river on your right (east). Natural mineral water flows into the upper pool at approximately 92° and then continues flowing into the lower pools. Some volunteers have lined the lower tub, which will hold six to eight people, with a tarp. During high water these pools are often underwater and need to be rebuilt annually.

Camping is possible near the springs.

Our RAM guides were not only experienced river guides, but very accomplished at storing all our gear in waterproof bags so that nothing would get wet.

We were very happy to see this first set of springs. Even though the day was warm, the water was cold and our feet were frozen!

While we were enjoying our soak, our RAM guides were busy across the river cooking up a delicious dinner.

702 B   RIVER RUN HOT SPRINGS

● **Near the town of Markleeville**

Natural mineral water emerges from several springs up the hillside at 110° or hotter and cools as it flows toward the river. The temperature of the water drops to approximately 100° by the time it reaches the large shallow pool near an eight-foot cliff at the river's edge. The small upper pools are quite hot and should be approached with caution. When the river water is low, it is possible to stand in your boat under the water coming off the cliffs.

There is a large open area available for camping, but there are no facilities except an outhouse near the springs.

This small waterfall is visible on the left (west) side of the river, approximately one-half mile from Riverside.

702 C   HOT SHOWERBATH

● **Near the town of Markleeville**

One mile downstream from River Run Hot Springs, a small pull out is visible on the left (west). Follow the warm ooze about 500 yards up into the canyon, where natural mineral water flows out of a spring at 110° and cools to approximately 98° before dropping over a twenty-foot bank into a warm, squishy-bottomed pool.

A refreshing warm shower was a perfect ending to a perfect two-day trip. We all talked about making this an annual event!

703   FALES HOT DITCH

●   **North of the town of Bridgeport**

A primitive pool on Hot Springs Creek in the sagebrush foothills of the Eastern Sierra. Elevation 7,200 feet. Open all year.

Natural mineral water emerges at 140° from a spring on the property of an old resort, now closed, and flows down Hot Springs Creek, gradually cooling as it goes. Volunteers have dammed the creek to form a thigh-deep, rock-and-sand pool on the east side of the highway .3 mile past the old resort (which is on the west side of the highway). Although the soaking pool is twenty feet below the highway and out of sight to passing vehicles, it is advisable to wear a bathing suit or have it close at hand.

There are no services on the premises. It is seven miles to a Forest Service campground and thirteen miles to all other services in Bridgeport.

Directions: From Bridgeport, drive north on US 395 for 13 miles to a boarded-up, fenced, brown wooden structure that used to be Fales Hot Springs Resort (on the west side of US 395). The gated property just north of the old resort is private and posted "no trespassing." However, from the old resort, drive .3 mile north and park along the shoulder of US 395 on the east side of the road. The creek and soaking pool are 20 feet below the highway (not visible until you park and look over the small cliff).

The large pools at the foot of the mineral-stained tufa mound are great fun for families. You can actually stand in the hot water and fish in Buckeye Creek. There is also a small cave under the overhang that makes a nice soak for two. The upper pool, with a beautiful view downriver, can hold two for romance or four very close friends.

704   BUCKEYE HOT SPRING

(see map)

● **Near the town of Bridgeport**

Delightful hot spring in a superb natural setting on the north bank of Buckeye Creek in Toiyabe National Forest. One of the best. Elevation 6,900 feet. Open all year; not accessible by road in winter.

Natural mineral water flows out of the ground at 135°, runs over a large cliff built up by mineral deposits, and drops into the creek. Volunteers have built loosely constructed rock pools along the edge of the creek below the hot waterfall. The pool temperature is controlled by admitting more or less cold water from the creek.

There is another small outflow of hot geothermal water on the bluff near the parking area. Volunteers have dug a shallow soaking pool that maintains a temperature of approximately 100°. It is near the foot of a tree located in the upstream direction from the parking area. The apparent local custom at both pools is clothing optional.

Three hundred yards upstream from the parking area are several acres of unmarked open space on which overnight parking is not prohibited. It is one mile to a Forest Service campground and nine miles to a restaurant, motel, store, and service station in Bridgeport.

There are no services on the premises. There is a parking turnout on the south side of the road on the bluff above the springs.

Directions: (This is the easier route.) At the north end of Bridgeport, take Twin Lakes Road west for 7.1 miles to Doc & Al's Resort. Turn right (north) onto FS 017, a two-lane, graded, washboard road, for 3 miles to the second bridge over the creek, where the road intersects with FS 038 toward Buckeye Campground to the left. Continue straight ahead for a few hundred yards up a short hill on the north branch of FS 017 to a large flat parking clearing on a big knoll. The upper pool is a few steps away (slightly downhill and to the right) under a tree, at the crest of the knoll overlooking Buckeye Creek. Several unofficial paths lead down the slope to the pools located along the creek at the foot of a large mound covered over by the mineral deposits.

Source maps: *Toiyabe National Forest*; USGS *Matterhorn Peak*.

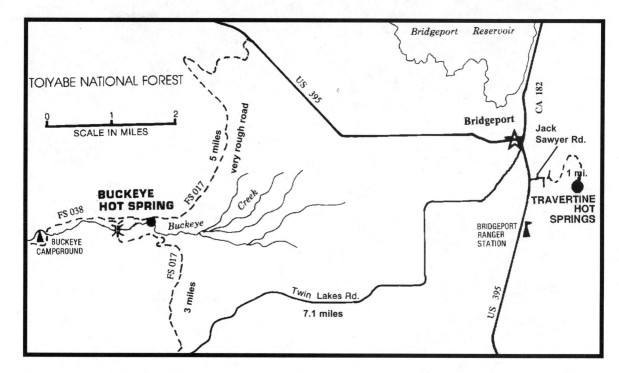

705 TRAVERTINE HOT SPRINGS
(see map)
● **Southeast of the town of Bridgeport**

An unusual group of volunteer-built soaking pools on large travertine ridges with commanding views of the High Sierra. Located two miles from the center of Bridgeport. Elevation 6,700 feet. Open all year.

The flow of natural mineral water (130-160°) out of several geothermal fissures can be interrupted or shifted to a new outlet by underground movement resulting from local earthquakes. The scalding water is channeled to a series of volunteer-built soaking pools in which the individual pool temperatures are controlled by temporarily diverting the hot water inflow as needed. The upper pool is handicap accessible with assistance. The apparent local custom is clothing optional.

At the upper ten- by five- by two-foot pool, scalding water bubbles up from under large rocks and is directed through a stepped channel with a "bear claw" configuration at pool's edge. The source can be capped to control pool temperature. There is a plug for draining and cleaning the pool, which is done fastidiously by volunteers. Overflow goes into a small adjoining foot bath for rinsing off before entering the pool. Since you can drive right up to this pool, it is handicap accessible with assistance.

Three lower rock-and-cement pools, one hundred yards below, are at the foot of a large granite boulder where water seeps up through the rock and gently trickles into the pools at 100°. A separate primitive 80° rock-and-mud pool nearby is fed by a separate underground source.

There are no services, but there is level ground on this BLM land on which overnight parking is not prohibited. Other primitive amenities include a large deck around the pools covered with old carpets for sunbathing, a wooden bench, and "but cans." There is no trash collection, so please pack it out. All other services are available within two miles in Bridgeport.

Directions: From the Ranger Station .5 mile south of Bridgeport, drive north on Hwy 395 for .2 mile. Turn right on Jack Sawyer Rd., the first paved road on your right. At .4 mile the paved road makes a 90-degree turn to the right. Do not bear right. Continue straight ahead on the unpaved, ungraded road for approximately 1 mile to the pools. On the way you will pass a sign on your left to Bridgeport Barrow Pit; continue straight to the forest service sign on your left. Across from this on the right is a turnoff to a flat camping area. If you continue straight, the second turnoff just ahead on the right leads to the lower pools. Or continue uphill to where the road curves around to the right to reach the upper cement pool.

The natural lower pools at *Travertine Hot Springs* (shown above) often need to be rebuilt because small earthquakes constantly cause the source springs to change location. The upper pool (shown at left) has been cemented in, and there is parking close by, making it easily handicap accessible.

"BIG HOT" WARM SPRINGS

●   **Near the town of Bridgeport**

This hot spring is located on private property and has now been closed to the public. People did not follow the simple request to shut the cattle gates to and from the spring. Trespassers will be shot.

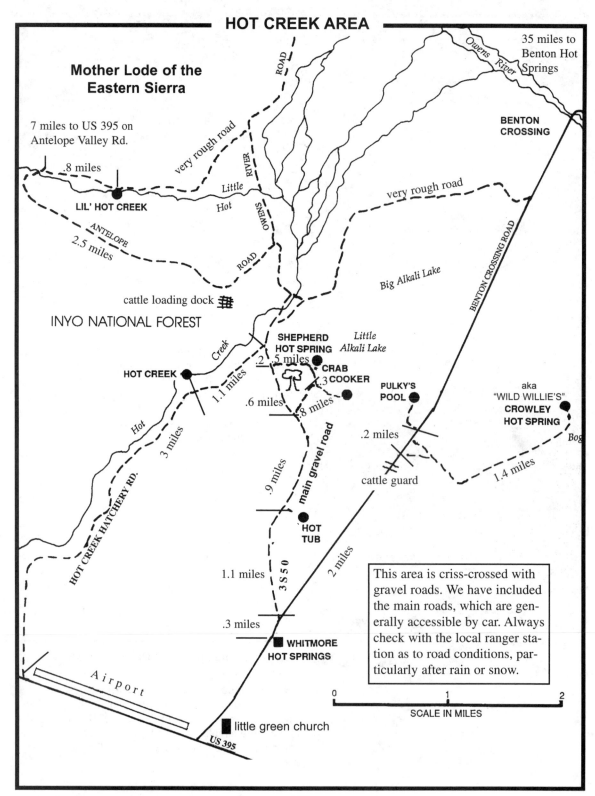

HOT CREEK AREA

Mother Lode of the Eastern Sierra

35 miles to Benton Hot Springs

BENTON CROSSING

7 miles to US 395 on Antelope Valley Rd.

ROAD

very rough road

.8 miles

LIL' HOT CREEK

RIVER

Little Hot

OWENS

ROAD

ANTELOPE
2.5 miles

very rough road

Owens River

BENTON CROSSING ROAD

cattle loading dock

INYO NATIONAL FOREST

Big Alkali Lake

Creek

SHEPHERD HOT SPRING

.2
.5 miles

Little Alkali Lake

HOT CREEK

1.1 miles

CRAB COOKER
.3

PULKY'S POOL

aka "WILD WILLIE'S" **CROWLEY HOT SPRING**

.6 miles

.8 miles

Bog

Hot

3 miles

.9 miles

main gravel road

.2 miles

cattle guard

1.4 miles

HOT CREEK HATCHERY RD.

HOT TUB

1.1 miles

3 S 5 0

2 miles

This area is criss-crossed with gravel roads. We have included the main roads, which are generally accessible by car. Always check with the local ranger station as to road conditions, particularly after rain or snow.

.3 miles

WHITMORE HOT SPRINGS

Airport

little green church

US 395

0   1   2

SCALE IN MILES

122

Hot Creek is one of the largest geothermal areas in the United States. The water is often scalding, so be particularly careful when wading in with children.

706 A   HOT CREEK

(see map on page 122)

● **East of the town of Mammoth Lakes**

Primarily a geologic observation and interpretive site with some limited use by bathers. Open daylight hours only.

Natural mineral water with a slight sulfur smell emerges from many fissures as steam or boiling water, and several danger areas have been fenced off for safety. Substantial amounts of boiling, geothermal water also flow up from the bottom of the creek. A bend in the creek provides a natural eddy in which the mixing of hot and cold water stays within a range of 50° to 110°. Those who venture into this confluence experience vivid thermal skin effects, but they must be careful to avoid the geothermal vents because of the danger of scalding. Bathing suits are required.

In the past, night use of this location has resulted in many injuries and some fatalities, so the area may be used only from sunrise to sunset. Citations are issued by the Forest Service to anyone found there after sunset or before sunrise. During the winter, when snow blocks the access road, skiers and hikers may still enter the area during daylight hours.

Facilities include men's and women's changing rooms, pit toilets, and an asphalt parking area with a paved, fenced pathway down to the creek, making the area handicap accessible with assistance. Overnight parking is prohibited. It is ten miles to all services in the town of Mammoth Lakes.

Directions: From US 395 3 miles south of the Mammoth Lakes turnoff, turn east on Hot Creek Hatchery Road/Airport. At .8 mile, turn right at the sign to "Hot Creek Geothermal Area." From this sign, it is 3 miles to the parking area for Hot Creek. Only the first 1.2 miles is paved. Or, from Benton Crossing Road, take 3S50, the main gravel road, for 2.8 miles. Turn left for .3 miles to the Hot Creek gate and another .8 mile to the parking area.

Source maps: *Inyo National Forest*, USGA *Mt. Morrison*.

706 B LIL' HOT CREEK
(see map on page 122)

● **East of the town of Mammoth Lakes**

A very hot flowing creek fed by a 180° geothermal spring. The name Lil' Hot Creek has been given to a large, squishy-bottom soaking pool located just below where the flow from several cold springs cools the hot stream to approximately 107°. The thigh-deep cement-and-rock pool has tiered seats so you can soak at different depths. Pool temperature can be controlled by opening or capping a four-inch plastic pipe that brings the water in from the nearby creek. There's a plug for draining and cleaning the pool. Spillover goes through a tiny channel back to the creek. As you leave, please shut the inflow of hot water so the next persons in will not be scalded.

Plenty of level ground, as well as hideaway spots among the pine trees in the nearby national forest, is available where overnight parking is not prohibited. The apparent local custom is clothing optional.

Directions: There are four routes, depending on your starting point.

1. From the main gravel road (3S50), drive a total of 3.3 miles to the sign for Owens River Road. (This is .7 mile past the turnoff to Shepherd.) You'll pass a cattle loading dock on the left just before Owens River Road. Turn left for .7 mile to Little Antelope Road. Turn left onto Antelope Road for 2.5 miles across a flat open area. At 2.5 miles, at the beginning of the pine forest, is a cattle guard. Make a sharp right just past the cattle guard and follow this very rough, ungraded dirt road for .8 mile to the springs on your right. Whenever the road forks, keep bearing right, following the fence until you come to a flat open area for parking. You'll see steam rising from the creek to your right as you follow the fence. At the parking area, look for a small wooden portion in the wire fence and a cattle-proof entrance. Go through the gate and over log planks across the creek to reach the hot soaking pool.

2. Take Hot Creek Hatchery Road from US 395 for 3 miles to the Hot Creek asphalt parking area. Continue past the parking area for another 1.1 miles to a fork in the unpaved road. Do not bear right, but continue straight ahead for another .1 mile to where the road ends at a wide gravel road. This is 3S50, the main gravel road. Turn left, and on your left you'll see the cattle loading dock mentioned above. Follow directions above.

3. A very beautiful but much longer drive begins at US 395. At the turnoff to Mammoth Lake, instead of heading west toward the lakes, turn east and follow the sign to Little Antelope Valley (not Chalk Hills). At 6.3 miles you will be at the cattle guard at the edge of the pine forest. Turn left onto the ungraded dirt road and follow the fence as described above to reach the soaking pool.

4. For those with 4WD vehicles, or at least with good clearance, continue past the turnoff to Antelope Road another 1.3 miles and turn left. Follow the washboard road 2 miles to the springs, which are now on the left.

These pipes travel quite a distance to bring the hot water into the pool below.

706 C   SHEPHERD HOT SPRING
(see map on page 122)

● **East of the town of Mammoth Lakes**

Natural mineral water flows out of a spring at 107° and through a hose to a twenty by twenty-four inch deep rock-and-cement tub. There are benches in the pool, which is large enough for three or four people. Pool temperature is controlled by diverting the hot water flow from the nearby source pool. The white plastic inflow pipe can be elevated by inserting the iron pipe underneath it. There is a plug for draining the pool, capped with a tennis ball. However, local volunteers prefer emptying the pool with a bucket before scrubbing. A scrub-brush is on site.

There are no facilities except a primitive campfire ring. A posted sign prohibits overnight parking. The apparent local custom is clothing optional.

Directions: From Benton Crossing Road, turn north on 3S50 (the main gravel road) .3 mile past the Whitmore Public swimming pool. Drive for 2.6 miles to a dirt road on your right. Follow this across an open bog for .5 mile to the pool on your left.

From Crab Cooker, follow the dirt road back the way you came in for .5 mile to a four-way, dirt-road intersection. To reach Shepherd, turn right at this intersection and go .2 mile to the small clearing where the pool is located.

706 D   CRAB COOKER
(see map on page 122)

● **East of the town of Mammoth Lakes**

Natural mineral water flows out of a spring at over 120° and through a pipe to a rock-and-cement soaking pool. The pool temperature can be controlled by turning off a valve in the pipe inside the pool when the desired soaking temperature is reached. (Please turn off this valve when leaving so as not to scald the next soakers.) Do not tamper with the pipes in the nearby well, as special plumbing equipment is required to fix them.

There are no facilities on the premises. The apparent local custom is clothing optional.

Directions: Follow the main gravel road for 2 miles from Benton Crossing Road (.9 mile past the turn off to Hot Tub). Watch for a lone juniper tree on the right side of the road. The road to Crab Cooker is on the right just before this tree. Two separate roads appear to head off to the right, but they merge after a short oval and continue as a rocky, one-lane dirt road for .1 mile to a large white mound of rocks. Follow the road around the left side of these rocks for another .2 mile to a four-way dirt-road intersection. Continue straight for another .5 mile across cow pastures to where the road ends at a flat open area where you will see the pool.

One of the many tubs in this area with an incredible view of the Sierra Mountains. With careful attention to road conditions, you can reach this pool after light snow as it is only one-quarter mile off the main road and you can walk in.

706 E   DAVE'S WARM TUB

● **East of the town of Mammoth Lakes**
        As of 1995, there was no longer a tub here and the existing water is only 80° in a shallow, algae-laden seep.

706 F   PULKY'S POOL
(see map on page 122)

● **East of the town of Mammoth Lakes**
    Natural mineral water flows out of a spring at 131° and through a pipe to a free-form, rock-and-cement pool with a spectacular view of the Sierras. Of recent construction, this pool features a very smooth surface and a drain to facilitate easy cleaning. Temperature is controlled by admitting cold water piped from a nearby pond.
    Primitive facilities include a small carpeted deck for undressing and sunbathing, and a cement bench. The area is posted for day use only; no overnight parking is permitted. The apparent local custom is clothing optional.

Directions: From US 395, drive 2 miles past Whitmore Pool to the cattle guard. The turnoff to Crowley, 706-G, is just past this cattle guard on the right (south). For Pulkey's, continue on Benton Crossing Road for another .2 mile to an unpaved road on the left (north). Follow this road as it curves around a large alkali field for .4 mile to a flat parking area. The pool is up on the plateau. Wooden planks form a path across the bog to prevent you from sinking in. Caution: Do not attempt to drive to the plateau; even 4WD vehicles have become stuck in the soft ground.

706 G CROWLEY HOT SPRING (also known as Wild Willie's)
(see map on page 122)
● **East of the town of Mammoth Lakes**

Natural mineral water flows out of a spring and down a small creek channel at 110°, then into a cement pool large enough for 30 people. Construction of such a pool was made possible by the 1983 earthquake, which substantially increased the flow of geothermal water in the creek. No temperature control is necessary because surface cooling keeps the pool temperature about 103° most of the year.

Fifty feet away, at the foot of a large rock outcropping, is a mud-bottom pool at approximately 100°, formed by a dam across the creek. Natural mineral water flows from a separate source near the rock into this knee-deep pool. The pool is large enough for a half-dozen people. The apparent local custom for both pools is clothing optional.

There are no facilities on the premises, but overnight parking is not prohibited in the large parking area.

Directions: From Benton Crossing Road, drive 2 miles past Whitmore Pool. Immediately past the cattle guard, two rough dirt roads cut off to the right. Take either one (they join up) and drive 1.1 mile to a large rock. Follow the road to the right side of the rock and take an immediate left at the fork. Drive .3 mile to a large level parking area fenced off by logs. Do not attempt to drive any farther. To reach the pools, follow the trail from the end of the parking area for approximately 250 yards to where it joins a trail from the opposite direction and a path leading down a small hill to your left. The primitive pool is under some trees near the big rock ahead on your left; the pool with the deck is ahead of you on the right.

Caution: Do not attempt to drive across the bog to the pool area. Even 4WD's have been trapped.

Applying the white mud from around the edges of the smaller pool feels wonderful on the skin as does the soak to then remove it.

706 H HOT TUB
(see map on page 122)

● **East of the town of Mammoth Lakes**

Natural mineral water flows out of a spring at 110° and through a hose to a three-foot-deep rock-and-cement pool. The pool temperature is controlled by diverting the hot water inflow whenever the desired soaking temperature has been reached. There is a plug for draining, and the pool is kept clean by a group of local volunteers. The thigh-high pool can hold about six people comfortably.

There are no facilities, but there is plenty of level area surrounding the pool, and overnight parking is not prohibited. Campers, please be considerate of others. Park away from the tubs, and keep the noise level down. The local custom is clothing optional.

Directions: From Benton Crossing Road, drive 1.1 miles on 3S50 (the main gravel road) to the second one-lane dirt road on the right. Turn right and go for .1 mile to a clearing, then bear left for another .1 mile to the pool.

Whether waiting for the pool to fill after a cleaning (upper right) or climbing into an already cleaned tub (below), soaking at the appropriately named *Hot Tub* is always enjoyable.

706 I WHITMORE HOT SPRINGS
(see map on page 122)
PO Box 1609   619 935-4222
■ **Mammoth Lakes, CA 93546**

Large, conventional public swimming pool jointly operated by Mono County and the town of Mammoth Lakes on land leased from the Los Angeles Department of Water and Power. Open during the day, Monday through Saturday, approximately mid-June to Labor Day.

Natural mineral water is pumped from a well at 90° and piped to the swimming pool where it is treated with chlorine. Depending on air temperature and wind conditions, the pool water temperature averages 82°. An adjoining shallow wading pool averages 92°. Bathing suits are required. No credit cards are accepted.

A small access fee includes showers (campers take note), a barbeque area. A full aquatic schedule is available on the premises. Parking is permitted only during hours of operation.

tubs. The four tubs, located under the trees, are drained and scrubbed with bleach after each use, then refilled. Each tub has a hot and cold faucet to adjust pool temperature. The five-foot diameter tubs are about three feet deep, have seats inside, and are large enough for four to six people. Bathing suits are optional in the tubs, which are separated by hedges. Owners request that nudity be discrete and only at the tubs.

Facilities include snacks and beverages. A gas pump is located across the street. No camping is permitted anywhere in the town of Benton Hot Springs, which is all privately owned. It is four miles to a campground/RV park and store in the town of Benton, and fifteen miles to a motel, restaurant, and casino north on US 6 at the state line.

Directions: From Bishop, take US 6 north for 36 miles to the tiny town of Benton. Turn west of CA 120 and drive 4 miles until you see the old green and white house on the north side of the street. Or, from US 395 in Lee Vining (Tioga Pass from Yosemite), take CA 120 east for 46 miles to Benton Hot Springs. If you are coming from the series of natural springs outside of Mammoth, take Benton Crossing Road south of the Mammoth Airport for 36 miles to where it ends at CA 120. Take 120 east for 3 miles to Benton Hot Springs.

707   THE OLD HOUSE AT BENTON HOT SPRINGS

Rte. 4, Box 58   619 933-2507
■   **Benton, CA 93512**

A group of old redwood tubs were cut from an old redwood pipeline that used to go to the generating plant. The tubs are on the property of an historic 1860s house now selling arts, crafts, antiques, and collectibles. The tubs are located in an oasis-type setting under cottonwood, Russian olive, tamarisk, and locust trees in high desert and sagebrush-type country along the eastern edge of California near the Nevada state line, with views of Montgomery and Boundary Peaks (highest point in Nevada). Elevation: 5,500 feet. Pools are rented by the hour, and reservations are suggested. Open all year.

Natural, soft, silky mineral water flows out of a spring at 135° and supplies water to the entire town of Benton Hot Springs. A cooling/evaporation tank at The Old House provides the only cool water in town. There is no chemical treatment of the water in the

Tom Reicheret, one of the owners at Benton Hot Springs, shows off one of the new tubs put in behind the Old House. The Old House itself, built in 1870, was moved to its present location by a team of horses.

708   RED'S MEADOW HOT SPRINGS

● **In Red's Meadow Campground near Devil's Postpile National Monument**

Tin-roof shed with six cement shower-over bath tubs in six small private rooms, on the edge of a mountain meadow campground. Elevation 7,000 feet. Open approximately Memorial Day to September 20.

Natural mineral water flows out of the ground at 100°, into a storage tank, and then by pipe into the bathhouse. Depending on the use, water temperature out of the shower heads will vary from 90-100°. No charge is made for the use of the tubs, which are available on a first-come, first-served basis.

In summer, all water from the spring is diverted into the bathhouse. During the winter, the cement hot water storage tank is used for soaking and can only be reached by snowmobile and cross-country skiers.

A Forest Service campground, open during the summer, adjoins the hot springs. It is four miles to a cafe, general store, rustic cabins, and pack station at Red's Meadow Resort, and twelve miles to an RV park and other services in Mammoth Lakes.

Directions: From the town of Mammoth Lakes ,take CA 203 west to the end, then follow signs through Minaret Pass to Devil's Postpile National Monument and to Red's Meadow Campground. Note: During the day in summer, private vehicles are prohibited beyond Minaret Pass. A frequent shuttle bus service originates at Mammoth Mountain Inn.

Source map: *Inyo National Forest.* USGS *Devil's Postpile.*

709   IVA BELL (FISH CREEK HOT SPRINGS)

● **South of Devil's Postpile National Monument**

A delightful cluster of volunteer-built soaking pools, some with spectacular views of the wilderness. Elevation 7,200 feet. Open all year.

This location adjoins the Iva Bell camp area which includes numerous camping sites separated by meadows and stands of pines. The two main soaking pools are not visible from the main camping area but are to be found fifty yards east, up and behind an obvious bare rock ledge.

The most popular pool has a nice sandy bottom and is nestled on the back side of this ledge, where a 106° trickle flows out of a fissure slowly enough to maintain a 101° pool temperature in the summertime. A 100° squishy-bottom pool may be reached by following a path thirty yards across a meadow.

From the first pool, another path leads due east for fifty yards to a cozy campsite. From this site, a steep one-hundred-yard path leads up to four more pools, ranging in temperature from 101° to 110°.

The twelve-mile hike (one way) from the road end at Reds Meadow involves an elevation change of 1,000 feet. Detailed directions to such a remote location are beyond the scope of this book. We recommend *Sierra North*, published by Wilderness Press; also consult with the Mammoth Ranger District of Inyo National Forest, 619 934-2505.

Source map: *USGS Devil's Postpile.*

710 A   MONO HOT SPRINGS
   (Summer) Mono Hot Springs, CA
   93642
■   (Winter) Lake Shore, CA 93634
●   Northeast of Fresno

A vacation resort offering fishing, hiking, and camping in addition to mineral baths. Located on the south fork of the San Joaquin River near Edison Lake, Florence Lake, and Bear Dam in the Sierra National Forest. Elevation 6,500 feet. Open May to October.

Natural mineral water flows from a spring at 107° and is piped to a bathhouse containing four two-person soaking tubs in private rooms. Tubs have geothermal water only, measuring 100-105°. Tubs are drained and refilled after each use, so no chemical treatment of the water is necessary. An outdoor hydrojet pool is maintained at 103-105° and is treated with chlorine. Bathing suits are required except in private rooms. Facilities are available on a day-use basis, as well as to registered guests, and are handicap accessible with assistance.

On the south side of the river directly across from the resort is a series of springs and soaking pools that are open all year, but only to cross-country skiers and snowmobilers in winter. Water from one spring feeds into a holding tank. From there it is piped across the river to the resort. This tank also feeds a nearby cement soaking tub called "The Coffin" due to its size and shape. A natural, hot water, outdoor shower flows continually from the tank spillover. Along the riverbank are several cement soaking tubs that remain from an historic bathhouse. A rock-and-mud pool is near the cement tubs, and another primitive pool, called "The Rock," is next to a large boulder ten feet up the hill from the cement tubs. Pool temperatures are approximately 101°. Bathing suits are advisable in the daytime.

Facilities include a cafe, store, service station, cabins, campground, and RV park. Massage is available on the premises. Visa and MasterCard are accepted.

Directions to the resort: From the city of Fresno on CA 99, go 80 miles northeast on CA 168 to the ranger station at the northeast side of Huntington Lake. Inquire here about road conditions before attempting to drive in. The one lane road is very narrow and winding. Allow at least one hour for this 15-mile stretch.

At 15 miles, you come to the High Sierra Ranger Station. Stop here for info and campfire permits,

needed even for cooking in your van. One mile past this station the road forks. Bear left to Mono Hot Springs. At 1 mile, you will cross a small bridge. Continue downhill to a second green bridge. Mono is less than .25 mile past the bridge on your left.

To reach the soaking pools on the south side of the river, park at the pullout just before the green bridge. Proceed through the yellow gate, walking north along the river for approximately 100 yards. "The Rock" is up a small hill to your left, the cement pools a few feet ahead at river level. These pools can also be reached by rock-hopping the San Joaquin River from the resort when the river level is low.

Only two of the soaking choices are shown here. Above are the remains from the old bathhouse. Below is the appropriately named "Coffin."

710 B   LITTLE EDEN

● **Northeast of Fresno**

A primitive, squishy-bottom, thigh-high pool surrounded by grass and large enough for a dozen people with a gorgeous view of the surrounding mountains and a real feeling that you are out in nature. Elevation 6,500 feet. Open all year; accessible to cross-country skiers and snowmobilers in the winter.

Natural mineral water bubbles up through the sandy pool bottom at around 100°. Because of its large size, pool temperatures measure only in the nineties. A heavy-duty plastic ladder aids in getting in and out, as the ground around the pool is very slippery. The apparent local custom is clothing optional.

There are no facilities on the premises, and any other services are less than a mile away at Mono Hot Springs Resort.

Directions: Follow directions given for Mono Hot Springs to the High Sierra Ranger station. One mile past the station, park in the turnout just beyond the steel bridge. A steep, unofficial trail to the pool begins on the left (north), approximately 50 feet before the bridge, and goes around a large rock outcropping, through some marshy spots, and down to the pool at the base of the rocks.

Some of the same source springs that feed *Mono Hot Springs* originate higher up the hill at *Little Eden*, one of those wonderful natural hot springs with just-right water and wonderful views.

711   BLANEY HOT SPRINGS

● **Southeast of Florence Lake**

A combination hot spring and mudbath in a grassy High Sierra meadow, 9.5 miles from the road's end at Florence Lake. Elevation 7,600 feet. Open all year.

Natural mineral water oozes up through the squishy bottom of a large pool, maintaining a temperature of approximately 102°, and then flows into a nearby small, warm lake. The apparent local custom is clothing optional.

There are no services at this location except nearby backpacker campgrounds. It is ten miles to a store, service station, etc.

The 9.5 mile trail from the road's end has an elevation gain of 1,000 feet and requires fording across the South Fork of the San Joaquin River. In the summer it is possible to avoid 3.5 miles of walking by riding the Sierra Queen across the lake. From this part of the John Muir Trail it is only a hike of 1.25 miles down the Florence Lake Trail to reach the springs.

We recommend *Sierra South*, published by Wilderness Press, for detailed directions, or consult the Pine Ridge Ranger District, 209 855-5360.

Nearby is Muir Trail Ranch, which offers rustic log cabin comfort to organized groups on a bring-your-own-food basis. Ranch guests enjoy private rock-and-tile mineral water pools. From the road end at Florence Lake, the hiking distance is eight miles, but summer guests can ride the Sierra Queen ferryboat across the lake and then ride ranch horses or four-wheel-drive vehicles the remaining five miles. For information, write the owner, Adeline Smith, Box 176, Lakeshore, CA 93634 from mid-June to October, or Box 269, Ahwanee, CA 93601 in other months.

Source map: USGS *Blackcap Mountain*.

712 A   KEOUGH HOT SPRINGS
Rte. 1, Box 9   619 872-1644
■   **Bishop, CA 93514**

Older hot springs resort in the Sierra foothills. The bathhouse is closed, and swimming pool access is extremely limited. It is advisable to phone for current information. Elevation 4,200 feet. Open only when owner is feeling well.

Natural mineral water flows out of the ground at 128° and into the enclosed swimming pool (87-95°) and the wading pool (100°), using flow-through mineral water so that no chlorine needs to be added. Bathing suits are required.

Nothing is available on the premises. No credit cards are accepted. It is eight miles to the nearest restaurant, motel, service station and store.

Directions: Go 7 miles south of Bishop on US 395, then follow signs west from US 395.

712 B KEOUGH HOT DITCH

● **Near Keough Hot Springs**

Runoff from Keough Hot Springs cools as it flows through a series of volunteer-built rock pools in a treeless foothill gully. Elevation 4,100 feet. Open all year.

Natural mineral water flows out of the ground at 128° on the property of Keough Hot Springs, then wanders northeast over BLM land for about a mile before joining with a cold water surface stream. Volunteer-built rock dams create several primitive soaking pools and swimming holes on both sides of the road, each one cooler than the preceding one upstream. The apparent local custom is clothing optional.

No services are available on the premises. The land is posted for day use only, no overnight parking, but reports are that parking for one night is not a problem as long as you leave nothing but tire tracks. Please do not bring any glass objects to the area, since broken glass is the biggest problem at Keough. It is one mile to an RV park and eight miles to a restaurant, store, and service station in Bishop.

Directions: Seven miles south of Bishop on US 395, turn west on Keough Hot Springs Road approximately .6 mile. At the only intersection with a paved road (old US 395), turn north 200 yards to where a cold stream crosses the road. (Note: There is an abundance of level parking space on the north side of the cold stream, but the stream must be forded with care.) Walk an additional 50 yards north to Keough Ditch. Either stream may be followed to where they join, forming a series of warm swimming pools.

As the hot water runs across the land, it forms several pools just ready for families or individuals to soak. There is plenty of room for privacy for those who wish to soak without a suit.

713   SALINE VALLEY HOT SPRINGS
(see map)
(see photos next page)
● **Northeast of the town of Olancha**

A sometimes crowded, spring-fed oasis located on a barren slope of BLM land in a remote desert valley that has recently been annexed to the western edge of Death Valley. Elevation 1,500 feet. Open all year, but access roads may become impassable during winter and heavy rainstorms.

Natural mineral water flows out of the two main source springs at 107°. Volunteers have installed pipes to carry this water to a variety of cement-and-rock pools for soaking, shampooing, dish washing, etc. By mutual agreement, no one bathes in the source pools. The rate of flow through the soaking pools is sufficient to eliminate the need for chemical treatment of the water. A third (upper) source spring flows into a natural, squishy-bottom pool that maintains an average temperature of 102°. All pools have valves and drains for controlling water flow and cleaning, except the natural upper warm spring. Most of the pools and facilities are handicap accessible with assistance. The apparent local custom in the entire area is clothing optional.

Services on the premises include delightfully decorated two-seater latrines, a shower with sunken porcelain bathtub, a sink for dishwashing, paperback library, central bonfire pit, shade trees and a lawn watered by the natural mineral water, and a goldfish pond to catch the runoff from the pools. There is an abundance of level space on which overnight parking is permitted for up to thirty days in any calendar year. There are two airstrips for small planes. It is more than 55 miles, mostly unpaved, to a store, cafe, service station, etc. Aluminum cans are collected for recycling. Everyone hauls out the remainder of their trash, and the entire area is kept spotless.

Temperatures regularly soar over the 110° mark in the summer, so this desert location with very little natural shade is preferred in the fall and spring. It becomes very crowded on major holidays and three-day weekends. The peace and quiet of the desert can best be enjoyed during the week.

Directions: The preferred route via Olancha is shown on the map. The unpaved portion of the road in from the south is county maintained. An alternate route starts at the north end of the town of Big Pine, on US 395. Drive northeast on CA 168 for 2.5 miles and turn right (southeast) on Death Valley Road. Drive approximately 15 miles and turn right on Waucoba-Saline Road. Drive 32 miles south to a large painted rock at a triangular intersection on the left (east) side of the road. Turn left (east) for 7 miles to the first group of springs. From US 395 it is approximately a 3-hour drive via either route. Either route may be temporarily washed out by infrequent but severe flash floods. Inquire about road conditions before making the trip.

Source maps: So. CA Auto Club *Death Valley*. USGS *Waucoba Wash and New York Butte*.

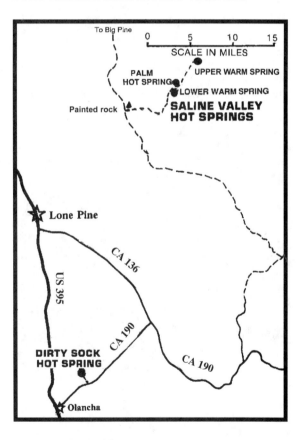

The "Wizard Pool" is at the Palm Hot Springs area.

Saline Hot Springs offers an abundance of choices. The pool at the upper warm spring has a natural squish bottom. At the pool below, crystals decorate the source pipe.

"Sunrise Pool" is a popular gathering place early in the day.

The palm trees at "Volcano" create a desert oasis.

Why would you really want to soak here?

A very long walk for a soak, but consider it your reward.

714   DIRTY SOCK HOT SPRING

● **Near the town of Olancha**

Large, shallow pool, green with algae, in an open desert area. Elevation 3,600 feet. Open all year.

Natural mineral water flows up from the bottom of a circular, cement-edged pool at 90° and flows out at various lower temperatures, depending on wind and air temperature. The murky water gives an uninviting appearance. The apparent local custom is clothing optional.

No services are available on the premises, and there are no remaining buildings. There are many acres of unmarked level space on which overnight parking is not prohibited. It is five miles to the nearest restaurant, motel, service station, and store.

Directions: From the intersection of US 395 and CA 190, go five miles northeast on CA 190. There are no signs on the highway, so look for a narrow, paved road on the northwest side and follow it 300 yards to the spring.

715   KERN HOT SPRING

● **On the upper Kern River**

A small concrete soaking pool offering a truly spectacular view in return for a truly strenuous three-day hike from the nearest road. Elevation 6,900 feet. Open all year.

Natural water flows out of the ground at 115° directly into a shallow soaking pool built at the edge of the Kern River. Water temperature is controlled by adding buckets of cold river water as needed. Bathing suit policy is determined by the mutual consent of those present.

There are no services available except a backpacker campground 100 yards away. The spring is 31.5 miles west from Whitney Portal and 37 miles east from Crescent Meadow. Situated in the mile-deep canyon of the upper Kern River, this spring has a magnificent view in all directions. Detailed directions to such a remote location are beyond the scope of this book. We recommend that you purchase *Sierra South*, published by Wilderness Press, and also consult with the Tule Ranger District of the Sequoia National Forest, 32588 Highway 190, Springville, CA 93265. 209 539-2607.

Source map: USGS *Kern Peak*.

716   JORDAN HOT SPRING

●   **Northwest of the town of Little Lake**

Hot water flows meet with cold creek water on Ninemile Creek in the southernmost part of the Golden Trout Wilderness. Elevation 6,500 feet. Open all year.

Natural mineral water flows out of a spring at approximately 120° and flows down to the river where it may be mixed with cold creek water to form casual pools. Permanent pools are not permitted. The old lodge has a caretaker in the summer but there are no longer any soaking pools available.

It is six miles to the nearest road's end at the end of paved Sequoia National Forest Road 21S03, reached via County Road J41 from south of Little Lake on US 395. The trail has an elevation change of 2,500 feet. Detailed directions to such a remote location are beyond the scope of this book. We recommend that you purchase *Exploring the Southern Sierra, East Side*, published by Wilderness Press, and also consult with the Mt. Whitney Ranger District of Inyo National Forest, Lone Pine, CA 93545. 619 876-6200.

717   CALIFORNIA HOT SPRINGS
        PO Box 146   805 548-6582
■   California Hot Springs, CA 93207

Historic resort that has been restored and expanded to offer family fun. Located in rolling foothills at the edge of Sequoia National Forest. Elevation 3,100 feet. Open all year except Thanksgiving and the week before Christmas.

Odorless natural mineral water flows out of several artesian wells at a temperature of 126° and is piped to the pool area where there are two large, tiled hydrojet spas maintained at 100° and 104°. A flow-through system eliminates the need for chemical treatment of the water. There is one large swimming pool containing filtered and chlorinated spring water that is maintained at 85° in the summer and 94° in the winter. Handicap access is at west end of pool. Bathing suits are required.

The restored main building contains an office, delicatessen, ice cream parlor, pizza stand, gift shop, and dressing room facilities. Massage is available on the premises. Full-hookup RV spaces are adjacent to the resort area. Visa and MasterCard are accepted. It is two miles to a motel, store, and gas station.

Directions: From CA 99 between Fresno and Bakersfield, take the J22 exit at Earlimart and go east 38 miles to the resort.

718   REMINGTON HOT SPRINGS
(see map)

●   **Near the town of Isabella**

A delightful, two-person cement tub and an adjoining river-level tub in an unspoiled, primitive, riverside setting of rocks and trees. Located in the Kern River Canyon down a steep trail from old Highway 178. Elevation 2,200 feet. Open all year, except during high water in the river.

Natural mineral water at 104° emerges from the ground at more than 100 gallons-per-minute. This flow comes directly up through the bottom of a volunteer-built, cement tub and provides a form of hydrojet action, maintaining the pool temperature at 104°. Twenty yards uphill is a drainable, one-person rock-and-cement pool that is fed by a smaller flow of 96° water, and has a valve for draining. There is a piece of old carpet along the edge of the pool to cover the marshy bog. The apparent local custom is clothing optional.

There are no services available on the premises. It is six miles to a motel, restaurant, and service station and two miles to a Forest Service campground.

Directions: From Bodfish (by Lake Isabella) drive west on Kern Canyon Road (old CA 178, now CA 214) to Hobo Forest Service Campground. Continue west 1.5 miles to a large turnout on the right with a telephone pole in the middle. (This is the second turnout with a telephone pole.) Overnight parking is not permitted. From the parking area, two trail heads down toward the river, 300 yards blow. A steep, narrow dirt trail on the left leads to a flat area along the river where camping is permitted. To reach the tubs, follow the very steep 4WD trail down to the rock foundation of an old building. Just before this foundation on your left is a footpath with some natural rock steps leading down toward the river. Under a tree on your left, a spur path leads to the shallow rock-and-cement pool. Follow the main path to the cement pools by the river. Please help keep this special place beautiful by packing out all trash.

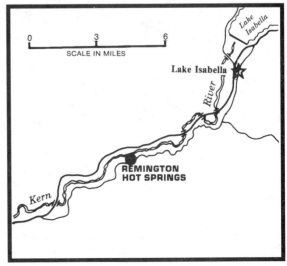

Remington Hot Springs is a delight. It is one of the most enjoyable hot springs in California, whether you choose to soak right on the river or in the lovely shaded spot under the trees. (See listing previous page.)

719   PYRAMID HOT SPRING

● **At the lower end of Kern River Canyon**

A delightful but hard-to-find, natural pool beneath a giant boulder at the edge of the Kern River. Open all year but not accessible during the high water of spring runoff. Elevation 1,900 feet.

Natural mineral water flows out of the ground at 109°, under a giant boulder, and into a sandy-bottom soaking pool large enough for two people, where it maintains a temperature of 103°. The apparent local custom is clothing optional, but you are visible to vehicles on CA 178.

There are no services available at the location. It is one mile west to a Forest Service Campground (Live Oak) and 15 miles to all other services in Bakersfield.

Directions: From Bakersfield, go east on CA 178 to the beginning of the Kern River Canyon. Continue 4 miles to a marked turnout on your left, containing a six-foot-high, pyramid-shaped boulder at its east end. From the center of the turnout, look across the river slightly eastward to locate a large, cube-shaped boulder on the opposite bank. The pool is under that boulder. To reach it, follow the trail from the east end of the turnout to the large downstream boulder where you can hop across the river. Then follow a faint unmarked path upstream to the pool. Stay low next to the river and beware of poison oak.

720   SESPE HOT SPRINGS

(see map)

● **Near the Sespe Condor Sanctuary**

A remote, pristine hot spring located in the rugged, desert mountains of a designated wilderness area. Elevation 2,800 feet. Open all year, subject to flash flooding and Forest Service closures.

Natural mineral water flows out of the side of a mountain at 185°, cooling as it flows through a series of shallow, volunteer-built, river-rock soaking pools. The apparent local custom is clothing optional.

There are no services on the premises. Access is via a nine-mile steep hiking trail from Mutau Flat or via a seventeen-mile hiking trail from Lion Campground. Horses and mules are also allowed on the trails. A Forest Service permit is required to enter the area at any time. Be sure to inquire at the Los Padres National Forest about fire-season closures, flood warnings, and the adequacy of your preparations for packing in and packing out.

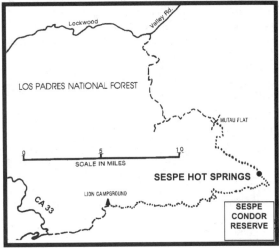

Lockwood

Valley Rd.

LOS PADRES NATIONAL FOREST

MUTAU FLAT

0   5   10

SCALE IN MILES

SESPE HOT SPRINGS

LION CAMPGROUND

CA 33

SESPE CONDOR RESERVE

721 WHEELER HOT SPRINGS
P.O. Box 250   **805 646-8131**
■   **Ojai, CA 93024**

A famed, historic, health resort in an exotic palm tree oasis in a rocky, wooded canyon in the Las Padres National Forest. Elevation 1,600 feet. Open all year.

Natural mineral water flows out of several springs at 101° and is piped to four private redwood tub rooms, each equipped with a skylight, hydrojet hot tub, and a cold tub. The mineral water is gas-heated to maintain a temperature of 105° and is chlorine treated. Water from a cold spring is also piped to the cold tubs and is chemically treated. The outdoor swimming pool, filled with chlorine-treated cold spring water and warmed by solar heat to 78°, is open all year.

Facilities include a gourmet restaurant in the original 1891 lodge. Live music is offered on the weekends and special concerts are often planned. Banquets and parties can be catered to your needs. Massage is available on the premises, and a hand-built cabin houses the new Skin Care Center. Visa, MasterCard, and American Express are accepted. It is seven miles to central Ojai and all other services. Phone for rates, reservations, and directions.

A soak in a hot tub is only one of the ways you can pamper yourself at *Wheeler Hot Springs*.

722 THE HOURGLASS
213 W. Cota   **805 963-1436**
□   **Santa Barbara, CA 93101**

Basic private-space, rent-a-tub facility located on a creekside residential street near downtown Santa Barbara.

Three private rooms with pools and eight private outdoor enclosures with pools are for rent to the public. Gas-heated tap water treated with chlorine is maintained at 104°.

A private sauna, a juice bar, and massage are available on the premises. Visa and MasterCard are accepted. Phone for rates, reservations, and directions.

723 A LITTLE CALIENTE HOT SPRINGS
(see map on page 144)

● **Near the city of Santa Barbara**

Two small, volunteer-built pools in a rocky canyon at the end of a wooded, winding, unpaved Forest Service road. Elevation 1,600 feet. Open all year, subject to fire-season and rain/mud closures.

Natural mineral water flows out of a spring at 105° and through a pipe into the upper six-foot by six-foot by eighteen-foot rock-and-cement soaking pool. From here it spills over into the lower slimy-bottom rock-and-mud pool where the temperature has cooled a degree or two. The pipe in the upper pool can be detached to stop the inflow and control water temperature. Remains of a volunteer-built wooden sunning deck and red wooden benches along the lower pool have collapsed due to erosion. The apparent local custom is clothing optional.

No services are available on the premises. It is one mile to a pack-in campground, six miles to a primitive National Forest campground, and twenty-seven miles to all other services.

Directions: See the directions to Big Caliente. At 3.2 miles past Juncal Campground, continue straight at the signed junction. After fording the creek, follow the graded unpaved road uphill for 3.7 miles to Mono Hill Gate and then park. From the gate it is 1 mile down a gradually descending graded road to Mono Campground (pack-in). It is another mile from here to the hot springs. At Mono Campground, continue straight. When the road forks, bear right at the gunshot wooden National Forest sign. When the path narrows, bear right again across a creekbed where you see primitive wooden steps. It is a few hundred feet along a narrow path to the springs. The brush becomes gradually greener as you get closer to the springs. Before heading to Little Caliente, it is advisable to check with the ranger station for information on how far the road is open and where to park. At times parking is near the turnoff to Big Caliente, making the hike more than 6 miles to Little Caliente.

Source map: *Los Padres National Forest.*

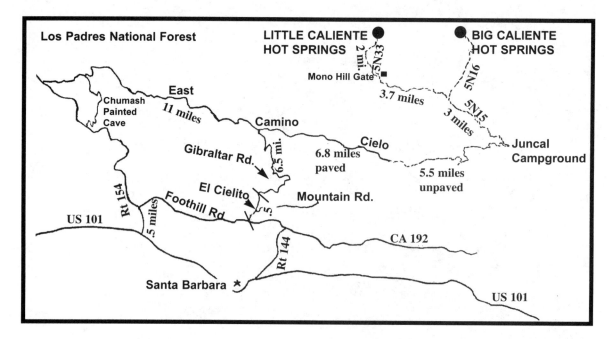

Map labels:

Los Padres National Forest

LITTLE CALIENTE HOT SPRINGS

BIG CALIENTE HOT SPRINGS

5N33 · 2 mi.

Mono Hill Gate

3.7 miles

5N16

5N15 · 3 miles

Chumash Painted Cave

East · 11 miles

Camino

Cielo

Juncal Campground

Gibraltar Rd. · 6.5 mi.

6.8 miles paved

5.5 miles unpaved

El Cielito

Foothill Rd · .5 miles

Mountain Rd.

US 101

Rt 154

Rt 144

CA 192

Santa Barbara ★

US 101

---

723 B   BIG CALIENTE HOT SPRINGS
(see map)

● **Near the city of Santa Barbara**

An improved, noncommercial hot spring located in a sparsely wooded canyon reached via ten miles of very windy, rocky, gravel road. Elevation 1,500 feet. Open all year, subject to fire closure and road conditions during rainy season. Check with Los Padres National Forest Ranger Station.

Natural mineral water flows out of a bluff at 115°, then through a faucet-controlled pipe to a six-foot by ten-foot concrete pool. Water temperature in the pool can be controlled by diverting the inflow hose or shutting off the faucet. As a courtesy to others, please close the valve and divert the hose out of the pool when leaving to prevent scalding others. When the valve is open, hot water showers up into the pool. Continual flow-through keeps the water clean. A galvanized pipe ladder leads into the pool, and concrete decks and benches are on two sides of the pool. The apparent local custom is clothing optional by mutual consent, although it is advisable to keep bathing suits handy for when rangers check. Since you can drive right up to the pool, it is handicap accessible with assistance.

A second primitive soaking pool is at creek level below the source spring. From the far end of the parking area, a marked trail leads off toward Big Caliente Debris Dam. Across the creek, water seeps down the mountain from a source spring under a cottonwood tree to the primitive 105° pool at creek level, which fills up with silt and mud and needs to be dredged periodically. This pool can be reached by rock-hopping where a pipe is visible underwater, approximately 100 yards from the trailhead.

Facilities include nearby changing rooms, very clean pit toilets across the level parking area, and a picnic table under the trees. A trail from the changing rooms leads down to the cold creek, which has small waterfalls and several small sunning beaches. There are no other services available on the premises. Several primitive Forest Service campgrounds are within three miles, and it is twenty-five miles to all other services in Santa Barbara.

Sign at Gibraltar Road and FS 5N12.

144

Directions: Coming from the south on Hwy 101 in Santa Barbara, take Milpas St. exit (Rte. 144). Follow Rte. 144 east through city, residential streets, and a five-point roundabout, for a total of 6.3 miles, to where it ends at Rte. 192. Turn left on Rte. 192 (Stanwood Drive) for 1.2 miles to El Cielito Rd. At .3 mile El Cielito crosses Mountain Drive. Continue straight uphill on El Cielito .5 mile to Gibraltar Rd. Turn right and follow Gibraltar for approximately 6.5 miles to where it ends at East Camino Cielo. Turn

While picknicking at *Big Caliente,* you can enjoy the sound of the water showering up from the open valve into the pool—just be sure to check the temperature before getting in. It could be very hot.

right on very windy East Camino Cielo, which is paved for the first 6.8 miles, then unsurfaced for the next 5.5 miles. At Juncal Campground, turn left on 5N15 for 3 miles to where the road forks. The right fork (5N16) ends at Big Caliente Hot Springs. (The left fork goes to Little Caliente.)

If coming from the north on Hwy 101, take Rte. 154 exit, heading east for .5 mile to Rte. 192 (called Foothill Rd.). At 4.7 miles you will come to a reservoir (Foothill has changed to Mountain Dr. and again to Mission Ridge). At .4 mile past the reservoir, Rte. 192 makes a sharp left at a fire station and becomes Stanwood Dr. Follow Stanwood to El Cielito Rd. and continue as described above.

Source map: *Los Padres National Forest.*

Measuring the temperature at the primitive creek-side pool makes sure that your soak will be comfortable.

724   LAS CRUCES HOT SPRINGS
(see map)

● **Near Gaviota State Park**

Two primitive, mud-bottom pools on a tree-shaded slope a few miles from the ocean. Elevation 500 feet. Open all year for day use only.

Natural mineral water emerges from the ground at 96° directly into a small, shallow, knee-deep rock-and-mud soaking pool with relatively clear water and large enough for six to eight people. The overflow forms a waterfall over the retaining earthen wall into the larger lower pool, which averages 80° and has a slimy-leaf bottom. The water is also a murky grey. Both of these volunteer-built pools have a slight sulfur smell. The apparent local custom is clothing optional by the mutual consent of those present.

There are no services available on the premises, and overnight parking is prohibited in the parking area at the trailhead, where a day-use self-parking fee is charged. Rangers check very frequently and cite vehicles without valid parking receipts. It is three miles to a campground with RV hookups and six miles to all other services.

Directions: On Hwy101 approximately 35 miles north of Santa Barbara is Gaviota State beach on the west with its landmark railroad bridge. From here it is 3 miles to the turnoff for CA 1, west toward Lompoc. Directly across from this turnoff is the small road paralleling the highway and heading south to the parking area for Las Cruces. After Gaviota State Beach you will have passed a rest area and gone through a tunnel. It is 1 mile past the tunnel to the turnoff.

From the parking area, follow the steep dirt 4WD trail to where it forks at a white sign saying "no horses past this point." Bear right on a narrow trail approximately .75 mile from the parking area to the pools.

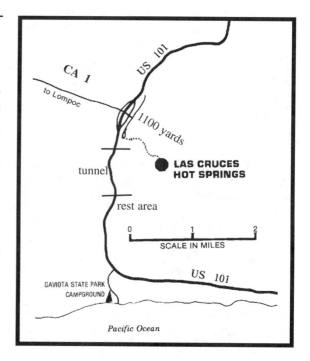

726   SYCAMORE MINERAL SPRINGS
1215 Avila Beach Dr.   805 595-7302
■   **San Luis Obispo, CA 93401**

This delightful resort offers dozens of secluded redwood hot tubs out under the oak trees and a private redwood hot tub on the balcony of every motel room. Located on a wooded rural hillside two miles from the ocean. Elevation 40 feet. Open all year, twenty-four hours per day.

Natural mineral water is pumped from a well at 110° and piped to the tubs on the hillside and on the motel balconies. Each tub has a hot mineral-water faucet and a cold tap-water faucet, so the temperature is controlled by the customer. Each tub also has its own jet pump, filter and automatic chlorinator. The swimming pool is filled with tap water treated with chlorine and maintained at 89° by a heat exchanger. A 102° natural-looking rock spa that will hold thirty people is located next to the pool. Bathing suits are required except in those outdoor tubs that are screened by shrubbery.

Facilities include a restaurant , motel rooms with hot tubs on the balcony (complete with Continental breakfast), new deluxe suites with spas and fireplaces, a one-bedroom cottage with its own hot tub in a private enclosure, dressing rooms, meeting space, a gift shop, and a sand volleyball court. Several varieties of massage are available. A half-hour soak in one of the outdoor tubs is included in each appointment. On request, directions to a nearby clothing-optional state beach will be provided. American Express, MasterCard, and Visa are accepted. Phone for rates and reservations.

Directions: From US 101 8 miles south of San Luis Obispo, take the Avila Beach exit, then go 1 mile west on Avila Beach Dr. and watch for the resort sign on the south side of the road.

725   AVILA HOT SPRINGS SPA & RV PARK
250 Avila Beach Drive   805 595-2359
■   **San Luis Obispo, CA 93405**

Combination hot spring and RV resort located in a foothill hollow at a freeway exit. Elevation 40 feet. Open all year.

Natural mineral water flows out of an artesian well at 130° and is piped to various pools. There are six indoor, tiled Roman tubs in which the water temperature is determined by the amount of hot mineral water and cold tap water admitted. These tubs are drained and refilled after each use so that no chemical treatment is needed. The outdoor soaking pool (105°) is drained and filled daily. The fifty-by one-hundred-foot outdoor swimming pool (86°) is filled with tap water and treated with chlorine. Bathing suits are required except in private tub rooms.

Massage, snack bar, RV hook-ups, lawn tenting spaces, and a small store are available on the premises. All major credit cards are accepted. It is one mile to a motel, restaurant, and service station.

Directions: From San Luis Obispo, drive south 8 miles on US 101, take the Avila Beach Drive exit (not San Luis Bay Drive), and go north 1 block to the resort entrance.

727 ESALEN INSTITUTE
Workshop, room reservation
408 667-3000

■ **Big Sur, CA 93920**

Primarily an educational/experiential center rather than a hot spring resort. Located on CA 1, 45 miles south of Monterey. Elevation 100 feet. Open all year.

Esalen specializes in residential programs that focus on education, philosophy, and the physical and behavioral sciences. Access to the grounds is by reservation only for those wishing to take workshops or for room and board. The hot springs are also open by reservation for up to 32 people each weekday morning from 1 AM to 3:30 AM at a charge. To make a bath reservation, please call 408 667-3047.

Natural mineral water flows out of the ground at 120° and into a bathhouse built on a cliff face, fifty feet above a rocky ocean beach. Within the bathhouse, which is open toward the ocean, are four concrete soaking pools and eight individual tubs. There are also two adjoining outdoor soaking pools. Water temperature is determined within each tub by admitting controlled amounts of hot mineral water and cold well water. This flow-through process, plus frequent cleaning of the pools, makes chemical treatment of the water unnecessary. Clothing is optional in and around the bathhouse. Handicap access is limited; make arrangements in advance.

Facilities include housing and a dining room for registered guests. It is eleven miles to a restaurant, store, and service station. Massage is available on the premises. Visa, MasterCard, and American Express are accepted for registered guests only.

728 TASSAJARA BUDDHIST MEDITATION CENTER
Tassajara Springs
Overnight Reservations
415 431-3771
Day Reservations   408 659-2229
■ **Carmel Valley, CA 93924**

Primarily a Buddhist Monastery with accommodations available to the public from early May to early September. Located in wooded mountains southeast of Monterey. Elevation 1,500 feet.

Please, no drop-in visitors. Prior reservations are required. Guests are expected to respect the spirit of a monastic community.

Natural mineral water flows out of the ground at 140° into two large, enclosed soaking pools that average 110° and two outdoor pools at 106°. This water, which is not chemically treated, cools as it flows into nearby streambed soaking areas. The outdoor swimming pool is maintained at approximately 75°. There are also steambaths in the separate men's and women's bathhouses. Bathing suits are required at the swimming pool only.

Rooms and meals are included as part of confirmed overnight reservation arrangements. The use of meditation facilities is also included. No credit cards are accepted. It is ninety minutes to a store, cafe, and service station. The road is steep and dangerous requiring good brakes and low gears.

730 SYKES HOT SPRING
(see map)

- **Near the village of Big Sur**

Remote, undeveloped hot spring on the Big Sur River in the Ventana Wilderness portion of the Los Padres National Forest. Elevation 1,110 feet. May be submerged during high water in the river.

Natural mineral water flows out of the ground at 100° from under a fallen tree and into a volunteer-built shallow soaking pool. This location involves a ten-mile hike on the Pine Ridge Trail, and a Wilderness Permit must be obtained from the Forest Service. The spring is near one of the most popular hiking routes, so the distance is no assurance of quiet or privacy during the summer months.

The Forest Service issues a trail map to those holding Wilderness Permits and, on request, will mark the hot-spring location on that map. Check your preparations, including water supply, with the ranger.

Source maps for trails: USGS *Ventana Cones, Partington Ridge* (springs not shown).

729 PARAISO HOT SPRINGS
408 678-2882

- **Soledad, CA 93960**

A quiet resort for adults, with several acres of tree-shaded grass areas, located on the west slopes of the Salinas Valley. Elevation 1,200 feet. Open all year.

Natural mineral water flows out of the ground at 115° and is piped to three pools: an indoor soaking pool with a temperature of 108°, an outdoor soaking pool with a temperature of 100°, and an outdoor swimming pool with a temperature of 80°. The swimming pool is treated with chlorine. Bathing suits are required. No cut-offs permitted.

Cottages, RV spaces, overnight camping, a snack bar, and a cocktail bar are available on the premises. No credit cards are accepted. It is eight miles to a restaurant and service station.

Directions: From US 101, exit on Arroyo Seco Rd., 1 mile south of Soledad. Go 1 mile west to stop sign, then go straight onto Paraiso Springs Rd. Continue uphill for 6 miles to resort at end of road.

731 DIFFERENT SOAKS
1157 Forest Ave.   408 646-8293
☐ Pacific Grove, CA 93950

Unusually spacious hot-pool rental and retail spa sales establishment located in a suburb of Monterey.

Five pools in private rooms are for rent to the public. One room has a tub large enough for ten persons, and rooms can be combined for larger groups. Gas-heated tap water treated with bromine is heated to 103°. Each room has a shower, dressing space, music speaker, and a landscaped, open-roof garden along one wall.

Massage is available on the premises. No credit cards are accepted. Phone for rates, reservations, and directions.

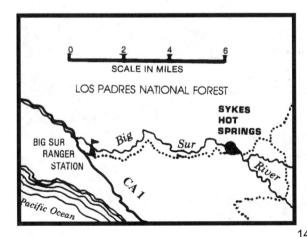

SCALE IN MILES
0   2   4   6

LOS PADRES NATIONAL FOREST

SYKES HOT SPRINGS

BIG SUR RANGER STATION

Big Sur River

CA 1

Pacific Ocean

One of the only things Santa Cruz doesn't have is a natural hot spring. However, *Kiva Retreat* (above) and *Heartwood Spa* (below) make two great substitutes with warm water pools and garden-like sunning areas.

732 A   HEARTWOOD SPA
3150A Mission Dr.   408 462-2192
☐   Santa Cruz, CA 95065

A clothing-optional, tree-shaded hot tub rental establishment located on a suburban side street.

A wooden hot tub, cold tub, sauna, and communal sunning areas are available for a day-rate charge. One private tub with a water temperature of 105° can be rented by the hour. All pools use gas-heated tap water treated with chlorine. The private tub area is wheelchair accessible. Bathing suits are optional everywhere except at the front desk.

Massage is available on the premises. The total facility may be reserved for private parties before and after regular business hours. No credit cards are accepted. Phone for rates, reservations, and directions. (Community area open on Sunday evenings for women only.)

732 B   KIVA RETREAT
702 Water St.   408 429-1142
☐   Santa Cruz, CA 95060

Trees, grass, and flowers lend a parklike setting to this unusual, clothing-optional, hot-pool rental establishment. Located near the city center.

A single day rate gives entry to the communal grass area, two large hot tubs, a cold-tub plunge, and a large sauna. Adjoining indoor dressing and social rooms are also available. Pools use gas-heated tap water and are treated with chlorine and ozone. Two private enclosures, rented by the hour, have water maintained at 102°. Bathing suits are optional everywhere except in the front entry.

Massage is available on the premises. Major credit cards are accepted. Phone for rates, reservations, and directions.

732 C WELL WITHIN
112 Elm St.   408 458-9355
☐   Santa Cruz, CA 95060

Beautiful hot pool and sauna rooms overlooking a Japanese bamboo garden, located in the heart of downtown Santa Cruz and available for rent by the hour.

Four private-space suites, consisting of a shower, changing area, and tub use bromine-treated tap water. The fiberglass pools offer a view of the garden and a sliding glass door can be opened. Two of the suites also offer a sauna. Water temperatures are maintained at 104°. Many of the tubs are handicap accessible. Herbal tea and large towels are provided.

Massage is available on the premises. No credit cards. Phone for rates and reservations.

733   LUPIN NATURIST CLUB
P.O. Box 1274   408 353-2250
☐   Los Gatos, CA 95031

A clothing-optional resort where both sexes are equal and the differences are accepted as natural. Located on 110 acres of tree-shaded tranquillity in the Santa Cruz mountains. Elevation 700 feet. Open all year.

Gas-heated spring water, chlorine-treated, is used in two outdoor fiberglass tubs available to all members and registered guests. Water temperature is maintained at 102-104°. Chlorine-treated well water is also used in two outdoor swimming pools, one of which is heated and covered with a plastic dome in the winter. Some facilities are handicap accessible. Bathing suits are prohibited in all pools. Clothing is optional elsewhere on the grounds.

RV , camping spaces, and yurts are available for overnight stays. A restaurant in a new, large clubhouse is available on the premises. Visa and MasterCard are accepted. It is seven miles to a motel, store, and service station.

Note: This is a private club not open to the public for drop-in visits. Phone first for information, guest passes, and directions.

734   GRAND CENTRAL SAUNA AND
**   HOT TUB CO.**
          376 Saratoga Ave.   408 247-8827
☐   San Jose, CA 95129

One of a chain of urban locations established by Grand Central, the pioneer in the room rent-a-tub business.

Twenty-one private indoor tubs are heated to 102-104° and treated with chlorine. The individual rooms each have a sauna and dressing room. Towels and soap are provided.

No credit cards or reservations are accepted. Phone for hours, rates, and directions.

Watercourse Way is an interesting combination of sleek modern and Oriental decor.

735   WATERCOURSE WAY
          165 Channing Way   415 462-2000
☐   Palo Alto, CA 94301

The beautiful oriental decor creates a comfortable and interesting environment offering a variety of enjoyable rooms and experiences.

Pools, for rent to the public, use gas-heated tap water treated with chlorine and muriatic acid. Ten individually decorated private rooms each have a different combination of hot pool, cold pool, sauna, and steambath. Water temperature in the pools is approximately 103°. In one of the rooms, special oils or bath salts can be added to the tub as the water is drained and refilled after each use. To accommodate larger groups, two rooms can be joined.

Facials, spa treatments, and massage are available on the premises. Visa and MasterCard are accepted. Phone for rates, reservations, and directions.

736   TROPICAL GARDENS
          200 San Pedro Rd.   415 755-8827
☐   Colma, CA 94105

Recreation-oriented rent-a-tub business sharing quarters with a racquetball facility and health club. Located a few blocks south of Daly City.

Ten private rooms have pools that use gas-heated tap water treated with chlorine. Water temperature is maintained at 102-104°. A sauna is included in seven of the rooms.

Other facilities include racquetball and handball courts, a tanning studio, Nautilus conditioning, swimming pool and locker rooms. Massage is available by appointment. No credit cards are accepted. Phone for rates, reservations, and directions.

737 A   THE HOT TUBS
          2200 Van Ness Ave.   415 441-TUBS
☐   San Francisco, CA 94109

One of the few stress-reduction establishments offering tile tubs and decks in a chrome and glass urban environment. Located on a main street just west of downtown.

Pools in 20 private rooms are for rent to the public. Gas-heated tap water treated with chlorine is maintained at 104°. A sauna, music, and rest area are included. Towels and soap are provided.

Massage and a juice bar are available on the premises. No credit cards are accepted. Phone for rates, reservations, and directions.

737 B   FAMILY SAUNA SHOP
          2308 Clement   415 221-2208
☐   San Francisco, CA 94121

One of the pioneer stress-reduction centers in San Francisco. Located in the Richmond District.

Two private rooms with pools for rent to the public use gas-heated tap water treated with chlorine. Water temperature is 104°.

Four private saunas are available for rent. Massage and facials are available on the premises. Visa and MasterCard are accepted. Phone for rates, reservations, and directions.

737 C   GRAND CENTRAL SAUNA AND HOT TUB CO.

15 Fell St.   415 431-1370

□   San Francisco, CA 94102

The first one of a chain of urban locations established by Grand Central, a pioneer in the private room rent-a-tub business.

Pools in 26 private rooms, each with a sauna, are for rent to the public. The pools use gas-heated tap water treated with chlorine and are maintained between 102-104°. Towels and soap are provided.

Tanning booths are available on the premises. Credit cards are not accepted. Reservations are not accepted. Phone for rates and directions.

738   F. JOSEPH SMITH'S MASSAGE THERAPY

158 Almonte Blvd.   415 383-8260

□   Mill Valley, CA 94941

A Marin healing center with two five-foot deep hot tubs nestled under redwood trees, located in a country setting.

Two private enclosures with water temperatures of approximately 104° and treated with chlorine are rented by the public. One of the tubs is available for communal use during the day. A sauna is also for rent. Bathing suits are optional in the tub and sauna area.

The prayer garden is open for relaxation and meditation. A crystal room also provides a space to meditate. Massage and advanced body therapy classes are available on the premises, as are chiropractic and acupuncture services. Massage classes and workshop space are available. Phone for rates, reservations, and directions.

Behind the flower and tree-lined entrance to *F. Joseph Smith's Massage Therapy* is a lovely garden with a waterfall, just perfect for meditation and relaxation before or after your massage.

739 SHIBUI GARDENS

19 Tamalpais Ave.   415 457-0283
☐   San Anselmo, CA 94960

An inviting blend of Marin County natural redwood hot tubs and Japanese landscaping. Located on a suburban side street.

Three privately enclosed hot tubs using bromine-treated, gas-heated tap water are for rent by the hour. Water temperatures range from 102-105°. One communal cold pool is also available to customers at no extra charge. Bathing suits are optional inside the pool and sauna spaces.

A private indoor sauna is for rent on the premises. Massage is available. Phone for rates, reservations, and directions.

740 FROGS

10B School St. Plaza   415 453-7647
☐   Fairfax, CA 94930

One of the first rent-a-tub facilities in the San Francisco Bay area. Located in a Marin County suburb and recently renovated by new ownership.

Wooden tubs for rent to the public use gas-heated tap water magnetically polarized, treated with chlorine, and maintained at 105°. There are two soaking tubs in private enclosures, plus a large communal hot tub and a cold plunge. There are two saunas (the hottest in the Bay area) and a clothing-optional sundeck.

Massage is available by appointment. Visa and MasterCard are accepted. Phone for rates, reservations, and directions.

741 ALBANY SAUNA AND HOT TUBS

1002 Solano Ave.   510 525-6262
☐   Albany, CA 94706

Established in 1934 as one of the earliest rent-a-tub establishments in the Bay Area, it has since been extensively remodeled. Located two blocks west of San Pablo Ave.

Three outdoor, privately enclosed pools for rent to the public use gas-heated tap water treated with chlorine. Water temperature is maintained at approximately 105°.

Four private rock-steam saunas, individually controlled for temperature with an outside air source for comfortable breathing, are available for rent. Swedish massage, and hair and skin care products are available on the premises. Major credit cards are accepted. Phone for rates, reservations, and directions.

Billy FROGS
School Street Plaza, Fairfax
(415) 453-7647

- ✦ Hot Tubs
- ✦ Saunas
- ✦ Cold Plunge
- ✦ Sundeck
- ✦ Massage

742 A   THE HOT TUBS
1915 University Ave.   510 843-4343
☐   Berkeley, CA 94704

One of two urban locations in Berkeley and San Francisco.

Twelve private rooms with pools use gas-heated tap water treated with chlorine. Water temperature varies between 102-104°. A sauna is included.

A juice bar is available on the premises. No credit cards or checks are accepted. Reservations are not accepted. Phone for rates and directions.

742 B   THE BERKELEY SAUNA
1947 Milvia St.   510 845-2341
☐   Berkeley, CA 94704

A stress-reduction establishment located a few yards north of University Avenue.

Three private rooms with gas-heated tap water pools are available for rent to the public. The bromine-treated water is maintained at temperatures from 104-106°.

Three private saunas are also for rent. Massage is available on the premises. Credit cards accepted. Phone for rates, reservations, and directions.

743 A   AMERICAN FAMILY HOT TUB
88 Trelany Lane   510 827-2299
☐   Pleasant Hill, CA 94523

Suburban rent-a-tub establishment located a few yards west of Contra Costa Blvd.

Twelve private outdoor pools are for rent by the hour. Gas-heated tap water treated with chlorine is maintained at 102-104°. A sauna and massage are available on the premises. Visa and MasterCard are accepted. Phone for rates, reservations, and directions.

743 B   SUNSHINE SPA
1948 Contra Costa Blvd.   510 685-7822
☐   Pleasant Hill, CA 94523

Funky, fun-loving rent-a-tub business located in the Pleasant Hill Plaza, fifteen miles east of Oakland.

Pools using gas-heated tap water treated with bromine are for rent to the public. There are seven private rooms, each with an in-ground hot tub, sauna, shower, massage table, and mural. Pool temperatures range from 90-102°. Handicap accessible.

Massage is available on the premises. Visa and MasterCard are accepted. Phone for rates, reservations, and directions.

744 ⸱⸱ PIEDMONT SPRINGS
3939 Piedmont   510 658-5697
☐   Oakland, CA 94611

Urban rent-a-tub establishment situated in downtown Oakland.

Four hot tubs, one in combination with a sauna, were built outdoors in private enclosures, complete with redwood decks, changing area, and shower. Water temperature is maintained at 106° but can be cooled down with hoses. All tubs are chlorine treated.

Massage, facials, salt scrubs, and other skin care treatments are available. Phone for rates, reservations, and directions.

745   HOT TROPICS
17389 Hesperion Blvd.   510 278-8827
☐   San Lorenzo, CA 94580

Seniors, families, singles, and couples are welcome at this rent-a-tub establishment just a couple of blocks off Hwy 880.

Twelve private indoor tubs are heated to 102-105° and treated with chlorine. Five rooms are also equipped with saunas, beds, and showers. Seven rooms do not have a sauna but do have large skylights that roll open when the weather permits. Special minerals are added to the tubs. Handicap accessible.

No credit cards or reservations are accepted. Phone for hours, rates, and directions.

746   PARADISE SPA
5168 Mowry Ave.   510 793-7727
☐   Fremont, CA 94538

Suburban rent-a-tub and tanning center located in a shopping center just off of Highway 880.

Eight private rooms, including one with special black lighting, come complete with tubs and showers. The water is heated to between 102-104° and is chlorine treated. Towels and radios are supplied.

Tanning booths are available. Visa and MasterCard are accepted. Phone for reservations.

SOUTHERN CALIFORNIA

This map was designed to be used with a standard highway map.

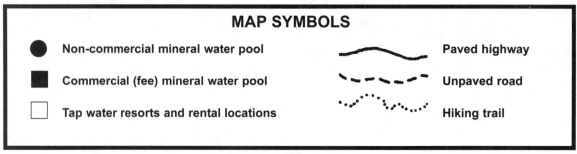

MAP SYMBOLS

● Non-commercial mineral water pool

■ Commercial (fee) mineral water pool

□ Tap water resorts and rental locations

〜 Paved highway

- - - Unpaved road

···· Hiking trail

801 A FURNACE CREEK INN RESORT
Box 1   619 786-2345
■ **Death Valley, CA 92328**

An historic resort built around a lush oasis on a barren hillside overlooking Death Valley. Elevation, sea level. Open mid-October to mid-May.

Natural mineral water flows out of a spring at 89°, into two outdoor pools, and through a large, palm-shaded arroyo. The swimming pool maintains a temperature of approximately 85°, and the flow-through rate is so great that no chemical treatment of the water is necessary. Bathing suits are required. Pools are for the use of registered guests only.

Facilities include two saunas, lighted tennis courts, rooms, two restaurants, live entertainment and dancing, and a bar. Major credit cards are accepted.

801 B FURNACE CREEK RANCH RESORT
Box 1   619 786-2345
■ **Death Valley, CA 92328**

A large, ranch-style resort in a green oasis setting. Located in the center of Death Valley, one mile west of Furnace Creek Inn. Elevation 178 feet. below sea level. Open all year.

Natural mineral water is piped from the 89° spring serving the inn to a swimming pool at the ranch. The rate of flow-through is so great that a temperature of approximately 85° is maintained and no chemical treatment is necessary. Pool use is open to the public as well as to registered guests. Most facilities are handicap accessible; handicap rooms are available. Bathing suits are required.

Facilities include rooms, three restaurants, bar, store, service station, RV hookups, golf course, and lighted tennis courts. Major credit cards are accepted.

These hundred-year-old palms at the *Furnace Creek Inn* provide a bit of shade during the hottest part of the day.

802 A SHOSHONE INN
Box 67   619 852-4335
■   Shoshone, CA 92384

Older resort located on CA 127 in desert foothills near the southern entrance to Death Valley. Elevation 1,600 feet. Open all year.

Natural mineral water flows out of a spring at 93° with such pressure that no pumps are needed to push it through the pipes to the outdoor swimming pool. The rate of flow-through is so great that a temperature of 92° is maintained and no chemical treatment of the water is necessary. A waterfall at the end of the pool cools the inflow for pool use in the summer. Pool use is available only to registered guests. Bathing suits are required.

Facilities include rooms, restaurant, bar, store, service station. RV hookups and overnight camping spaces are available at the Shoshone RV Park (802 B). Major credit cards are accepted.

Location: Shoshone is 28 miles south of Death Valley Junction and 58 miles north of Baker on CA 127.

802 B SHOSHONE RV PARK
Box 67   619 852-4569
■   Shoshone, CA 92348

Lush, green, tree-shaded oasis RV park one hundred yards north of the Shoshone Inn on the main street (CA 127) in Shoshone.

The natural mineral water outdoor swimming pool described at left is adjacent to the RV park and is for the use of registered guests of either facility and for local residents (all forty of them) who purchase a season's membership. Non-guests may use the pool by paying a day-use fee (which is the same as the overnight RV park fee).

Half of the hot geothermal well water supplies the RV park's showers, the inn, and the pool; the other half is used for the town water supply. All water must be brought to a rolling boil for at least a minute before being used for drinking or cooking.

No credit cards are accepted at the RV park.

803 A   DELIGHT'S HOT SPA
   Box 368   **619 852-4343**
■ **Tecopa, CA 92389**

One of the original hot spring spas in the arid, alkali desert east of Death Valley, originally established in the early 1940s. For adults only (ages 21-101). Elevation 1,400 feet. Open all year.

Hundreds of warm mineral springs supply geothermal water to the entire region. Delight's sits on the dome of the mineral springs area and has four, large, three-foot-deep, private, coed cement tubs that hold two to three people. Water flows from a 285-foot artesian well into three of the tubs. The fourth pool is fed by a small spring that comes up directly into the spring house. Water cools as it flows through pipes into the pool, where it measures 106°. Pools are open from 5 AM to 9 PM and are drained and scrubbed nightly. Pools have stairs and bars and are handicap accessible with assistance. Pool use is for registered guests only. No suits are allowed in the pools to prevent contamination from fabric dyes.

Facilities include rustic housekeeping cottages with refrigeration (no TVs, radios, or phones), full hookup RV spaces, showers, rest rooms, and laundromat. The clubhouse has a stage, pool table, and fireplace and is large enough for banquets and weddings. It is two miles to all other services in Tecopa.

Directions: From CA 127, 5 miles south of Shoshone or 50 Miles north of Baker, drive east on Tecopa Hot Springs Rd. for 3 miles. A red windmill and sign to the spa are on the east side of the street.

803 B   TECOPA HOT SPRINGS RESORT
   Box 420   **619 852-4373**
■ **Tecopa, CA 92389**

RV park and pools located on the Tecopa loop of CA 127 in desert foothills near the Dumont sand dunes. Elevation 1,400 feet. Open all year. (Motel units scheduled to open in 1996.)

Natural mineral water flows from an artesian well at 108° and is piped to seven hydropools in private rooms. Continuous flow-through maintains a temperature of approximately 107°, and no chemical treatment of the water is necessary. Posted signs require nude bathing in these pools, which are for the use of registered guests only.

Facilities include mini-mart, RV hookups, and overnight camping spaces. It is one mile to a service station. No credit cards are accepted.

803 C   TECOPA HIDE-A-WAY (ALI BABA'S)
   Box 101   **619 852-4438**
■ **Tecopa, CA 92389**

Small RV park located on the Tecopa loop off CA 127. Elevation 1,400 feet. Open all year. (Reopening in 1996; inquire about status.)

Natural mineral water flows out of an artesian well at 118° and is piped to two indoor soaking pools where the temperature is controlled between 100-108°, depending on the season. The rate of flow-through is so great that no chemical treatment of the water is necessary. The pools are available to the public as well as to registered guests.

Facilities include RV hookups and camping spaces. No credit cards are accepted. It is one mile to a motel, restaurant, store, and service station.

Even though *Tecopa Desert Pond* is only one mile from the developed resorts, it feels secluded and remote.

803 D   TECOPA HOT SPRINGS
(operated by Inyo county)
PO Box 158   619 852-4264
■   Tecopa, CA 92389

A county-operated trailer park, bathhouse, and campground located on the Tecopa loop off CA 127. Elevation 1,400 feet. Open all year, seven days a week, twenty-four hours a day; free to park users and the general public.

Natural mineral water flows out of a spring at 108° and is piped to separate men's and women's bathhouses. Each one has two gravel-bottom, three-foot-deep soaking pools maintained at 100° and 105°, plus an enclosed outdoor sunbathing area. The indoor pool is twelve by twelve and the enclosed outdoor pool is eight by -twelve; both pools have steps and grab bars for handicap access. Posted signs required nude bathing. Mixed bathing is not permitted.

RV hookups and overnight spaces are available on the premises. There is an air-conditioned community center with library, exercise classes, and social activities. No credit cards are accepted. It is two miles to a store and service station.

803 E   TECOPA DESERT POND

●   **Near the town of Tecopa**

A cement-bottom rectangular tub with cement steps, protected on three sides by wooden barriers. Located on an open stretch of flat white alkali BLM desert, next to the only palm tree and greenery in the area. Elevation 1,400 feet. Open all year.

Natural 98° mineral water flows from an artesian well just next to the tub, with overflow running off the far side of the pool in a continual flow-through pattern. The apparent local custom is clothing optional.

There are no facilities on the premises. Overnight parking for one night is not prohibited on BLM desert. Partying remains are evident near the pool, but the tub itself is relatively clean. Slimy algae is scrubbed away by volunteers. It is one mile to all services.

Directions: Located on the Tecopa loop of CA 127, 5 miles south of Shoshone, 50 miles north of Baker, and 27 miles southwest of Pahrump, NV on CA 178/NV 372.

One block south of Delight's Hot Spa on Tecopa Hot Springs Rd. and just north of the county-run Tecopa Hot Springs bathhouse, turn east at the sign saying "Slow, Entering County Park, Co. in Inyo." At .3 mile you pass a large duck pond on your left, and the gravel road bears right. Do not bear right, but continue straight ahead on the ungraded, unsurfaced road across the flat alkali desert. At .2 mile farther on, go around to the left of the log barrier and keep driving on the rough road toward the only cluster of green foliage in the area. The tub is at the foot of the small, low palm tree, a total of .9 mile from Hot Springs Rd. During the rainy season, the road to this pool may be muddy and impassable.

804 SILVER VALLEY SUN CLUB
48382 Silver Valley Road

619 257-4239

☐ Newberry Springs, CA 92365

Southern California's first clothing-optional lake resort, located on a paved road in the high desert 26 miles east of Barstow. Sunshine 355 days per year. Elevation 1,800 feet. Open all year.

Electric-heated well water, treated with bromine, is used in an outdoor hydropool that is maintained at a temperature of 104°. Clothing is optional everywhere on the grounds, but bathing suits are prohibited in the lake, pool, and showers.

Facilities include a two and one-half acre lake, air-conditioned clubhouse, restaurant, snack bar, rental rooms, RV hookups, tent sites, and exercise equipment. Volleyball, shuffleboard, horseshoes, children's games, theme parties and bingo are available on the premises. Visa and MasterCard are accepted. It is seven miles to a service station and store, twenty-five miles to a motel.

This is a commercial resort affiliated with the American Sunbathing Association and open to the public. Phone for rates, reservations, and directions.

805 A BASHFORD'S HOT MINERAL SPA
10590 Hot Mineral Spa Rd.

619 354-1315

■ Niland, CA 92257

Primarily an RV winter resort for adults, located on a desert slope overlooking the Salton Sea. Elevation 50 feet below sea level. Open October 1 to May 30.

Natural mineral water flows out of an artesian well at 150° and into two cooling tanks from which it is piped to an outdoor swimming pool maintained at 84° and to an outdoor hydropool maintained at 102°. The water in both pools is chlorine-treated. Mineral water is also piped to six outdoor soaking tubs with temperatures from 101-105°. These tubs are drained and refilled after each use so that no chemical treatment is needed. Bathing suits are required.

RV hookups, overnight spaces, and a laundry room are available on the premises, and catfish fishing (no license required) is about one mile away. Discover cards are accepted. It is seven miles to a motel, restaurant, and service station.

805 C IMPERIAL SEA VIEW HOT SPRINGS
10595 Hot Mineral Spa Rd.

619 354-1204

HCO 1, Box 20 (mailing address)

■ **Niland, CA 92257**

The original "Old Spa" location, with the first hot well drilled in this area. Located on a desert slope overlooking the Salton Sea. Elevation fifty feet below sea level. Open all year.

Natural mineral water flows out of an artesian well at 165° and into a large holding and cooling tank from which it is piped to seven outdoor pools. Five hydropools are maintained at a variety of temperatures from 96-104°. Two mineral-water soaking pool are maintained at 96° and 88°. All pools are treated with chlorine. Bathing suits are required.

RV hookups, overnight camping spaces, and a store are on the premises. No credit cards accepted. It is six miles to a service station on CA 111 across from the border patrol and seven and one-half miles north to a restaurant and motel in Bombay Beach.

805 B FOUNTAIN OF YOUTH SPA
10249 Coachella Canal Rd.

619 348-1340

Rte.1, Box 12 (mailing address)

■ **Niland, CA 92257**

The largest of the RV parks in this area, located on a desert slope overlooking the Salton Sea. Elevation sea level. Open all year.

Natural mineral water flows out of an artesian well on the property at 137°, is cooled by heat exchangers, and is piped to two pool areas, one of which is reserved for adults. The two outdoor swimming pools range in temperature from 85-90°. The five outdoor hydropools range in temperature from 100-107°. The water in all pools is chlorine treated. The pools are available to registered overnight campers only. No day use. Bathing suits are required.

The facilities include a laundromat, store, cafe, RV hookups, overnight camping spaces, recreation rooms, library, exercise and fitness room, and car wash facility. Services include massage and beauty and barber shops. Church services and activity programs are also offered. No reservations are taken. If no hookup spaces are available, it is possible to dry camp and get on a waiting list. It is two and one-half miles south to a service station across from the border patrol on CA 111 and four and one-half miles north to a motel and restaurant at Bombay Beach.

Directions: from CA 111, 3 miles south of Bombay Beach, drive east on Hot Mineral Spa Rd. for 1.5 miles, then right onto Spa Rd. for 1.1 miles.

805 D LARK SPA
HCO-1, Box 10   619 354-1384

■ **Niland, CA 92257**

Mobile home and RV winter resort for adults, located on a desert slope overlooking the Salton Sea. Elevation fifty feet below sea level. Open all year.

Well water and mineral water, gas heated and chlorine treated, are used in an outdoor hydropool maintained at 102°. Bathing suits are required.

Overnight spaces and RV hookups are available on the premises. No credit cards are accepted. It is one mile to a store and service station and four miles to a motel and restaurant.

Directions: From Niland, drive 10.5 miles north to Frink Rd. and turn right (east) for 1 mile. Frink Rd. is 3 miles south of the border patrol station on CA 111.

806   FIVE PALMS WARM WELL OASIS

● **Near the city of Brawley**

An exotic, picturesque, true desert oasis surrounded by palm trees and tall bullrushes inn the otherwise flat, arid, sparsely vegetated Imperial Valley desert south of the Salton Sea. Elevation 113 feet below sea level. Open all year.

Natural 92° mineral water bubbles up from an artesian well through a three-inch pipe in the middle of a large, clean, sandy-bottom soaking pond that is eighteen inches deep and large enough for a dozen people. In winter, the bullrushes and palms keep the pool in the shade, cooling it down. The apparent local custom is clothing optional.

There are no services available except plenty of open BLM desert where overnight parking is permitted with a fourteen-day limit. Caution: Choose your parking space carefully; vehicles have been know to get stuck in the soft sand underneath a deceptively firm crust. Please help by cleaning up any party trash. All services are available in Brawley, approximately sixteen and one-half miles.

Directions: From Brawley, drive 15 miles east on CA 78, cross the Highline Canal, and take the second dirt road right (l4 miles past the canal). Follow the one-lane road for 1.6 miles to the five tall palms, the only greenery in the area. At 1.5 miles, where the road forks, either fork will lead you to the oasis. The one-lane, graded, unsurfaced road has some soft sandy spots that can usually be handled by normal passenger vehicles.

Alternate directions: From I-8 take the CA 115 exit and drive north for 20 miles to CA 78. Turn right (east) for 6 miles to the canal, and follow the directions above.

807   HIGHLINE SOUTH HOT WELL

● **Near the town of Holtville**

Two cement soaking pools and a large pond fed by an artesian well, located just off the I-8 right-of-way on the east edge of Holtville. Elevation sea level. Open all year; closed midnight to 5 AM.

Natural mineral water flows out of an artesian well at 125° and splashes on the edge of a six-foot by six-foot by three-foot deep cement cistern. Hot water showers in through holes in an overhead swing-arm horizontal pipe, which can be diverted when the desired pool temperature is reached. A smaller, cement, bathtub-size pool is right next to the larger tub. There is very little self-cleaning action, and algae growth is rapid. Volunteer snowbirds regularly scrub the pools with bleach, which also removes the green algae smell. Because the pools are visible from I-8, bathing suits are recommended. A four-step ladder makes the tub handicap accessible with assistance. A sign reminds campers that "soap is prohibited in spa/pond." The area is posted for day-use only and the sheriff patrols regularly.

Overflow from the tub goes into a large, shallow, sandy-bottom "olde swimming hole" that used to be stocked with fish. Water temperature measures 90°, and fan palms offer a spot of shade.

Facilities include wooden benches, a cement deck, trash cans, nearby BLM pit toilets, and a fenced-off parking area where overnight parking is prohibited. A primitive BLM campground with a fourteen-day limit is located twenty yards north of the well, across the road. All other services are in Holtville.

Directions: At the east end of Holtville, take the Van Der Linden exit (CA 115) from I-8. Go north and immediately take the first right turn onto a frontage road paralleling I-8. At approximately 1 mile you will cross over the Highline Canal. Just past the canal on the right (south) is a flat, fenced parking area with pit toilets. The pools are just ahead toward I-8.

The pools are located inside this corrugated tin hut, and with the desert sun beating down, you often get a free sauna along with your soak.

808 AGUA CALIENTE COUNTY PARK
For reservations call   619 565-3600

■ **Located in the Anza Borego Desert**

A county-operated, desert campground located in a wildlife refuge area near the Anza Borego Desert. A wide range of animals and beautiful spring wildflowers and succulents are native to this area. No pets are permitted at any time! Elevation 1,300 feet. Open September through May.

Natural mineral water flows out of several springs at 96° and is then piped to two pools where it is filtered and chlorinated. The outdoor swimming pool with a water temperature between 90-92° is available for families and children. The large indoor hydropool for adults only is located in a corrugated tin quonset hut. The chlorine-treated mineral water is solar and gas heated to 104°. The hydropool, showers, restrooms, and dressing area are all handicap accessible. Bathing suits are required. Pool facilities are available to the public for day use, as well as to registered campers.

Facilities include RV hookups and overnight camping spaces, hiking trails, picnic and barbeque area, horseshoe pits, shuffleboard, and a children's play area. No credit cards are accepted. It is one-half mile to a small general store, cafe and phone, twenty-five miles to a gas station, and thirty-five miles to a motel. There is a nearby airstrip for small planes.

Directions: Take the Ocotillo exit off I-8, 27 miles east of El Centro and 95 miles west of San Diego. Follow Imperial Co. Rd. S-2 for 25 miles into the Anza Borego desert to the sign for Agua Caliente springs. Bear left .1 mile to the general store and left again for about .5 mile to the campground.

809 JACUMBA HOT SPRINGS SPA LODGE AND RESORT
Box 371   619 766-4333

■ **Jacumba, CA 92034**

An older motel spa located just off I-8, 80 miles east of San Diego. Elevation 2,800 feet. Open all year.

Natural mineral water with a slight sulfur smell flows out of a spring at 140-150 gallons per minute at a temperature of 97° and is then piped to an indoor hydropool and an outdoor swimming pool. Continuous flow-through maintains a temperature of 95° in the hydropool and 85° in the swimming pool, with no chemical treatment of the water required. Hot mineral water showers are in the spa room. The pools are available to the general public for a use fee. Pools are handicap accessible, with assistance. Bathing suits are required.

Facilities include rooms, rustic Alpine restaurant, bar, sauna, tennis and shuffleboard courts, a German "biergarten patio" with Mexican sculpture and pottery, and a lawn area with shade trees. Horseback riding and guided hikes can be arranged. Massage is available on the premises. Visa, MasterCard and American Express are accepted. It is one block to a store and service station and .5 mile to RV hookups.

Directions: Take the Jacumba exit off I-8 and go 3 miles to the tiny town of Jacumba. The spa is located on the north side of Old Highway 80, the main street through town.

810 SWALLOWS/SUN ISLAND NUDIST RESORT
1631 Harbison Canyon Rd.
619 445-3754
☐ El Cajon, CA 92021

A large, well-equipped, traditional nudist park located in a tree-shaded canyon 15 miles east of San Diego. Elevation 500 feet. Open all year.

Gas-heated well water, chlorine treated, is used in an outdoor swimming pool with a temperature range of 75-80° and in an outdoor hydropool with water temperature maintained at 104°. Bathing suits are not permitted in pools, and clothing is prohibited everywhere, weather permitting.

Facilities include rooms, restaurant, tennis and volleyball courts, RV hookups, and overnight camping. Visa and MasterCard are accepted. It is one mile to a store and eight miles to a service station.

Note: This is a membership organization not open to the public for drop-in visits, but prospective members may be issued a guest pass by prior arrangement. Resort rules prohibit guns, cameras, drugs, and erotic behavior. Telephone or write for information and directions.

811 THE TUBS
7220 El Cajon Blvd.   619 698-7727
☐ San Diego, CA 92115

San Diego's original rent-a-tub establishment, located on a main suburban street near San Diego State University.

Eleven spa suites for rent to the public use gas-heated tap water that is treated with chlorine and maintained at 102°. Saunas are included in all rooms. The VIP Suite, large enough for 12 persons, has a bathroom and steambath, plus a sauna.

A juice bar is available on the premises. Visa and MasterCard are accepted. Phone for rates, reservations, and directions.

812 PALM SPRINGS SPA HOTEL AND CASINO, RESORT...
100 N. Indian Canyon Dr.   619 325-1461
☐ Palm Springs, CA 92262

A major destination resort with an elaborate mineral-water spa located in downtown Palm Springs. Elevation 500 feet. Open all year.

Natural mineral water flows out of historic Indian wells on the property at a temperature of 106°. The spa has separate men's and women's sections, each containing 14 marble tubs with mineral-water temperature separately controllable up to 104°. These tubs are drained and refilled after each use so that no chemical treatment of the water is necessary. Each spa also has vapor-inhalation rooms, a steam-bath and a dry sauna. Handicap rooms are on the ground floor. Bathing suits are required in the outdoor pool area, optional in the bathhouse and solarium. Prices are discounted for hotel guests.

Services and facilities on the premises include massage, barber and beauty shop, rooms, restaurant and lounge, pool bar, snacks, airport pickup, and group conference rooms. Also available is an Indian gaming casino, open twenty-four hours. All major credit cards are accepted. Pool and spa facilities are available to the public as well as to registered guests.

Directions: Take the Indian Ave. exit from I-10 and drive south 6.5 miles to the resort.

GOING NATURAL IN PALM SPRINGS

The following listings covers a growing industry in Palm Springs—going uncovered in lush, upscale surroundings. These clothing optional resorts have varying amenities, but all of them will arrange for airport pickup, are open all year, and accept credit cards. The pools use tap water and are gas heated and chlorine treated. Phone for rates, reservations, and directions.

813 A   LE PETIT CHATEAU BED AND BREAKFAST INN

1491 Via Soledad   619 325-2686

☐   Palm Springs, CA 92264

This small, intimate retreat was the nation's first clothing optional B&B. It's unique residential, wind-free cove location is within walking distance to famous Tahquitz Canyon, with waterfalls and natural swimming pools.

The lush grounds of this quiet enclave are lovingly maintained in pristine condition. All of the rooms have a Country French decor and are complete with every amenity including private patios for most. The soaking tub is set on its own patio surrounded by grapefruit and lemon trees and features a choice of two heat settings. The central courtyard pool is solar heated to between 85-92°.

813 B   MORNINGSIDE INN/PARADISE DESERT RESORT

888 N. Indian Canyon   619 325-2668

☐   Palm Springs, CA 92263

Exclusive, secluded, clothing-optional resort in the heart of Palm Springs.

Suites and cabana rooms are available. Suites contain fully equipped kitchens, and some have private patios. The pool and the spa are heated to 86° and 102° respectively. A misting system operates to keep customers comfortable all year around. An outdoor barbeque area on a covered patio is available for guest use.

813 C RAFFLES PALM SPRINGS HOTEL
619 320-3949

☐　　Palm Springs, CA

An exotic clothing-optional oasis named for the Singapore Raffles and located in the northern part of Palm Springs.

A large hydrojet pool is maintained at 102°, and a swimming pool is maintained at 87°. Clothing is optional throughout the grounds.

Facilities and services include rooms with kitchenettes, a beautifully landscaped central patio garden, cooled by an automatic misting system in the summer, outdoor barbeque area, and continental breakfast.

813 D DESERT SHADOWS INN
1533 Chaparral　　　619 325-6410

☐　　Palm Springs, CA 92262

A secluded retreat for the discerning naturist with a magnificent view of the San Jacinto Mountains. Only minutes away from downtown Palm Springs

Two full-size pools are heated to 86°. The main pool has a waterfall created by jets of water flowing from three stone lions. The "quiet" pool has classical music playing softly in the background. A one-hundred-foot square soaking pool, heated to 102°, is open twenty-four hours a day.

The thirty-four designer-decorated rooms have color cable TV, direct dial phone, and refrigerators. A full-service restaurant and bar overlooks the unique wave fountain in the main courtyard. Private courtyards are found amid the acres of lushly landscaped and totally private grounds. Daily continental breakfast is included. Massage, facials, manicures, hair styling, and herbal body wraps are offered. A handicap accessible room is available.

Desert Hot Springs has been called "The Mineral Water Capital of the World," with natural crystal-clear, tasteless, odorless geothermal water throughout the entire town. Close to fifty hotels, motels, spas, resorts, swimming pools, RV parks, and mobile home communities have therapeutic hot mineral water facilities. Elevation 1,185 feet. Most facilities are open all year.

All of the establishments listed below are in or near the city of Desert Hot Springs, which is ten miles north of Palm Springs. All of them pump natural mineral water from their own wells and offer at least one chlorine-treated (except where noted) swimming pool and one hyrdopool. Many have handicap facilities; inquire at each-specific location. Bathing suits are required.

It is one mile or less to a store, restaurant, or service station. Most locations take credit cards, except where noted. For additional information contact the Chamber of Commerce, PO Box 848, Desert Hot Springs, CA 92240. Phone 619 329-6403, or contact the individual locations directly.

Mailing address for all locations is Desert Hot Springs, CA 92240.

---

813 E   THE TERRA COTTA INN
2388 E. Racquet Club Road
619 322-6059

☐   Palm Springs, CA 92262

A premier clothing-optional resort for couples surrounding secluded, romantic gardens. Situated on a private, colorful acre with magnificent mountain vistas.

A large, pristine pool is heated year round, and the fifteen-person hydropool spa is maintained at 102°. Both pool and spa are available twenty-four hours a day, with wonderful views. The pool patio is micro-mist cooled for relaxing sunbathing in all temperatures.

The seventeen luxurious rooms are lavishly appointed. The charming grounds feature a private shady fountain retreat and several sun patios. A special suite is available with a private patio, sunken tub, and terrarium bathroom garden. A clubhouse, barbeque facilities, and bicycles are available for your use. Amenities include a sumptuous poolside breakfast, hot hors d'oeuvres in the afternoon, and pampering services such as massage and spa treatments. Phone for a free brochure, 800 SUNNY FUN.

---

814 A   AMBASSADOR ARMS AND HEALTH
SPA MOTEL
12921 Tamar Dr.   619 329-1909
■   800 569-0541

Indoor and outdoor 104° therapy pools 90° outdoor swimming pool, all with fresh mineral water on a flow-through basis. Also 200-250° dry sauna. Kitchens available.

---

814 B   ATLAS HI LODGE
■   13-336 Avenida Hermosa   619 329-5446

Heated mineral water pool, enclosed, jacuzzi. Rooms with kitchens. No credit cards.

---

814 C   BROADVIEW LODGE MOTEL-SPA
■   12-672 Eliseo Rd.   619 329-8006

Indoor therapy pool, outdoor swimming pool, sauna. Rooms with connecting kitchens.

---

814 D   CARAVAN SPA MOTEL
■   66810 Fourth St.   619 329-7124

Hot mineral spa, outdoor swimming pool.

814 E   DAVID'S SPA MOTEL
■   11-220 Palm Drive   610 329-6202

Indoor and outdoor hydropool, swimming pool, steam and dry sauna. Massage.

814 F   DESERT HOT SPRINGS SPA
■   10805 Palm Dr.   619 329-6495

Largest full-service spa resort in the area. Seven mineral water soaking pools ranging from 80-106° and the Olympic-size pool are open for day use.

Facilities include a restaurant, bar, and gift shop. Various types of massage, facials, beauty treatments, and classes in water aerobics are available. to guests and the general public for day-use.

814 G   DESERT PALMS SPA MOTEL
■   67485 Hacienda Ave.   619 329-4443

Six pools on two and one-half acres, enclosed indoor and outdoor spas, sauna. Acu-massage.

814 H   DESERT SPRINGS INN
■   12-697 Eliseo Road   619 251-1668

A 90° swimming pool, 104° sauna, enclosed sunbathing area. Rooms with kitchens. Reservations required. No children or pets.

814 I   DOM'S FLAMINGO MOTEL & SPA
■   67-221 Pierson Blvd.   619 251-1455

Six mineral pools and swimming pool. Kitchens available. Texas-style barbeque restaurant on premises.

814 J   DR. PORTEOUS' HEALING WATERS
■   SPA AND...ARTHRITIS CARE CLINIC
      68-061 Calle Azteca   714 474-2188

Mineral water is used throughout this quiet, secluded retreat and in the pool and spa. Week long residential programs for rejuvination, arthritis, and chronic pain held Nov.-May. Chiropractic care, nutrional counseling, and herbal body wraps offered. Pamper yourself.

814 K   EL REPOSO
■   66-334 W. Fifth St.   619 329-6632

Enclosed hot mineral pool, outdoor swimming pool. Recreation room, apartments with kitchens.

814 L   HACIENDA RIVIERA SPA
■   67-375 Hacienda Ave.   619 329-7010

Day use only. Outdoor swimming pool, enclosed hot pool. Water temperatures vary with the season.

814 M   HILLVIEW MOTEL
■   11-740 Mesquite Ave.   619 329-5317

Enclosed hot mineral therapeutic jet pool; large outdoor heated pool.

814 N   HIGHLANDER LODGE
■   68-187 Club Circle Dr.   619 251-0189

Indoor spa, outdoor pool.

814 O   ILONA'S HEALTH & FITNESS
      AT EMERALD SPRINGS RESORT
      68-055 Club Circle Dr.   619 329-1151

A 90° swimming pool, 102° outdoor spa, 106° indoor spa, and sauna. Health, fitness, and nutrition classes and programs.

814 P   KISMET LODGE
■   13340 Mountain View   619 329-6451

Swimming pool, hot therapy pool.

814 Q   LAS PRIMAVERAS RESORT AND SPA
■   66-659 Sixth St.   619 251-1677

104° indoor hot tub, 92° outdoor swimming pool, sauna. State-of-the-art outdoor cooling system cools outdoor temperature fifteen to twenty degrees. Luxury units with jet tubs, kitchens.

814 R   LIDO PALMS SPA MOTEL
■   2801 Tamar Dr.   619 329-6033

Two outdoor pools, large indoor spa, dry sauna. Kitchenettes. Massage.

814 S   LINDA VISTA LODGE
■   67200 Hacienda Ave.   619 329-6401

104° outdoor pool, two enclosed therapy pools, sauna. Rooms with kitchens.

814 T   LORANE MANOR
■   67-751 Hacienda Ave.   619 329-9090

Enclosed hot tub, outdoor swimming pool. No credit cards accepted.

814 U   MA-HA-YAH LODGE & HEALTH SPA
■   66-111 Calle Las Tiendas   619 329-5420

Two indoor hot tubs, 100° and 102° (one has special handicap access), one body-temperature outdoor hot tub, outdoor swimming pool, sauna. Kitchenettes. Sauna, massage, and reflexology. No credit cards accepted.

814 V MINERAL SPRINGS
■   11-000 Palm Drive   619 329-6484

Pool, spa, mineral springs waterfall. Rooms with private spas. Bar. Salt rubs.

814 W MIRACLE MANOR SPA-TEL
■   12-589 Reposo Way   619 329-6641

Enclosed hot pool, outdoor pool. Therapeutic massage, psychic facials.

814 X THE MIRAGE SPRINGS HOTEL, CASINO AND SPA
■   10-625 Palm Drive   619 251-3399

The *Mirage Springs Hotel* is a beautiful upscale resort.

Eight outdoor hot spas at different temperatures, including an eighteen-inch deep "champagne" bubbling spa and two dry saunas. Whirlpool bathtubs in separate men's and women's areas. Massage. Restaurant, banquet facilities, approved gaming.

814 Y MISSION LAKES COUNTRY CLUB
■   8484 Clubhouse Blvd. 619 329-6481

Residential country club with eight-unit motel. Swimming pool, spa, and golf course open to public.

814 Z MONTE CARLO
■   67-840 Hacienda Ave.   619 329-9058

Small motel with heated pool, spa.

814 AA THE MOORS MOTEL AND SPA
■   12-637 Reposo Way   619 329-7121

Family oriented. Swimming pool and hot therapy pool are wheelchair accessible.

814 BB PYRAMID SPA MOTEL
■   66-563 East Fifth St.   619 329-5652

A 90° swimming pool and 105° mineral water hydrojet pool. Kitchenettes.

814 CC ROYAL FOX INN
■   14-500 Palm Dr.   619 329-4481

Indoor and outdoor therapeutic hot pools with hydrojets, large swimming pool, sauna. Rooms with private hot mineral swimming pool. RV park. Exercise room, massage.

814 DD ROYAL PALM INN
■   12-885 Eliseo Road   619 329-7975

Covered outdoor twelve-foot spa. Seven units.

814 EE SAHARA SPA MOTEL
■   66700 E. Fifth St.   619 329-6666

Indoor spa, indoor swimming pool, sauna, hot waterfall.

814 FF SAM'S FAMILY SPA HOT WATER RESORT
■   70-875 Dillon Rd.   619 329-6666

One of largest, multi-service resorts with all facilities open to the public for day use as well as to registered guests. Large outdoor swimming pool uses chlorinated mineral water. Gazebo-enclosed wading pool and four covered hydropools use flow-through mineral water, requiring no chemical treatment.

Coed sauna, motel rooms, restaurant, RV hookups, overnight spaces, store, laundromat, playground, exercise room. Barbeque area. Handicap accessible with assistance.

814 GG SANDPIPER INN & SPA
■   12-800 Foxdale Dr.   619 329-6455

Large swimming pool, therapeutic hot spa, dry and steam sauna.

814 HH SKYLINER SPA
■   12-840 Inaja St.   619 251-0933

Mineral pool with spa; covered citrus patio.

814 II SPA TOWN HOUSE MOTEL
■   66-540 E. Sixth St.   619 329-6014

814 JJ STARDUST MOTEL
■   66-634 Fifth St.   619 329-5443

Hydrojet pool, swimming pool.

814 KK SUNSET INN
■   67-585 Hacienda Ave. 619 329-4488

Pool, two hydrojet spas, dry sauna, wet sauna. Some rooms with kitchens. Massage.

814 LL SWISS HEALTH SPA
■   66-729 Eighth St.   619 329-6912

A 100° indoor mineral pool, 104° hydropool, 80-90° outdoor mineral pool, all flow-through, requiring no chlorine. Various kinds of massage. No children or pets.

814 MM TAMARIX SPA
■   66-185 Acoma   619 329-6615

Smaller motel with heated mineral pool.

814 NN TRAVELLERS REPOSE
BED & BREAKFAST
■   66-290 First St.   619 329-6615

Travellers Repose resembles a traditional Victorian

Outdoor pool and covered spa. No credit cards.

814 OO TROPICAL MOTEL & SPA
■   12-962 Palm Dr.   619 329-6610

Outdoor hydropool, enclosed hydropool, long "lap" mineral swimming pool. Pools, showers, and picnic area available for day-use fee.

DESERT HOT SPRINGS RV AND MOBILE HOME RESORTS
No credit cards are accepted except where noted. All locations have their address as Desert Hot Springs, 92240.

MEMBERSHIP RV PARKS

815 A AMERICAN ADVENTURE
    70-405 Dillon Rd.   619 329-5371

One swimming pool, three hydropools and a sauna. Family-oriented. Not open to the public for drop-in visits except during the summer.

815 B CATALINA RV SPA
    13-800 Corkill Rd.   619 329-4431

Hot mineral swimming pool, therapy pool. Clubhouse with activities. Family oriented.

815 C TWO SPRINGS RESORT
    14-200 Indian Ave.   619-251-1102

MOBILE HOME AND RV PARKS

815 D CALIENTE SPRINGS
    70-200 Dillon Rd.   619 329-2970

Four hot spas, 168-foot mineral water swimming pool. Tennis courts. Overnighters welcome.

815 E CORKILL RV AND MOBILE HOME PARK
    17-989 Corkill Rd.   619 329-5976
                         800 982-3714

One swimming pool, one hydropool, one soaking pool, and two cold pools, enclosed and covered.

815 F COUNTRY SQUIRE PARK
    66-455 Dillon Rd.   619 329-1191

Swimming pool, spa, clubhouse. Family oriented. Overnighters welcome.

815 G DESERT HOT SPRINGS TRAILER PARK
    66-434 W. Fifth   619 329-6041

815 H DESERT VIEW ADULT MOBILE PARK
18555 Roberts Rd.   619 329-7079

Outdoor swimming pool and two indoor hydropools. Strictly a mobile home park with no RVs and no overnighters.

815 I DESERT OASIS MOBILE HOME PARK
71-850 Corkill Rd.   619 329-7346

Large swimming pool, three enclosed hydropools. RVs also welcome.

815 J DESERT SPRINGS SPA
17-325 Johnson Rd.   619 329-1384

Large swimming pool, hydropool, RV park.

815 K GOLDEN LANTERN MOBILE VILLAGE
17-300 Corkill Rd.   619 329-6633

One outdoor swimming pool, three enclosed soaking pools. Mobile home spaces, RV hookups, overnight spaces. Used mobile homes for sale. Restaurant, store, and service station next-door.

815 L HEALING WATERS PARK
13-131 Langlois Rd.   619 329-5306

One outdoor swimming pool, three therapy pools. Overnighters welcome.

815 M HOLMES HOT SPRINGS MOBILE PARK
69530 Dillon Rd.   619 329-7934

One outdoor swimming pool, one outdoor soaking pool. RV hookups and overnight spaces.

815 N MAGIC WATERS MOBILE HOME PARK
17551 Mt. View Rd.   619 329-2600

Outdoor swimming pool and indoor hydropool use hot mineral water. Mobile homes, RV hookups, overnight spaces.

815 O MOUNTAIN VIEW MOBILE HOME PARK
15525 Mt. View Rd.   619 329-5870

One outdoor swimming pool, one semi-enclosed hydropool. Mobile homes, RV hookups, overnight spaces.

815 P ROYAL FOX RV PARK
14500 Palm Dr.   619 329-4481

Swimming pool, two hydropools, and two saunas available to registered guests in the RV park as well as to motel guests.

815 Q SAM'S FAMILY SPA
70875 Dillon Rd.   619 329-6457

See entry 814 FF for full description.

Sam's has it all: motel rooms, RV hookups, swimming pools, and soaking pools.

815 R SANDS RV COUNTRY CLUB
16-400 Bubbling Wells 619 251-1030

Swimming pool, two hydropools. Registered guests only. Nine-hole golf course open to the public.

815 S SKY VALLEY EAST
74-711 Dillon Rd.   619 329-2909

One swimming pool, an outdoor hydropool, an enclosed hydropool on separate patio reserved for adults. Adjoining patio contains outdoor swimming pool and outdoor hydropool for family use. Men's and women's saunas. Mobile homes, RV hookups, and overnight spaces.

815 T SKY VALLEY PARK
74-565 Dillon Rd.   619 329-7415

Two outdoor swimming pools, one outdoor hydropool, two enclosed hydropools, one indoor hydropool. Men's and women's saunas. Mobile homes, RV hookups, overnight spaces.

815 U SPARKLING WATERS PARK
17-800 Langlois Rd.   619 329-6551

Mineral water swimming pool, two spas at 100° and 104°. For senior adults. Overnighters welcome.

815 V TAMARISK MOBILE PARK
18-075 Langlois Rd.
Covered swimming pool, hot tub. RV hookups. Overnighters welcome. Visa and MasterCard.

815 W VISTA GRANDE SPA
17-625 Langlois Rd.   619 329-5424
Swimming pool, two spas. Senior adults. Overnighters welcome.

MOBILE HOME COMMUNITIES

815 X CORKILL PALMS
17-640 Corkill Rd.
Natural hot mineral water pool and spa. Senior adults.

815 Y DESERT CREST COUNTRY CLUB
69-400 Country Club
Swimming pool, spa. Senior adults.

815 Z DESERT VIEW ADULT MOBILE PARK
18-555 Roberts Rd.   619 329-7079
Outdoor swimming pool, two indoor hydropools. Mobile homes only.

815 AA DESERT WILLOWS
65-565 Acoma Ave.   619 329-4471
Swimming pool, two spas, two saunas. Clubhouse, lake with waterfall, lighted tennis courts.

815 BB JOSHUA MOBILE HOME PARK
18-080 Langlois Rd.   619 329-3277
Swimming pool, two enclosed hot pools. Senior adults.

815 CC LA POSADA PARK
17-555 Corkill Rd.   619-329-7113

815 DD PALM DRIVE TRAIL PARK
14-881 Palm Dr.   619 329-8341

815 EE QUAIL HOLLOW MOBILE HOME PARK
15-300 Palm Dr.   619 329-2921

815 FF RAINBOW SPA, INC.
17-777 Langlois Rd.   619 329-7165
Mineral water swimming pool, two hydropools at 98-100° and 100-104°. Senior adults.

815 GG SKY HAVENS MOBILE PARK
14-777 Palm Dr.   619-329-5001

815 HH WAGNER MOBILE HOME PARK
18801 Roberts Rd.   619 329-6043
One outdoor swimming pool, two indoor hydropools, two indoor cold pools. Mobile homes and RV hookups. No overnighters.

815 II WHISPERING SANDS MOBILE HOME PARK
15-225 Palm Dr.   619 329-7210
Swimming pool, hydropool. Clubhouse, library, laundry.

816　PAN HOT SPRINGS
420 E. North Shore Blvd.
909 585-2757
■ 　Big Bear City, CA 92314

Historic indoor and outdoor swimming pools with adjoining health club, located in the Big Bear recreation area. Elevation 6,700 feet. Open weekends in May and then every day through September 15.

Natural mineral water is pumped from a well at 90° and piped to an indoor pool that maintains a temperature of 85°. The water then flows on through to the outdoor pool, which maintains a temperature of 78°. Both pools are treated with chlorine. Bathing suits are required.

Facilities include dressing rooms, health club, arcade games, and a snack bar. All other services are available within five miles. No credit cards are accepted. Phone for rates and directions.

Whether you hike in the long way or the short way there are many wonderful places to soak at *Deep Creek*.

817　DEEP CREEK HOT SPRINGS
(see map)
● 　Near the town of Hesperia

Beautiful, remote springs on the south bank of Deep Creek at the bottom of a spectacular canyon in the San Bernardino National Forest. Elevation 3,000 feet. Open all year.

Natural mineral water flows out of several rock fissures at 108° and directly into volunteer-built, rock-and-sandbag pools on the edge of Deep Creek, which flows all year. Water temperature in any one pool will depend on the amount of creek water admitted. The apparent local custom is clothing optional.

There are no services, and overnight camping is prohibited in the canyon near the springs. It is seven miles by an all-year trail to an overnight parking area. There is also a steep, two and one-half mile, slippery trail of decomposed granite down the north side of the canyon from Bowen Ranch, where a fee is charged for admission to the ranch and for overnight parking. From either parking area it is ten miles to a store, restaurant, service station, and all other services. Note: The trail from Bowen Ranch ends on the north bank of Deep Creek, which runs so high during spring runoff that it is not safe to ford.

Directions: From I-15, take the Hesperia exit and drive for 8 miles along Main Street to a major Y in the road, where Main St. becomes Rock Spring Rd. To reach Deep Creek via Bowen Ranch, continue another 1.1 miles, bear left on Kiowa Rd. for .4 mile, then right on Roundup for 4.2 miles (the last 1.2 miles are unpaved). Turn right (south) on Bowen Ranch Rd., a wide, unpaved, washboard road, and drive 5.5 miles to the ranch. Whenever you come to a fork, bear right to reach the ranch.

Directions to the all-year trail: Follow directions above to Deep Creek Rd. Turn right (south) for 5 miles to where the pavement ends. Bear left across the open space, heading toward the earthen dam. Park at the southeast end of the earthen dam near the overflow ramp. To reach the trailhead, go up the paved service road next to the overflow. From the top of the service road you can look down to the right and see a bathing beach at the creek and to the left, the trailhead marked with a rusty tin sign. There is short, steep ascent to the trail, which hugs the side of the mountain for 6 miles to the springs.

Source maps: *San Bernardino National Forest.* USGS *Lake Arrowhead.*

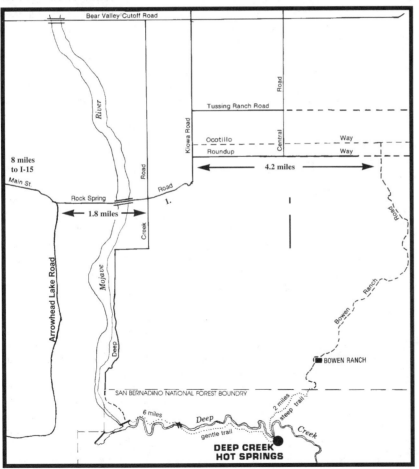

At Bowen Ranch, illustrated, hand-drawn maps of the trails are available, reminding you that at Bowen Ranch there are "no fireworks, no guns, no tan lines?"

818 PUDDINGSTONE HOT TUBS
1777 Camper View Rd.   909 592-2222
□   San Dimas, CA 91773

A unique, modern rent-a-tub facility that offers both privacy and a spectacular view. Located in Bonelli County Regional Park overlooking Puddingstone Reservoir, twenty-five miles east of Los Angeles.

Sixteen outdoor pools using chlorine-treated tap water heated by a combination of propane and electricity, are for rent to the public. The very large community tub has a 360° view with spacious decking, fire pit and barbecue. The smaller tubs offer a beautiful view, tub temperature controls, and a three-sided enclosure for privacy.

A wedding gazebo is available on the premises. An RV park, golf course, picnic area, horse stables, boat rentals, and Raging Waters recreation area are available in the adjoining regional park. Phone for rates, reservations, and directions.

819 OLIVE DELL RANCH
26520 Keissel Rd.   909 825-6619
□   Colton, CA 92324

A pioneer, Southern California nudist park located on a dry and sunny hilltop sixty miles east of Los Angeles. Elevation 2,000 feet. Open all year.

Gas-heated well water, chlorine treated, is used in an outdoor hydropool maintained at 105° and in a swimming pool maintained at 75°. Clothing is prohibited in the pools and in the main recreation area, optional elsewhere.

Cabins, cafe, overnight camping, and RV hookups are available on the premises. It is three miles to a store and service station. No credit cards are accepted.

Note: This is a membership organization, so please call first if you are interested in visiting. Telephone or write for information.

820 A LAKE ELSINORE HOT SPRINGS MOTEL

316 N. Main   909 674-2581
■ Lake Elsinore, CA 92330

Older motel and spa located several blocks north of downtown Lake Elsinore. Elevation 1,300 feet. Open all year.

Natural sulphur water flows out of an artesian well at 100° and is piped to three pools and to the bathtubs in all rooms. The outdoor swimming pool is maintained at 104°. All pools are chlorine treated and are available to the public as well as to registered guests. Bathing suits are required.

Facilities include a sauna and a recreation room. Rooms and massage are available on the premises. Visa and MasterCard are accepted. It is five blocks to a restaurant, store, and service station.

820 B HAN'S MOTEL AND MINERAL SPA

215 W. Graham   909 674-3551
■ Lake Elsinore, CA 92330

An older motel in downtown Lake Elsinore. Elevation 1,300 feet. Open all year.

Natural mineral water flows out of an artesian well at 133° and is piped to two pools and to the bathtubs in every room. The outdoor swimming pool is maintained at 86°, and the indoor hydropool at 105°. The water in both pools is chlorine treated. There is also a dry sauna and outdoor shower. Bathing suits are required.

Rooms are available on the premises. No credit cards are accepted. It is two blocks to a restaurant, store, and service station.

821 GLEN EDEN SUN CLUB

25999 Glen Eden Rd.   909 277-4650
☐ Corona, CA 91720

Large, well-equipped, traditional nudist park located on the dry side of the Santa Ana mountains, 70 miles from Los Angeles. Elevation 1,200 feet. Open all year.

Gas-heated well water is used in an outdoor hydropool maintained at 105° and an indoor soaking pool maintained at 85°. The solar-heated swimming pool averages 75° from May to November. All pools have automatic filters and chlorinators. Bathing suits are prohibited in the pools and sauna. Nudity is expected in warm weather. Dress conforms to the majority or the weather. Nights are usually cool.

Facilities include tennis and volleyball courts, sauna, restaurant, RV hookups, camping sites, rental trailers, laundry room, and a recreation center. Visa and MasterCard are accepted. It is eight miles to a motel, store, and service station.

Note: This is a membership organization not open to the public for drop-in visits, but prospective members may visit by prior arrangement. Telephone or write for information and directions.

822   GLEN IVY HOT SPRINGS SPA
25000 Glen Ivy Road   909 277-3529
■   Corona, CA 91719

Large, well-equipped, beautifully landscaped day-use resort and spa located on the dry east side of the Santa Ana mountains, 70 miles from Los Angeles. Elevation 1,300 feet. Open all year, except Thanksgiving and Christmas.

Natural mineral water from two wells at 90° and 110° is mixed and piped to a wide variety of pools. There are seven sunken hydrojet tubs with temperatures of 104-106°, using continuous flow-through, unchlorinated mineral water. The other pools have automatic filters and chlorinators. An outdoor swimming pool is maintained at 85°, a covered soaking pool at 103°, two outdoor hydropools at 101° and 104°, two outdoor shallow bubble pools at 103° and 100°, a large outdoor floating pool at 90°, and a California red clay-bath pool at 100°. (Guests should bring an old bathing suit to wear in the mud bath as the clay does stain some fabrics.) Two hydrojet pools are situated in a patio reserved for adults. Bathing suits are required.

Facilities include men's and women's locker rooms equipped with hair blowers, a coed dry sauna, and two outdoor cafes. Spa treatments include Swedish, shiatsu, and aromatherapy massage, eucalyptus wraps, apricot body scrubs, European facials, manicures, pedicures and waxings. Entrance to the spa facilities and restroom are handicap accessible, but no attendants are provided or lifts for the pools. Advance reservations are highly recommended. Visa and MasterCard, ATMs and personal checks are accepted.

Directions: Eight miles south of Corona on I-15, exit right onto the Temescal Canyon Rd. exit. Go 1 mile south to Glen Ivy Rd., turn right and go 1 mile to the resort at the end of the road.

Be sure to bring an old bathing suit so that you can treat yourself to this incredible mud application. You then lie down on lounges in the sun and enjoy the feeling of your skin tickling as the mud dries. The last step is to rinse off all the mud and feel how soft your skin is now. *Glen Ivy's* other name is "Club Mud."

The assortment of pools at *Glen Ivy* (as shown on these two pages) provides something for everyone, whether you like to soak indoors or out, in a deep or shallow pool, by yourself or with a group. There is even a pool for adults

824 BEVERLY HOT SPRINGS
308 N. Oxford Ave.   213 734-7000
■ **Los Angeles, CA 90004**

A modern, Korean-style, indoor spa built over a hot water artesian well a few miles west of downtown Los Angeles. Elevation 300 feet. Open all year.

From a well drilled in the early 1900s, mineral water flows out at a temperature of 105° and is piped to large, tiled, soaking pools equipped with hydrojets in the women's section (first floor) and the men's section (second floor). Each section also has a pool of cooled mineral water. All pools operate on a continuous flow-through basis so that no chemical treatment of the water is necessary. Bathing suits are not required in pool rooms.

Facilities include a dry sauna and a steam sauna in each section, plus a restaurant and beauty salon. Shiatsu massage, cream massage, and body scrubs are available on the premises. Visa and MasterCard are accepted. Phone for rates, reservations, and directions.

823 NEPTUNES LAGOONS
2784 W. Ball Rd.   714 761-8325
□ **Anaheim, CA 92804**

Modern, suburban pool-rental facility near Disneyland and Knott's Berry Farm. Open seven days.

Private-space hot pools using gas-heated tap water are treated with chlorine. There are six indoor fiberglass pools with water temperatures maintained at 99-101°. Three of the rooms have a sauna.

Each room has a hydrojet tub with jets and bubble controls, a dimmer for lights, air conditioning, relaxation bed, shower, towels, hair dryer, tape player, and sky light. TV and VCR are available.

Massage, acupressure, and a choice of scrubs and skin therapies are offered. All major credit cards are accepted. Phone for rates, reservations, and directions.

825A-B SPLASH, THE RELAXATION SPA

10932 Santa Monica Blvd.   310 479-4657
☐   Los Angeles, CA 90025

8054 W. 3rd St.   213 653-4412
☐   Los Angeles, CA 90048

Eighteen beautifully decorated, romantic, very private suites located in two urban Los Angeles locations.

All rooms feature a chlorinated hydrojet tub with controls for bubbles, water temperature, and cool-off mists. Also included are dimmer controls for room and tub lights, air conditioning, relaxation bed, and fully equipped dressing room with shower and herbal soaps and towels. Many of the more exotically decorated suites offer additional amenities such as saunas, waterfalls, aquariums, skylights, etc.

Gift certificates, in-suite catering, corporate memberships and overnight stays are available. Group discounts for private parties are also available, as well as help in arranging the party.

Major credit cards are accepted. Phone for rates, reservations, and directions.

One of the biggest hot tubs at any resort can be found at *Elysium Institute*. There is room for all your friends.

Just two of the beautifully decorated rooms at *Splash*.

826   ELYSIUM INSTITUTE

814 Robinson Rd.   310 455-1000
☐   Topanga, CA 90290

Tree-shaded, rolling lawns are part of a ten-acre, clothing-optional growth center located in smog-free Topanga Canyon, 30 miles west of Los Angeles. Elevation 1,000 feet. Open all year.

Gas-heated tap water, chlorine treated, is used in a large outdoor hydropool maintained at a temperature of 105°. Chlorine-treated tap water is also used in a gas-heated swimming pool. Clothing is optional everywhere on the grounds.

Massage, sauna, tennis, volleyball, recreation room, and educational/experimental workshops and seminars are available on the premises. There is also a seasonal snack bar on weekends. Visa and MasterCard are accepted. It is two miles to a store, cafe, and service station and seven miles to a motel room.

Note: This is a membership organization, but nonmembers are welcome to attend all seminars and to visit. Phone or write for a copy of the *Elysium Journal of the Senses* (JOTS), and *Elysium Living Newsletter,* which describes all programs.

BAJA CALIFORNIA
BAJA NORTE

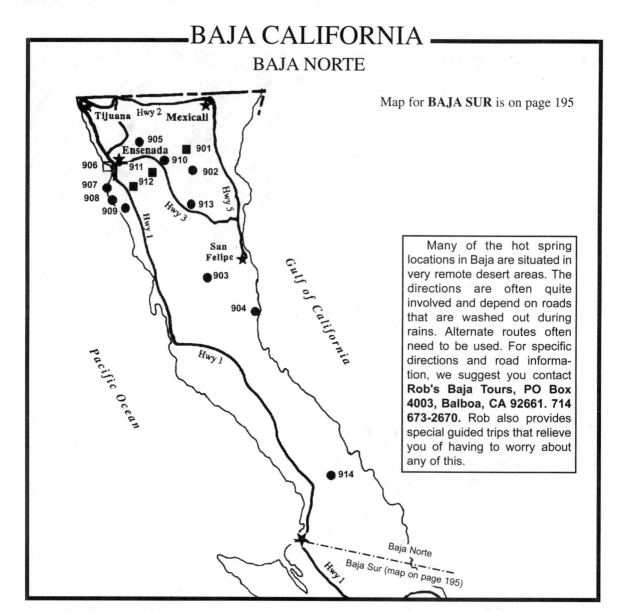

Map for **BAJA SUR** is on page 195

Tijuana Hwy 2 Mexicali

● 905
Ensenada ■ 901
906 ☆ ● 910
911 ● 902
■ 912
907 ●
908 ● ● 913
909 ● Hwy 3 Hwy 5

Hwy 1

San Felipe ☆

● 903

904 ●

Gulf of California

Pacific Ocean

Hwy 1

Many of the hot spring locations in Baja are situated in very remote desert areas. The directions are often quite involved and depend on roads that are washed out during rains. Alternate routes often need to be used. For specific directions and road information, we suggest you contact **Rob's Baja Tours, PO Box 4003, Balboa, CA 92661. 714 673-2670.** Rob also provides special guided trips that relieve you of having to worry about any of this.

● 914

Baja Norte
Baja Sur (map on page 195)

Hwy 1

This map was designed to be used with a standard highway map.

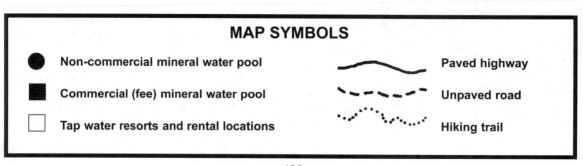

MAP SYMBOLS

● Non-commercial mineral water pool

■ Commercial (fee) mineral water pool

□ Tap water resorts and rental locations

〜 Paved highway

- - - Unpaved road

····· Hiking trail

901 GUADALUPE CANYON HOT SPRINGS

■ **Southwest of Mexicali**

Beautiful mineral water soaking pools, waterfalls, and campsites in a remote palm canyon on the east slope of the Sierra Juarez Mountains. Elevation 1,300 feet. Open all year, but summer temperatures often reach 110°. For campground reservations call Rob's Baja Tours at 714 673-2670.

Natural mineral water emerges from several springs at 125° and flows through man-made aqueducts to pools and flush toilets. More than twenty drainable soaking pools, built of rocks and cement, are scattered through palm forests and piles of boulders. Bathing suits are required except at night.

A limited number of campsites at Campo 1, each with its own parking area, palapas, pool, and picnic table, can be rented by the day, week, or month. Reservations require two weeks notice. This Campo has new rest rooms and some newer tubs.There is no electricity or telephone at this location. All services are sixty miles away in Mexicali, but there is a restaurant and a small store that sells cold beer and soft drinks. Ancient Indian caves, cascading waterfalls, and thick palm forests are within hiking distance. Other palm canyons in the mountain range may be explored for primitive hot springs, but the use of an experienced guide is recommended.

Directions (via Tecate): From San Diego go East on Hwy 94 approximately 40 miles. Turn south on Tecate Road (188) and go 1.3 miles to the border crossing (open 6:00 AM to midnight). Four blocks past the border, turn left on Mexico Hwy 2. Travel east 41 miles to La Rumorosa (last chance for gas). Just east of La Rumorosa you will begin the winding descent to the desert. At approximately 65 miles (200 yards past the K28 marker) there will be signs for "Cannon De Guadalupe." Turn right onto a graded dirt road. This dirt road has a great number of "washboards" and some bad dips. Ten miles down the road you will see signs for The Canyon at Rancho Ponderosa. (Ignore any signs that say to turn left. This is an alternate route only in dry weather). At 27 miles, turn right at the sign for the canyon. This last part is 7 miles of good but winding dirt road. The last mile is rough (take it slow). Campo 1 is on the left across the road from a sign which says "BIENVENIDOS."

● **Southwest of Mexicali**

Small wilderness hot springs in a remote palm canyon on the east slope of the Sierra Juarez Mountains, 45 miles from the nearest paved road. Elevation 1,500 feet. Open all year, but summer temperatures often reach 110°.

Natural mineral water bubbles out of three small source pools at 98° and then sinks into the sand as it flows down the canyon. No soaking pools have yet been built. At this remote location, the apparent local clothing custom is the mutual consent of those present.

There are no facilities or services, but there is an all-year cold water stream in the canyon and excellent camping locations for backpackers. Four-wheel drive is required on the last few miles of the access road, and the springs are a two-hour hike up the canyon beyond the end of the road.

Directions to such a remote location are beyond the scope of this book. The use of a guide service is recommended.

"'El Sol" hot tub and campsite at *Guadalupe Canyon* with a view of the Sierra Juarez mountains in the back and a sixty-mile view of the desert in front.

903   VALLE CHICO HOT SPRINGS

● **Southwest of San Felipe**

A remote, primitive hot spring in a barren canyon in the eastern escarpment of the Sierra San Pedro Martir. Elevation 1,500 feet. Open all year, but summer temperatures often exceed 110°.

Natural mineral water bubbles out of a large source pool at 144° and flows across the canyon into an all-year cold water stream. Volunteers could build a soaking pool at that confluence but have not yet done so. At this remote location, the apparent clothing custom is the mutual consent of those present.

There are no services at this location.

Directions to such a remote location are beyond the scope of this book. The use of a guide service is recommended.

In such remote areas it is not unusual to find the hot water simply flowing across the ground. This area could use volunteers to help build more permanent pools.

A series of three soaking pools is revealed for a few hours each day at low tide. Located between the volcanic rocks, the pools need the cool ocean water to make the water temperatures comfortable.

The tiny pueblo of Puertecitos does provide such necessary services as gas, vehicle repair, a small store, campsites, a restaurant, fishing, and boat ramps.

904   PUERTECITOS HOT SPRINGS
On the Gulf of California

● **South of San Felipe**

Geothermal water bubbles up from under volcanic rock along the edge of the Sea of Cortez and collects in waist-deep soaking pools that are under water during high tide and useable only several hours each day during low tide. Elevation sea level. Open all year, although summer air temperature can soar above 110°.

Natural mineral water flows up through the gravel bottom of several soaking pools that have been blasted out of the volcanic rock. Two rectangular pools are large enough for at least a dozen people each; a third round pool can accommodate at least six people. Pool temperatures vary widely, depending on the mix of geothermal water and sea water. There is only a brief time each low tide when the mixture makes it possible to soak. Bathing suits are recommended.

There are no services at this location. It is .25 miles to all services in the tiny pueblo of Puertecitos. Services include gas (honk your horn 8 AM to 8 PM for service), vehicle repair, a four-room hotel, small store for provisions, and a string of campgrounds all along the Sea of Cortez south from San Felipe.

Directions: From the round-about at the Pemex Station just past the arches in San Felipe, follow Hwy 5, which is the road toward the airport. At 6.4 miles take the turnoff toward Laguna Chapal, Percebu, and El Faro. Pay careful attention to signs along this road warning of "vados" (dips), which are deep, steep, and imperceptible until you are upon them. It is 53 miles from the round-about in San Felipe to the town of Puertecitos, where the paved road ends.

In Puertecitos, just before the Pemex station, turn left toward the pink entranceway marked "Private Property: Puertecitos Hot Springs, boat ramp..." The owners collect a fee of $1.00 per person to go to the springs. At .2 miles past the gate, on the left is "Taller Panama," a large tin building where the dirt road veers to the right up a hill past the boat ramp. Follow this road for .6 miles to a cul-de-sac and turn around. The hot springs are in the tide pools on your right below a green building. There are parking turnouts on both sides of the road. There is a cement walkway through the volcanic rock down to the pools.

ENSENADA REGION

To Tecate

LA MISION

Rio San Miguel

GUADALUPE

Guadalupe

805 **905 Russian Valley Hot Springs**

EL SAUZAL

ENSENADA

△ Cerro de Ensenada

906 Las Rosas Hotel and Spa

Arroyo de Ensenada

PIEDRAS GORDAS

910 Marconi Warm Springs

Bahia de Todos Santos

Punta Banda

OJOS NEGROS

Rio San

AGUA CALIENTE

907 Punta Banda Hot Springs

Carlos

908 Cantu Hot Springs

911 Agua Caliente Hot Springs

GATE

EJIDO URUAPAN

912 Uruapan Hot Springs

3

Continue southeast to:
913 Valle La Trinidad

909 Rancho Gilberto Hot Springs

✝ (RUINS)

★ SANTO TOMAS

This map shows in more detail those springs whose travel starting place is in or near Ensenada. For full details, use this map with a detailed road map.

As arid as this land appears, less than a quarter of a mile away is a lovely cold stream and waterfall.

905   RUSSIAN VALLEY HOT SPRINGS
(see map on page 187)
● **South of Tecate**

Several undeveloped wilderness hot springs near a beautiful waterfall in a remote valley that was named for an historic Russian settlement. Elevation 1,500 feet. Open all year.

Natural mineral water flows from two main source springs at 125°. In one sandy-bottom pool, the geothermal water bubbles up from below and is cooled by evaporation to maintain the pool temperature at approximately 110°. The other source spring flows out of a sandy bank into a rock-lined pool where it is mixed with creek water, and the temperature is controlled by moving rocks to admit cold water. In this remote location, the apparent local clothing custom is the mutual consent of those present.

There are no services on the premises, but there is a delightful cold pool and waterfall beside the access trail a quarter mile from the springs. All services are twenty five miles away in Ensenada.

The hot springs area is located fifty miles south of Tecate and ten miles east of Hwy 3. See map at right for detailed directions.

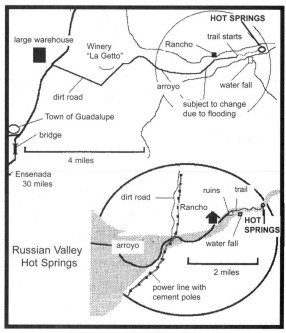

906 LAS ROSAS HOTEL & SPA

(see map on page 187)

Post Office Box 316

011-52-617-4-43-10

☐ Ensenada, Baja California, Mexico

A charming, upscale, small hotel/resort on the magnificent shoreline north of Ensenada. Elevation sea level. Open all year.

Tap water, heated with propane, is used in a seaside pool maintained at 80° and in a hydrojet spa maintained at 104°. Bathing suits are required. Pools are available for day use except during the busiest summer months. Inquire by telephone to determine current status.

Rooms, restaurant, fitness center, and racquetball court are available on the premises. It is two miles to all other services in Ensenada. Visa and MasterCard are accepted.

Directions: From Tijuana, take the Hwy 1 toll road south for 60 miles to Las Rosas, which is two miles north of Ensenada.

907 **PUNTA BANDA HOT SPRINGS**

Estero Beach (see map on page 187)

● **On the Punta Banda Peninsula**

A unique opportunity to literally dig your own hot spring pool at low tide on an easily accessible beach south of Ensenada. Elevation sea level. Open all year.

Natural mineral water (up to 170°) bubbles up through many yards of beach sand. During high tide swimmers can feel the extra warmth in the surf. During low tide it is possible to dig pools in the beach sand. These fill with a soakable combination of hot mineral water and cold sea water. Bathing suits are required.

Parking is available in the adjoining trailer camp, which offers its tenants hot mineral water piped from geothermal wells on the premises. It is eight miles to all other services in Ensenada.

Directions: From Ensenada, drive south on Hwy 1 to Hwy 23 Maneadero. Turn right on the paved road for approximately eight miles to the Agua Caliente Trailer Camp. This beach is also known as La Jolla and is near the Baja Beach and Tennis Club.

Soakers must travel thirteen miles of very scenic, improved, dirt road, climbing to 2,000 feet before crossing the Punta Banda ridge and dropping to a remote beach on the Pacific Coast.

908 CANTU HOT SPRINGS
(see map on page 187)
● **South of the Punta Banda Peninsula**

A small pool on the edge of the ocean on a remote rocky beach just past Rancho Cantu. Elevation 20 feet. Open all year.

Natural mineral water flows from a small, 90° stream down an arroyo to a shallow, hand-made pool about 100 yards from the beach. You may need to do some further digging to enlarge the pool to your specifications. Due to the remote location, clothing is optional.

There is free camping on the windswept bluffs, fifty feet above the beach. There are no services on the premises, and it is thirty miles, one hour driving time, back to Ensenada. This is a good area for fishing, diving, and surfing.

Directions: Take Hwy 23 .5 miles past La Jolla Beach and turn left onto graded dirt road. There is a sign for Ej. Cantu. The dirt road winds up the mountain and crosses over the top, then drops down to the Pacific Coast. There are no other signs on the dirt road, but there are kilometer markers (small cement posts on the side of road).

909 RANCHO GILBERTO/ST. TOMAS HOT SPRINGS
(see map on page 187)
● **South of Ensenada**

Hot water comes up in several locations in a small stream which flows down into a valley near Santo Tomas and is surrounded by farming areas and tree-covvered hillsides. Elevation 500 feet. Open all year.

Natural mineral water flows up from under the stream at 100° in several places. You will need to dig your own pool and place rocks and sand around the edge to hold the water. Temperatures are regulated by mixing hot water with cold stream water. Bathing suits are required.

There are no services on the premises, but overnight parking is available at the farm house one-hundred yards away. It is fifteen miles to a campground at La Bocana Beach and four miles to a store and restaurant.

Directions: From Ensenada, travel 20 miles south on Highway 1. Turn right on the dirt road with a sign for La Bocana. Drive 4.1 miles on graded dirt road toward the ocean. Rancho is on the left side, no sign.

The only way to find out where the hot water comes up in this stream is to feel for it. Then, build yourself a pool to soak in.

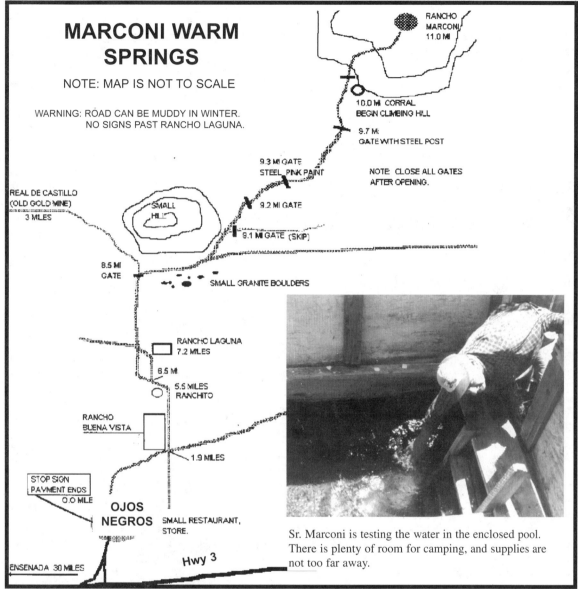

MARCONI WARM SPRINGS

NOTE: MAP IS NOT TO SCALE

WARNING: ROAD CAN BE MUDDY IN WINTER.
NO SIGNS PAST RANCHO LAGUNA.

RANCHO MARCONI 11.0 MI

10.0 MI CORRAL
BEGIN CLIMBING HILL

9.7 MI
GATE WITH STEEL POST

NOTE: CLOSE ALL GATES
AFTER OPENING.

9.3 MI GATE
STEEL PINK PAINT

9.2 MI GATE

9.1 MI GATE (SKIP)

REAL DE CASTILLO
(OLD GOLD MINE)
3 MILES

SMALL HILL

8.5 MI GATE

SMALL GRANITE BOULDERS

RANCHO LAGUNA
7.2 MILES

6.5 MI

5.5 MILES
RANCHITO

RANCHO
BUENA VISTA

1.9 MILES

STOP SIGN
PAVMENT ENDS
0.0 MILE

OJOS NEGROS
SMALL RESTAURANT, STORE.

Hwy 3

ENSENADA 30 MILES

Sr. Marconi is testing the water in the enclosed pool. There is plenty of room for camping, and supplies are not too far away.

910   MARCONI WARM SPRINGS

(see map on page 187)

- **East of Ensenada**

Located in the foothills of the Sierra Juarez Mountains at the northern end of the Ojos Negros Valley. Elevation 1,500 feet. Open all year.

Natural mineral water at 80° fills one enclosed six-foot by four-foot by three-foot deep pool. Considering the hot summers in this area, this water temperature should feel quite good. Clothing may be required outside the enclosed area even though there are very few tourists. However, this is a farming community.

There is one shelter for camping plus many open areas where camping is permitted. There is a $10 charge per night per car. The nearest food and gas are in Ojos Negros, and all other services are found in Ensenada.

Directions: Take Hwy 3 east of Ensenada for 30 miles and turn left at the sign to Ojos Negros. Pavement ends one mile later in the center of town. It is 11 miles to the springs (see detailed map above).

Relaxing, waiting for the pool to refill with fresh water.

911   AGUA CALIENTE HOT SPRINGS
(see map on page 187)
■   **East of Ensenada**

An older commercial hot springs "resort" located in an arid valley five miles south of Hwy 3. Elevation 1,500 feet. Open all year, but the bar and restaurant are open only during April, May, June, July, and August.

Natural mineral water flows out of several springs at temperatures ranging from 80 to 108°. The warmest source spring supplies 108° water to the bathhouse tubs, which are drained and filled after each use. It also flows directly into a large concrete outdoor soaking pool where it maintains a temperature of 97°. Water from the coolest spring is piped to a large swimming pool that is drained and filled every week, resulting in a temperature of 75°. No chemical treatment is added to the mineral water. Water from a third spring (97°) is piped to the motel rooms, bar, and restaurant as tap water. Bathing suits are required except in private-space individual tubs.

Motel rooms are available on the premises, with bar and restaurant service during spring and summer months only. It is sixteen miles to all other services in Ensenada.

Directions: (Do not attempt in wet weather.) From Ensenada, drive east on Hwy 3 to marker KM 26. Watch for "AGUA CALIENTE" sign and turn right on a 5-mile dirt road that ends at the resort that is not recommended for trailers or low clearance vehicles.

Since this location does not have a telephone or mailing address, it is not possible to secure reservations. It is usually very crowded during Easter vacation.

912   URUAPAN HOT SPRINGS
(see map on page 187)
■   **South of Ensenada**

A well-worn combination bathhouse and laundry in a green fertile valley at the base of coastal scrub foothills two miles from Hwy 1. Elevation 500 feet. Open all year.

Natural mineral water flows out of many pastureland springs at temperatures ranging from 118 to 138° and is piped to a cistern that supplies a fifty-year-old building with five individual bathtub rooms and five outdoor washing machines. Clearly, the tubs are for cleanliness bathing, not recreational soaking, and clothing is optional only in the private-space bathtub rooms.

There are no services available, but overnight camping is permitted. It is two miles to a comfortable campground at Hwy 1 and ten miles to all other services in Ensenada.

Directions: From Ensenada, drive south on Hwy 1 to marker KM 42. Turn left (east) at Uruapan sign on the dirt road, drive 2 miles through the village of Uruapan, and watch for "Banos Thermales" signs. The hard-pack dirt road is in fair condition until it crosses the river; it may be impassable in winter.

913 VALLE LA TRINIDAD/RANCHO LOS POZITOS

(see map on page 187)

● **Southeast of Ensenada**

Sandy bottom pools, semi-developed, at the head waters of a stream in an open valley. Surrounded by small hills, low mountains, and agricultural lands in the midst of old ranchos. Elevation 2,800 feet. Open all year.

Natural mineral water flows up from the bottom of the first pool at 105°. This eight-foot square pool has a sandy bottom, brick walls, and tin roof. The second pool is lined with rocks and located in the middle of the stream. In the third, water flows into a six-foot square brick pool. Bathing suits are required.

Overnight parking is permitted at the farm house-about one-hundred yards away. It is five miles to a store, restaurant and other services.

Directions: Go east out of Ensenada on Highway 3 about 60 miles. Turn right toward Valle De Trinidad on paved road. Go 1 mile and turn right onto dirt road at church. Continue 2 miles toward west end of valley and follow dirt road about 5 miles with some signs for San Isidoro. Look for Rancho Los Pozitos, Family Arballo.

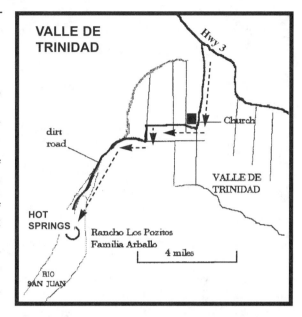

While it is always fun to soak out in the middle of nature having a pool with a bit of covering to offer protection from the sun is often welcome in this hot, arid valley.

914   MISSION SAN BORJA HOT SPRINGS

●   **East of the town of Rosarito**

A small, historic source pool on the grounds of a well-preserved mission in a remote and enchanting part of the Sierra La Libertad. Elevation 2,200 feet. Open all year.

Natural mineral water at 96° flows out of a rock-lined source pool built by the missionaries in the early 1800s. It is located at the edge of the mission cornfields, a five-minute walk southeast from the main building. The runoff from the spring was com-mingled with a nearby cold stream to water the mission's fields. Bathing suits are required.

There are no facilities or services, but camping is permitted anywhere among the ruins of the old mission buildings.

Directions: At Rosarito, from Hwy 1, turn east on a dirt road for 21 miles. There will be no sign for the mission, but there are two ranchos on the way, and the road ends in a remote valley where the mission is located.

The hot spring water was mixed with water from several cold streams to water the fields when the mission was in use in the 1800s.

BAJA SUR

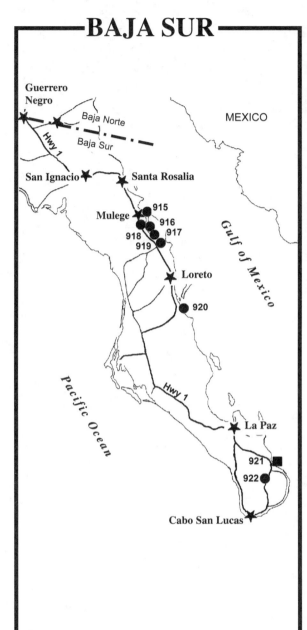

Guerrero Negro

Baja Norte

Baja Sur

MEXICO

Hwy 1

San Ignacio

Santa Rosalia

915

Mulege

916

918 917

919

Gulf of Mexico

Loreto

920

Pacific Ocean

Hwy 1

La Paz

921

922

Cabo San Lucas

---

915   MULEGE MISSION WARM SPRINGS

● **Near the town of Mulege**

Warm water springs found in middle of a stream that creates a jungle-like oasis complete with fan palms and ponds surrounded by desert and a view of the mountains. Elevation 50 feet. Open all year.

Natural mineral water bubbles up through the sand into the cool stream bed at 90° creating an interesting effect as you sit in the stream. Bathing suits are required.

There are no services on the premises. It is two miles to a campground and one mile to all other services in Mulege.

Directions: Park at the mission and walk down hill. Cross stream in front of the dam. Continue 100 yards downstream; gas bubbles can be seen rising in the stream. Suggestion: On Hwy 1 at Mulege, ask for Arcadio Valle Somora at the ABC Bus Station and hire him to guide you.

This squishy-bottom pool at Santispac Beach is located above the tide line, so it is available for soaking all day.

916 SANTISPAC BEACH
Concepcion Bay
● **South of Mulege**

Two squishy-bottom soaking pools built by volunteers near a mangrove swamp on the edge of the Bay. Elevation sea level. Open all year.

Natural mineral water oozes up through the rock-encircled mud bottom of one source spring, maintaining a temperature of 106° except when flooded by high tide. A second source spring, on slightly higher ground, has been excavated by volunteers to create a squishy-bottom pool that maintains a temperature of 102°. Bathing suits are required.

Santispac beach is a popular RV and camping destination on the Sea of Cortez. Camping is $5 per car per night, and there is a small restaurant on the beach. All other services are ten miles north in Mulege.

Directions: From Mulege, drive 10 miles south on Hwy 1 and turn left into the commercial parking and camping ground. Drive to the far right side of the cove, to a small area for parking, and walk approximately 100 yards on a dirt trail around the mangrove swamp to the two pools.

917 CONCEPCION BEACH
Concepcion Bay
● **South of Mulege**

On the edge of a beautiful bay, very hot water flows from rock fissures into rock-and-sand pools which are usable only when the high tide brings cold water for mixing. Elevation sea level. Open all year.

Natural mineral water flows out of cracks above the high tide line at more than 135° into volunteer-built soaking pools on the beach below. Twice a day the high tide supplies enough cold water to bring the pool temperatures down to tolerable soaking levels. Bathing suits are required.

Directions: There are no direct routes down the steep cliffs that border this beach. Therefore, it is necessary to hike south along the tide pools from Santispac Beach (see 917) or north from Los Cocos Beach.

Since these pools require cold ocean water to cool them down to a soakable temperatur,e it would be a good idea to bring along a tide table to figure out when to expect a high tide.

● **South of Mulege, on Concepcion Bay**

A small permanent soaking pool in a fantastic setting on the edge of Concepcion Bay. Elevation sea level. Open all year.

Natural mineral water seeps into a tide pool at the base of a cliff. Volunteers have built a rock-and-concrete wall around the tide pool, which maintains a temperature of 86° at low tide. Small shrimp have been observed in the warm, partly salty water. Bathing suits are required.

The camping fee at El Coyote Beach is $10 per night, but there is no additional fee for using the hot spring. There are no other facilities at the beach, but there is a restaurant at Rancho El Coyote across the highway. All other services are seventeen miles away in Mulege.

Directions: From Mulege, drive 17 miles south on Hwy 1 to the El Coyote Beach commercial campground. Park and follow a rocky trail 100 yards to the pool.

Waiting for the tide to go out so that you can build a pool where the hot water seeps up through the sand.

---

919   BUENA VENTURA HOT SPRINGS

● **South of Mulege, on Concepcion Bay**

Build your own pool in Concepcion Bay as hot water flows up through the sand at low tide on this beach twenty-five miles south of Mulege. Elevation sea level. Open year round.

Natural mineral water at 100° pushes up through various spots in the sand at low tide, just waiting for someone to build a small soaking pool with the available rocks. The apparent local custom is clothing optional.

The Playa Buenaventura Hotel and Restaurant is right nearby, and it is twenty-five miles to all other services in Mulege.

Suggestion: See Mike at the Playa Buenaventura Hotel and Restaurant for boat rentals and for progress on future plans to build a hot pool.

920   AGUA VERDE HOT SPRINGS

● **Near Agua Verde, south of Loreto**

Two pools in the Sea of Cortez, surrounded by the volcanic, rocky coastline and panoramic ocean views. Elevation sea level. Open all year.

Natural mineral water percolates up through the sand into two large eight-foot and ten-foot rock pools. The temperature at low tide in the upper pool is 110° and 105° in the lower pool. High tide covers the pools. The apparent local custom is clothing optional.

There are no services available on the premises, but overnight parking is permitted (watch the tides). It is two hundred yards to the nearest campground and thirty miles to all other services. This is a very good area for snorkeling.

Directions: Go 29 miles south of Loreto and turn at sign for Agua Verde. Go another 12 miles and take first turn onto the beach. Go north on beach 1 mile. You must wait for low tide to drive to the site.

Along with some of the best diving, spectacular views, and an oceanside campground, there are two large soaking pools available at low tide.

921 HOTEL BUENA VISTA RESORT
PO Box 574   800 731-4914
■ La Paz, Baja California Sur, Mexico

This full destination resort is located on the coast between the Baja desert and the Sea of Cortez, southeast of La Paz. Elevation sea level. Open all year.

Natural mineral water flows up from several wells at 180° into pools that are drained and refilled once a week. The large swimming pool, with a swim-up bar, is maintained at 80°, and a smaller swimming pool is 80-100°. There is also a hydropool. All three use an ion filtration system. Also hot water seeps up on the beach next to the hotel at low tide. The pools are open to the public for day use for a charge. Bathing suits are required.

Luxurious rooms, tennis courts, gift shop, a restaurant, and entertainment on Saturday nights are available on the premises. The hotel also has its own fishing fleet. Deep sea fishing is legendary in this area. Major credit cards are accepted. Phone for rates, reservations, and directions.

922 AGUA CALIENTE (SANTIAGO) HOT SPRINGS

● Near the town of Santiago

Mountains and trees surround two small hot pools located in a canyon with fresh-water streams and cold pools. Elevation 900 feet. Open all year.

Natural mineral water at 115° flows into a two-foot by three-foot source pool and then through a ditch to a three-foot by four-foot pool big enough for one or two people, where the water has cooled to 108°. The only way to further cool this tub is to block up or divert the water flow. The apparent local custom is clothing optional.

There are no services on the premises, but there is room for three or four cars to park overnight. It is seven miles to all other services.

Directions: From the town of Santiago, go east 5 miles to the town of Agua Caliente. Continue east 1.5 miles to Rancho El Chorro. Pass the nature preserve (El Santuario) .5 miles, then go .3 miles further to the end of the road and the springs.

INDEX

This index is designed to help you locate a listing when you start with the location name. The description of the location will be found on the page number given for that name.

Within the index the abbreviations listed below are used to identify the specific state or geographical area of the location. The number shown after each state listed below is the page number where the KEY MAP of that state will be found.

AZ = Arizona / 80
BJ = Baja (Mexico) / 182
CCA = Central California / 114
CO = Colorado / 38
NV = Nevada / 18
NM = New Mexico / 62
NCA = Northern California / 94
SCA = Southern California / 156
TX = Texas / 58
UT = Utah / 30

NUBP = Not Usable By the Public

	Order Quan.	Amount
Name		
Street		
City	State	Zip
Hot Springs and Hot Pools of the Northwest $16.95		
Hot Springs and Hot Pools of the Southwest $16.95		
Day Trips in Nature: California $14.95		
Postage: $3 first book, $2 each additional book		

Canadians: Please send in US dollars

BOOK Make check to: AQUA THERMAL ACCESS (408) 426-2956
MAIL ORDER Mail to: 55 Azalea Lane, Santa Cruz, CA 95060   TOTAL

	Order Quan.	Amount
Name		
Street		
City	State	Zip
Hot Springs and Hot Pools of the Northwest $16.95		
Hot Springs and Hot Pools of the Southwest $16.95		
Day Trips in Nature: California $14.95		
Postage: $3 first book, $2 each additional book		

Canadians: Please send in US dollars

BOOK Make check to: AQUA THERMAL ACCESS (408) 426-2956
MAIL ORDER Mail to: 55 Azalea Lane, Santa Cruz, CA 95060   TOTAL

If you discover that the description of a location needs to be revised, or you find a location not in the book, jot down the pertinent information below and send it to:

ATA Directory Editor
55 Azalea Lane
Santa Cruz, CA 95060
408 426-2956